ISBN 978-1-333-29989-7
PIBN 10485841

1 MONTH OF
FREE
READING

at
www.ForgottenBooks.com

By purchasing this book you are eligible for one month membership to ForgottenBooks.com, giving you unlimited access to our entire collection of over 700,000 titles via our web site and mobile apps.

To claim your free month visit:
www.forgottenbooks.com/free485841

English
Français
Deutsche
Italiano
Español
Português

www.forgottenbooks.com

Mythology Photography **Fiction**
Fishing Christianity **Art** Cooking
Essays Buddhism Freemasonry
Medicine **Biology** Music **Ancient
Egypt** Evolution Carpentry Physics
Dance Geology **Mathematics** Fitness
Shakespeare **Folklore** Yoga Marketing
Confidence Immortality Biographies
Poetry **Psychology** Witchcraft
Electronics Chemistry History **Law**
Accounting **Philosophy** Anthropology
Alchemy Drama Quantum Mechanics
Atheism Sexual Health **Ancient History**
Entrepreneurship Languages Sport
Paleontology Needlework Islam
Metaphysics Investment Archaeology
Parenting Statistics Criminology
Motivational

POETICAL WORKS OF
ELLA WHEELER WILCOX

To Marry
or
Not to Marry—

POETICAL WORKS OF ELLA WHEELER WILCOX

WITH INDEX OF TITLES

AND

INDEX OF FIRST LINES

ILLUSTRATED BY ALICE ROSS

EDINBURGH

W. P. NIMMO, HAY, & MITCHELL

Printed by BALLANTYNE, HANSON & Co.
at the Ballantyne Press, Edinburgh

INTRODUCTORY VERSES

OH, you who read some song that I have sung—
What know you of the soul from whence it sprung?

Dost dream the poet ever speaks aloud
His secret thought unto the listening crowd?

Go take the murmuring sea-shell from the shore—
You have its shape, its colour—and no more.

It tells not one of those vast mysteries
That lie beneath the surface of the seas.

Our songs are shells, cast out by waves of thought;
Here, take them at your pleasure; but think not

You've seen beneath the surface of the waves,
Where lie our shipwrecks, and our coral caves.

INDEX OF TITLES

INDEX OF TITLES

INDEX OF TITLES

INDEX OF TITLES

INDEX OF TITLES

INDEX OF TITLES

INDEX OF TITLES

INDEX OF TITLES

INDEX OF TITLES

POEMS OF PASSION

LOVE'S LANGUAGE

HOW does Love speak ?
    In the faint flush upon the tell-tale cheek,
And in the pallor that succeeds it ; by
The quivering lid of an averted eye—
The smile that proves the parent to a sigh—
  Thus doth Love speak.

  How does Love speak ?
By the uneven heart-throbs, and the freak
Of bounding pulses that stand still and ache,
While new emotions, like strange barques, make
Along vein-channels their disturbing course ;
Still as the dawn, and with the dawn's swift
    force—
  Thus doth Love speak.

  How does Love speak ?
In the avoidance of that which we seek—
The sudden silence and reserve when near—
The eye that glistens with an unshed tear—
The joy that seems the counterpart of fear,

ELLA WHEELER WILCOX

As the alarmèd heart leaps in the breast,
And knows, and names, and greets its god-like guest—
　Thus doth Love speak.

　How does Love speak ?
In the proud spirit suddenly grown meek—
The haughty heart grown humble ; in the tender
And unnamed light that floods the world with splendour,
In the resemblance which the fond eyes trace
In all fair things to one belovèd face ;
In the shy touch of hands that thrill and tremble ;
In looks and lips that can no more dissemble—
　Thus doth Love speak.

　How does Love speak ?
In the wild words that uttered seem so weak
They shrink ashamed to silence ; in the fire
Glance strikes with glance, swift flashing high and
　　higher,
Like lightnings that precede the mighty storm ;
In the deep, soulful stillness ; in the warm,
Impassioned tide that sweeps through throbbing veins,
Between the shores of keen delights and pains ;
In the embrace where madness melts in bliss,
And in the convulsive rapture of a kiss—
　Thus doth Love speak.

IMPATIENCE

HOW can I wait until you come to me ?
    The once fleet mornings linger by the way ;
Their sunny smiles touched with malicious glee
  At my unrest, they seem to pause, and play
  Like truant children, while I sigh and say,
     How can I wait ?

How can I wait ? Of old, the rapid hours
  Refused to pause or loiter with me long ;
But now they idly fill their hands with flowers,
  And make no haste, but slowly stroll among
  The summer blooms, not heeding my one song,
     How can I wait ?

How can I wait ? The nights alone are kind ;
  They reach forth to a future day, and bring
Sweet dreams of you to people all my mind ;
  And time speeds by on light and airy wing.
  I feast upon your face, I no more sing,
     How can I wait ?

How can I wait ? The morning breaks the spell
  A pitying night has flung upon my soul.
You are not near me, and I know full well
  My heart has need of patience and control ;
  Before we meet, hours, days, and weeks must roll,
     How can I wait ?

ELLA WHEELER WILCOX

How can I wait ?   Oh, Love, how can I wait
  Until the sunlight of your eyes shall shine
Upon my world that seems so desolate ?
    Until your hand-clasp warms my blood like wine ;
  Until you come again, oh, Love of mine,
      How can I wait ?

COMMUNISM

WHEN my blood flows calm as a purling river,
    When my heart is asleep and my brain has
    sway,
It is then that I vow we must part for ever,
  That I will forget you, and put you away
Out of my life, as a dream is banished
  Out of the mind when the dreamer awakes ;
That I know it will be when the spell has vanished,
  Better for both of our sakes.

When the court of the mind is ruled by Reason,
  I know it is wiser for us to part ;
But Love is a spy who is plotting treason,
  In league with that warm, red rebel, the Heart.
They whisper to me that the King is cruel,
  That his reign is wicked, his law a sin,
And every word they utter is fuel
  To the flame that smoulders within.

4

POEMS OF PASSION

And on nights like this, when my blood runs riot
　With the fever of youth and its mad desires,
When my brain in vain bids my heart be quiet,
　When my breast seems the centre of lava-fires,
Oh, then is the time when most I miss you,
　And I swear by the stars and my soul and say
That I will have you, and hold you, and kiss you,
　Though the whole world stands in the way.

And like Communists, as mad, as disloyal,
　My fierce emotions roam out of their lair;
They hate King Reason for being royal—
　They would fire his castle, and burn him there.
O Love! they would clasp you, and crush you, and kill
　　you,
　In the insurrection of uncontrol.
Across the miles, does this wild war thrill you,
　　That is raging in my soul?

THE COMMON LOT

IT is a common fate—a woman's lot—
　To waste on one the riches of her soul,
Who takes the wealth she gives him, but cannot
　Repay the interest, and much less the whole.

As I look up into your eyes, and wait
　For some response to my fond gaze and touch,
It seems to me there is no sadder fate
　Than to be doomed to loving overmuch.

5

ELLA WHEELER WILCOX

Are you not kind ?   Ah, yes, so very kind—
  So thoughtful of my comfort, and so true.
Yes, yes, dear heart ; but I, not being blind,
  Know that I am not loved, as I love you.

One tenderer word, a little longer kiss,
  Will fill my soul with music and with song ;
And if you seem abstracted, or I miss
  The heart-tone from your voice, my world goes
    wrong.

And oftentimes you think me childish—weak—
  When at some thoughtless word the tears will start :
You cannot understand how aught you speak
  Has power to stir the depths of my poor heart.

I cannot help it, dear—I wish I could,
  Or feign indifference where I now adore ;
For if I seemed to love you less you would,
  Manlike, I have no doubt, love me the more.

'Tis a sad gift, that much applauded thing,
  A constant heart ; for fact doth daily prove
That constancy finds oft a cruel sting,
  While fickle natures win the deeper love.

POEMS OF PASSION

INDIVIDUALITY

O YES, I love you, and with all my heart ;
　　Just as a weaker woman loves her own,
Better than I love my belovèd art,
　　Which, till you came, reigned royally, alone,
My king, my master.　Since I saw your face
I have dethroned it, and you hold that place.

I am as weak as other women are—
　　Your frown can make the whole world like a tomb
Your smile shines brighter than the sun, by far ;
　　Sometimes I think there is not space or room
In all the earth for such a love as mine,
And it soars up to breathe in realms divine.

I know that your desertion or neglect
　　Could break my heart, as women's hearts do break,
If my wan days had nothing to expect
　　From your love's splendour, all joy would forsake
The chambers of my soul.　Yes, this is true,
And yet, and yet—one thing I keep from you.

There is a subtle part of me, which went
　　Into my long pursued and worshipped art ;
Though your great love fills me with such content
　　No other love finds room now, in my heart.
Yet that rare essence was my art's alone.
Thank God you cannot grasp it ; 'tis mine own.

7

ELLA WHEELER WILCOX

Thank God, I say, for while I love you so,
  With that vast love, as passionate as tender,
I feel an exultation as I know
  I have not made you a complete surrender.
Here is my body ; bruise it, if you will,
And break my heart ; I have that *something* still

You cannot grasp it.   Seize the breath of morn,
  Or bind the perfume of the rose as well.
God put it in my soul when I was born ;
  It is not mine to give away, or sell,
Or offer up on any altar shrine.
It was my art's ; and when not art's, 'tis mine.

For love's sake, I can put the art away,
  Or anything which stands 'twixt me and you.
But that strange essence God bestowed, I say,
  To permeate the work He gave to do :
And it cannot be drained, dissolved, or sent
Through any channel, save the one He meant.

FRIENDSHIP AFTER LOVE

AFTER the fierce midsummer all ablaze
    Has burned itself to ashes, and expires
  In the intensity of its own fires,
There come the mellow, mild, St. Martin days
Crowned with the calm of peace, but sad with haze.

8

POEMS OF PASSION

So after Love has led us, till he tires
Of his own throes, and torments, and desires,
Comes large-eyed Friendship : with a restful gaze,
He beckons us to follow, and across
Cool verdant vales we wander free from care.
Is it a touch of frost lies in the air ?
Why are we haunted with a sense of loss ?
We do not wish the pain back, or the heat ;
And yet, and yet, these days are incomplete.

OLD AND NEW

LONG have the poets vaunted, in their lays,
Old times, old loves, old friendship, and old wine
Why should the old monopolise all praise ?
Then let the new claim mine.

Give me strong new friends, when the old prove weak,
Or fail me in my darkest hour of need ;
Why perish with the ship that springs a leak,
Or lean upon a reed ?

Give me new love, warm, palpitating, sweet,
When all the grace and beauty leaves the old ;
When like a rose it withers at my feet,
Or like a hearth grows cold.

Give me new times, bright with a prosperous cheer,
In place of old, tear-blotted, burdened days ;
I hold a sunlit present far more dear,
And worthy of my praise.

9

ELLA WHEELER WILCOX

When the old creeds are threadbare, and worn through,
   And all too narrow for the broadening soul,
Give me the fine, firm texture of the new,
   Fair, beautiful and whole.

ATTRACTION

THE meadow and the mountain with desire
   Gazed on each other, till a fierce unrest
  Surged 'neath the meadow's seemingly calm breast,
And all the mountain's fissures ran with fire.

A mighty river rolled between them there.
   What could the mountain do but gaze and burn ?
   What could the meadow do but look and yearn,
And gem its bosom to conceal despair ?

Their seething passion agitated space,
   Till lo ! the lands a sudden earthquake shook,
   The river fled : the meadow leaped, and took
The leaning mountain in a close embrace.

AD FINEM

ON the white throat of the useless passion
   That scorched my soul with its burning breath,
I clutched my fingers in murderous fashion,
   And gathered them close in a grip of death ;

POEMS OF PASSION

For why should I fan, or feed with fuel,
  A love that showed me but blank despair ?
So my hold was firm, and my grasp was cruel—
  I meant to strangle it then and there !

I thought it was dead. But with no warning,
  It rose from its grave last night, and came
And stood by my bed till the early morning,
  And over and over it spoke your name.
Its throat was red where my hands had held it
  It burned my brow with its scorching breath
And I said, the moment my eyes beheld it,
  " A love like this can know no death."

For just one kiss that your lips have given
  In the lost and beautiful past to me,
I would gladly barter my hopes of Heaven
  And all the bliss of Eternity.
For never a joy are the angels keeping
  To lay at my feet in Paradise,
Like that of into your strong arms creeping
  And looking into your love-lit eyes.

I know, in the way that sins are reckoned,
  This thought is a sin of the deepest dye
But I know, too, if an angel beckoned,
  Standing close by the Throne on High,
And you, adown by the gates infernal,
  Should open your loving arms and smile,
I would turn my back on things supernal,
  To lie on your breast a little while.

ELLA WHEELER WILCOX

To know for an hour you were mine completely—
  Mine in body and soul, my own—
I would bear unending tortures sweetly,
  With not a murmur and not a moan.
A lighter sin or a lesser error
  Might change through hope or fear divine
But there is no fear, and hell has no terror
  To change or alter a love like mine.

UPON THE SAND

ALL love that has not friendship for its base,
  Is like a mansion built upon the sand.
Though brave its walls as any in the land,
And its tall turrets lift their heads in grace ;
Though skilful and accomplished artists trace
  Most beautiful designs on every hand,
  And gleaming statues in dim niches stand,
And fountains play in some flow'r-hidden place,
Yet, when from the frowning east a sudden gust
  Of adverse fate is blown, or sad rains fall
  Day in, day out, against its yielding wall,
Lo ! the fair structure crumbles to the dust.
Love, to endure life's sorrow and earth's woe,
Needs friendship's solid mason-work below.

POEMS OF PASSION

REUNITED

LET us begin, dear love, where we left off ;
    Tie up the broken threads of that old dream ;
  And go on happy as before ; and seem
Lovers again, though all the world may scoff.

Let us forget the graves, which lie between
    Our parting and our meeting, and the tears
    That rusted out the goldwork of the years ;
The frosts that fell upon our gardens green.

Let us forget the cold malicious Fate
    Who made our loving hearts her idle toys,
    And once more revel in the old sweet joys
Of happy love. Nay, it is *not* too late !

Forget the deep-ploughed furrows in my brow ;
    Forget the silver gleaming in my hair ;
    Look only in my eyes ! Oh ! darling, there
The old love shone no warmer then than now.

Down in the tender depths of thy dear eyes,
    I find the lost sweet memory of my youth,
    Bright with the holy radiance of thy truth,
And hallowed with the blue of summer skies.

Tie up the broken threads, and let us go,
    Like reunited lovers, hand in hand,
    Back, and yet onward, to the sunny land
Of our To Be, which was our Long Ago.

ELLA WHEELER WILCOX

YOU WILL FORGET ME

YOU will forget me. The years are so tender,
  They bind up the wounds which we think are
    so deep ;
This dream of our youth will fade out as the splendour
  Fades from the skies when the sun sinks to sleep ;
The cloud of forgetfulness, over and over
  . Will banish the last rosy colours away,
And the fingers of time will weave garlands to cover
  The scar which you think is a life-mark to-day.

You will forget me. The one boon you covet
  Now above all things will soon seem no prize,
And the heart, which you hold not in keeping to prove it
  True or untrue, will lose worth in your eyes.
The one drop to-day, that you deem only wanting
  To fill your life-cup to the brim, soon will seem
But a valueless mite ; and the ghost that is haunting
  The aisles of your heart will pass out with the dream.

You will forget me ; will thank me for saying
  The words which you think are so pointed with pain.
Time loves a new lay ; and the dirge he is playing
  Will change for you soon to a livelier strain.
I shall pass from your life—I shall pass out for ever,
  And these hours we have spent will be sunk in the
    past.
Youth buries its dead ; grief kills seldom or never—
  And forgetfulness covers all sorrows at last.

PROGRESS

LET there be many windows to your soul,
　　That all the glory of the universe
May beautify it.　Not the narrow pane
Of one poor creed can catch the radiant rays
That shine from countless sources.　Tear away
The blinds of superstition ; let the light
Pour through fair windows broad as Truth itself
And high as God.
　　　　　　　　Why should the spirit peer
Through some priest-curtained orifice, and grope
Along dim corridors of doubt, when all
The splendour from unfathomed seas of space
Might bathe it with the golden waves of Love ?
Sweep up the débris of decaying faiths ;
Sweep down the cobwebs of worn-out beliefs,
And throw your soul wide open to the light
Of Reason and of Knowledge.　Tune your ear
To all the wordless music of the stars
And to the voice of Nature, and your heart
Shall turn to truth and goodness, as the plant
Turns to the sun.　A thousand unseen hands
Reach down to help you to their peace-crowned heights,
And all the forces of the firmament
Shall fortify your strength.　Be not afraid
To thrust aside half-truths and grasp the whole.

ELLA WHEELER WILCOX

NEW AND OLD

I AND new love, in all its living bloom,
  Sat *vis-à-vis*, while tender twilight hours
Went softly by us, treading as on flowers.
Then suddenly I saw within the room
The old love, long since lying in its tomb.
  It dropped the cerecloth from its fleshless face
  And smiled on me, with a remembered grace
That, like the noontide, lit the gloaming's gloom.

Upon its shroud there hung the grave's green mould,
  About it hung the odour of the dead ;
  Yet from its cavernous eyes such light was shed
That all my life seemed gilded, as with gold ;
  Unto the trembling new love " Go," I said,
" I do not need thee, for I have the old."

THE TRIO

WE love but once. The great gold orb of light
  From dawn to eventide doth cast his ray ;
But the full splendour of his perfect might
  Is reached but once throughout the live-long day.

We love but once. The waves, with ceaseless motion,
  Do day and night plash on the pebbled shore ;
But the strong tide of the resistless ocean
  Sweeps in but one hour of the twenty-four.

16

POEMS OF PASSION

We love but once.   A score of times, perchance,
   We may be moved in fancy's fleeting fashion—
May treasure up a word, a tone, a glance,
   But only once we feel the soul's great passion.

We love but once.   Love walks with death and birth
   (The saddest, the unkindest of the three) ;
And only once while we sojourn on earth
   Can that strange trio come to you or me.

WHAT SHALL WE DO ?

HERE now, for evermore, our lives must part.
   My path leads there, and yours another way.
What shall we do with this fond love, dear heart ?
   It grows a heavier burden day by day.

Hide it ?   In all earth's caverns, void and vast,
   There is not room enough to hide it, dear ;
Not even the mighty storehouse of the past
   Could cover it, from our own eyes, I fear.

Drown it ?   Why, were the contents of each ocean
   Merged into one great sea, too shallow then
Would be its waters, to sink this emotion
   So deep it could not rise to life again.

ELLA WHEELER WILCOX

Burn it ?   In all the furnace flames below,
  It would not in a thousand years expire.
Nay ! it would thrive, exult, expand and grow,
  For from its very birth it fed on fire.

Starve it ?   Yes, yes, that is the only way.
  Give it no food, of glance, or word, or sigh,
No memories, even, of any bygone day ;
  No crumbs of vain regrets—so let it die.

" THE BEAUTIFUL BLUE DANUBE "

THEY drift down the hall together ;
  He smiles in her lifted eyes.
Like waves of that mighty river,
  The strains of the " Danube " rise.
They float on its rhythmic measure,
  Like leaves on a summer stream ;
And here, in this scene of pleasure,
  I bury my sweet, dead dream.

Through the cloud of her dusky tresses,
  Like a star, shines out her face ;
And the form his strong arm presses
  Is sylph-like in its grace.
As a leaf on the bounding river
  Is lost in the seething sea,
I know that for ever and ever
  My dream is lost to me.

POEMS OF PASSION

And still the viols are playing
  That grand old wordless rhyme ;
And still those two are swaying
  In perfect tune and time.
If the great bassoons that mutter,
  If the clarinets that blow,
Were given a voice to utter
  The secret things they know,

Would the lists of the slain who slumber
  On the Danube's battle-plains
The unknown hosts outnumber
  Who die 'neath the " Danube's " strains ?
Those fall where cannons rattle,
  'Mid the rain of shot and shell ;
But these, in a fiercer battle,
  Find death in the music's swell.

With the river's roar of passion
  Is blended the dying groan ;
But here, in the halls of fashion,
  Hearts break, and make no moan.
And the music, swelling and sweeping,
  Like the river, knows it all ;
But none are counting or keeping
  The lists of those who fall.

ELLA WHEELER WILCOX

THE DUET

I WAS smoking a cigarette ;
  Maud, my wife, and the tenor McKey,
Were singing together a blithe duet,
And days it were better I should forget
  Came suddenly back to me.
Days when life seemed a gay masque ball,
And to love and be loved was the sum of it all.

As they sang together the whole scene fled,
The room's rich hangings, the sweet home air,
Stately Maud, with her proud blonde head,
And I seemed to see in her place instead
  A wealth of blue-black hair,
And a face, ah ! your face,—yours, Lisette,
A face it were wiser I should forget.

We were back—well, no matter when or where,
But you remember, I know, Lisette,
I saw you, dainty, and débonnaire,
With the very same look that you used to wear
  In the days I should forget.
And your lips, as red as the vintage we quaffed,
Were pearl-edged bumpers of wine when you laughed.

Two small slippers with big rosettes,
Peeped out under your kilt-skirt there,
While we sat smoking our cigarettes

The Duet

POEMS OF PASSION

(Oh, I shall be dust when my heart forgets !)
  And singing that self-same air ;
And between the verses for interlude,
I kissed your throat, and your shoulders nude.

You were so full of a subtle fire,
You were so warm and so sweet, Lisette ;
You were everything men admire,
And there were no fetters to make us tire,
  For you were—a pretty grisette.
But you loved, as only such natures can,
With a love that makes heaven or hell for a man.

.   .   .   .   .   .

They have ceased singing that old duet,
Stately Maud and the tenor McKey.
" You are burning your coat with your cigarette,
And *qu'avez vous*, dearest, your lids are wet,"
  Maud says, as she leans o'er me.
And I smile, and lie to her, husband-wise,
" Oh, it is nothing but smoke in my eyes."

LITTLE QUEEN

DO you remember the name I wore—
  The old pet-name of Little Queen—
In the dear, dead days that are no more,
  The happiest days of our lives, I ween ?

ELLA WHEELER WILCOX

For we loved with that passionate love of youth
    That blesses but once with its perfect bliss,—
A love that, in spite of its trust and truth,
    Seems never to thrive, in a world like this.

I lived for you, and you lived for me;
    All was centred in " Little Queen ";
And never a thought in our hearts had we
    That strife or trouble could come between.
What utter sinking of self it was!
    How little we cared for the world of men!
For love's fair kingdom, and love's sweet laws,
    Were all of the world and life to us then.

But a love like ours was a challenge to fate;
    She rang down the curtain and shifted the scene;
Yet sometimes now, when the day grows late,
    I can hear you calling for Little Queen;
For a happy home and a busy life
    Can never wholly crowd out our past;
In the twilight pauses that come from strife,
    You will think of me while life shall last.

And however sweet the voice of fame
    May sing to me of a great world's praise,
I shall long sometimes for the old pet-name
    That you gave to me in the dear, dead days;
And nothing the angel band can say,
    When I reach the shores of the great Unseen,
Can please me so much as on that day
    To hear your greeting of " Little Queen."

POEMS OF PASSION

WHEREFORE

WHEREFORE in dreams are sorrows born anew,
   A healed wound opened, or the past revived ?
Last night in my deep sleep I dreamed of you—
   Again the old love woke in me, and thrived
On looks of fire, and kisses, and sweet words
   Like silver waters purling in a stream,
Or like the amorous melodies of birds :
        A dream—a dream.

Again upon the glory of the scene
   There settled that dread shadow of the cross
That, when hearts love too well, falls in between—
   That warns them of impending woe and loss.
Again I saw you drifting from my life,
   As barques are rudely parted in a stream ;
Again my heart was torn with awful strife :
        A dream—a dream.

Again the deep night settled on me there,
   Alone I groped, and heard strange waters roll.
Lost in that blackness of supreme despair
   That comes but once to any living soul.
Alone, afraid, I called your name aloud—
   Mine eyes, unveiled, beheld white stars agleam,
And lo ! awake, I cried, " Thank God, thank God,
        A dream—a dream."

ELLA WHEELER WILCOX

DELILAH

IN the midnight of darkness and terror,
  When I would grope nearer to God,
With my back to a record of error
  And the highway of sin I have trod,
There come to me shapes I would banish—
  The shapes of the deeds I have done;
And I pray and I plead till they vanish—
  All vanish and leave me, save one.

That one, with a smile like the splendour
  Of the sun in the middle-day skies—
That one, with a spell that is tender—
  That one with a dream in her eyes—
Cometh close, in her rare Southern beauty,
  Her languor, her indolent grace;
And my soul turns its back on its duty,
  To live in the light of her face.

She touches my cheek, and I quiver—
  I tremble with exquisite pains;
She sighs—like an overcharged river
  My blood rushes on through my veins;
She smiles—and in mad-tiger fashion,
  As a she-tiger fondles her own,
I clasp her with fierceness and passion,
  And kiss her with shudder and groan.

24

POEMS OF PASSION

Once more, in our love's sweet beginning,
   I put away God and the World ;
Once more, in the joys of our sinning,
   Are the hopes of eternity hurled.
There is nothing my soul lacks or misses
   As I clasp the dream-shape to my breast ;
In the passion and pain of her kisses
   Life blooms to its richest and best.

O ghost of dead sin unrelenting,
   Go back to the dust, and the sod !
Too dear and too sweet for repenting,
   Ye stand between me and my God.
If I, by the Throne, should behold you,
   Smiling up with those eyes loved so well,
Close, close in my arms I would fold you,
   And drop with you down to sweet Hell !

LOVE SONG

ONCE in the world's first prime,
   When nothing lived or stirred,
Nothing but new-born Time,
   Nor was there even a bird—
The Silence spoke to a Star,
   But I do not dare repeat
What it said to its love afar :
   It was too sweet, too sweet.

ELLA WHEELER WILCOX

But there, in the fair world's youth,
  Ere sorrow had drawn breath,
When nothing was known but Truth,
  Nor was there even death,
The Star to Silence was wed,
  And the Sun was priest that day,
And they made their bridal-bed
  High in the Milky Way.

For the great white star had heard
  Her silent lover's speech ;
It needed no passionate word
  To pledge them each to each.
O lady fair and far,
  Hear, oh, hear, and apply !
Thou the beautiful Star—
  The voiceless Silence, I.

TIME AND LOVE

TIME flies. The swift hours hurry by
  And speed us on to untried ways ;
New seasons ripen, perish, die,
  And yet love stays.
The old, old love—like sweet at first,
  At last like bitter wine—
I know not if it blest or curst,
  Thy life and mine.

POEMS OF PASSION

Time flies. In vain our prayers, our tears,
　　We cannot tempt him to delays ;
Down to the past he bears the years,
　　And yet love stays.
Through changing task and varying dream
　　We hear the same refrain,
As one can hear a plaintive theme
　　Run through each strain.

Time flies. He steals our pulsing youth,
　　He robs us of our care-free days,
He takes away our trust and truth,
　　And yet love stays.
O Time ! take love ! When love is vain,
　　When all its best joys die—
When only its regrets remain—
　　Let love, too, fly.

CHANGE

CHANGED ? Yes, I will confess it—I have changed.
　　I do not love you in the old fond way.
I am your friend still—time has not estranged
　　One kindly feeling of that vanished day.

But the bright glamour which made life a dream,
　　The rapture of that time, its sweet content,
Like visions of a sleeper's brain they seem—
　　And yet I cannot tell you how they went.

27

ELLA WHEELER WILCOX

Why do you gaze with such accusing eyes
   Upon me, dear ? Is it so very strange
That hearts, like all things underneath God's skies,
   Should sometimes feel the influence of change ?

The birds, the flowers, the foliage of the trees,
   The stars which seem so fixed, and so sublime,
Vast continents, and the eternal seas,—
   All these do change, with ever-changing time.

The face our mirror shows us year on year
   Is not the same ; our dearest aim, or need,
Our lightest thought, or feeling, hope, or fear,
   All, all the law of alternation heed.

How can we ask the human heart to stay,
   Content with fancies of Youth's earliest hours ?
The year outgrows the violets of May,
   Although, maybe, there are no fairer flowers.

And life may hold no sweeter love than this,
   Which lies so cold, so voiceless, and so dumb.
And will I miss it, dear ? Why yes, we miss
   The violets always—till the roses come !

POEMS OF PASSION

DESOLATION

I THINK that the bitterest sorrow or pain
  Of love unrequited, or cold death's woe,
  Is sweet, compared to that hour when we know
That some grand passion is on the wane.

When we see that the glory, and glow, and grace
  Which lent a splendour to night and day,
  Are surely fading, and showing the grey
And dull groundwork of the commonplace.

When fond expressions on dull ears fall,
  When the hands clasp calmly without one thrill,
  When we cannot muster by force of will
The old emotions that came at call.

When the dream has vanished we fain would keep,
  When the heart, like a watch, runs out of gear,
  And all the savour goes out of the year,
Oh, then is the time—if we could—to weep !

But no tears soften this dull, pale woe ;
  We must sit and face it with dry, sad eyes.
  If we seek to hold it, the swifter joy flies—
We can only be passive, and let it go.

NOT QUITE THE SAME

NOT quite the same the springtime seems to me,
　　Since that sad season when in separate ways
　　Our paths diverged.　There are no more such days
As dawned for us in that last time when we
Dwelt in the realm of dreams, illusive dreams ;
Spring may be just as fair now, but it seems
　　　　Not quite the same.

Not quite the same in life, since we two parted,
　　Knowing it best to go our ways alone.
　　Fair measures of success we both have known,
And pleasant hours ;　and yet something departed
Which gold, nor fame, nor anything we win,
Can all replace.　And either life has been
　　　　Not quite the same.

Love is not quite the same, although each heart
　　Has formed new ties, that are both sweet and true ;
　　But that wild rapture, which of old we knew,
Seems to have been a something set apart
With that lost dream.　There is no passion, now,
Mixed with this later love, which seems, somehow,
　　　　Not quite the same.

Not quite the same am I.　My inner being
　　Reasons and knows that all is for the best.
　　Yet vague regrets stir always in my breast,

30

POEMS OF PASSION

As my soul's eyes turn sadly backward, seeing
The vanished self, that evermore must be,
This side of what we call eternity,
    Not quite the same.

A WALTZ-QUADRILLE

THE band was playing a waltz-quadrille,
   I felt as light as a wind-blown feather,
As we floated away, at the caller's will,
  Through the intricate, mazy dance together.
Like mimic armies our lines were meeting,
Slowly advancing, and then retreating,
  All decked in their bright array ;
And back and forth to the music's rhyme
We moved together, and all the time
  I knew you were going away.

The fold of your strong arm sent a thrill
  From heart to brain as we gently glided
Like leaves on the wave of that waltz-quadrille ;
  Parted, met, and again divided—
You drifting one way, and I another,
Then suddenly turning and facing each other,
  Then off in the blithe chassé,
Then airily back to our places swaying,
While every beat of the music seemed saying
  That you were going away.

31

ELLA WHEELER WILCOX

I said to my heart, " Let us take our fill
  Of mirth and music, and love, and laughter ;
For it all must end with this waltz-quadrille,
  And life will be never the same life after.
Oh, that the caller might go on calling !
Oh, that the music might go on falling
  Like a shower of silver spray,
While we whirled on to the vast Forever,
Where no hearts break, and no ties sever,
  And no one goes away."

A clamour, a crash, and the band was still,
  'Twas the end of the dream, and the end of the
    measure :
The last low note of that waltz-quadrille
  Seemed like a dirge o'er the death of Pleasure.
You said good-night, and the spell was over—
Too warm for a friend, and too cold for a lover—
  There was nothing else to say ;
But the lights looked dim, and the dancers weary,
And the music was sad, and the hall was dreary,
  After you went away.

BEPPO

WHY art thou sad, my Beppo ? But last eve,
  Here at my feet, thy dear head on my breast,
I heard thee say thy heart would no more grieve
  Or feel the olden ennui and unrest.

What troubles thee ?   Am I not all thine own—
  I, so long sought, so sighed for and so dear ?
And do I not live but for thee alone ?
  " *Thou hast seen Lippo, whom I loved last year !* "

Well, what of that ?   Last year is naught to me—
  'Tis swallowed in the ocean of the past.
Art thou not glad 'twas Lippo, and not thee,
  Whose brief bright day in that great gulf was cast ?

Thy day is all before thee.   Let no cloud,
  Here in the very morn of our delight,
Drift up from distant foreign skies, to shroud
  Our sun of love whose radiance is so bright.

" Thou art not first ? "   Nay, and he who would be
  Defeats his own heart's dearest purpose then.
No truer truth was ever told to thee—
  Who has loved most, he best can love again.

If Lippo (and not he alone) has taught
  The arts that please thee, wherefore art thou sad ?
Since all my vast love-lore to thee is brought,
  Look up and smile, my Beppo, and be glad.

ELLA WHEELER WILCOX

CONVERSION

I HAVE lived this life as the sceptic lives it,
  I have said the sweetness was less than the gall ;
Praising, nor cursing, the Hand that gives it,
  I have drifted aimlessly through it all.
I have scoffed at the tale of a so-called heaven,
  I have laughed at the thought of a Supreme Friend ;
I have said that it only to man was given
  To live, to endure ; and to die was the end.

But now I know that a good God reigneth,
  Generous-hearted, and kind and true :
Since unto a worm like me He deigneth
  To send so royal a gift as you.
Bright as a star you gleam on my bosom,
  Sweet as a rose that the wild bee sips ;
And I know, my own, my beautiful blossom,
  That none but a God could mould such lips.

And I believe, in the fullest measure
  That ever a strong man's heart could hold,
In all the tales of heavenly pleasure
  By poets sung, or by prophets told ;
For in the joy of your shy, sweet kisses,
  Your pulsing touch and your languid sigh,
I am filled and thrilled with better blisses
  Than ever were claimed for souls on high.

34

POEMS OF PASSION

And now I have faith in all the stories
   Told of the beauties of unseen lands ;
Of royal splendours and marvellous glories
   Of the golden city not made with hands ,
For the silken beauty of falling tresses,
   Of lips all dewy and cheeks aglow,
With—what the mind in a half trance guesses
   Of the twin perfection of drifts of snow.

Of limbs like marble, of thigh and shoulder,
   Carved like a statue in high relief—
These, as the eyes and the thoughts grow bolder
   Leave no room for an unbelief.
So my lady, my queen most royal,
   My scepticism has passed away ;
If you are true to me, true and loyal,
   I will believe till the Judgment Day.

LOVE'S COMING

SHE had looked for his coming as warriors come.
   With the clash of arms and the bugle's call ;
But he came instead with a stealthy tread,
   Which she did not hear at all.

She had thought how his armour would blaze in the sun,
   As he rode like a prince to claim his bride ;
In the sweet dim light of the falling night
   She found him at her side.

35

ELLA WHEELER WILCOX

She had dreamed how the gaze of his strange, bold eye
  Would wake her heart to a sudden glow:
She found in his face the familiar grace
  Of a friend she used to know.

She had dreamed how his coming would stir her soul,
  As the ocean is stirred by the wild storm's strife:
He brought her the balm of a heavenly calm,
  And a peace which crowned her life.

AN ANSWER

IF all the year was summer-time,
  And all the aim of life
Was just to lilt on like a rhyme—
  Then I would be your wife.

If all the days were August days,
  And crowned with golden weather,
How happy then through green-clad ways
  We two could stray together!

If all the nights were moonlit nights,
  And we had naught to do
But just to sit and plan delights,
  Then I would wed with you.

POEMS OF PASSION

If life was all a summer fête,
  Its soberest pace the " glide,"
Then I would choose you for my mate,
  And keep you at my side.

But winter makes full half the year,
  And labour half of life,
And all the laughter and good cheer
  Give place to wearing strife.

Days will grow cold, and moons wax old,
  And then a heart that's true
Is better far than grace or gold—
  And so, my love, adieu !
  I cannot wed with you.

ANSWERED

GOOD-BYE—yes, I am going.
    Sudden ? Well, you are right.
But a startling truth came home to me
  With sudden force last night.
What is it ? shall I tell you—
  Nay, that is why I go.
I am running away from the battlefield,
  Turning my back on the foe.

ELLA WHEELER WILCOX

Riddles ?   You think me cruel !
   Have you not been most kind ?
Why, when you question me like that
   What answer can I find ?
You fear you failed to amuse me,
   Your husband's friend and guest,
Whom he bade you entertain and please—
   Well, you have done your best.

Then why am I going !
   A friend of mine abroad,
Whose theories I have been acting upon,
   Has proven himself a fraud.
You have heard me quote from Plato
   A thousand times no doubt ;
Well, I have discovered he did not know
   What he was talking about.

You think I am speaking strangely ?
   You cannot understand ?
Well, let me look down into your eyes,
   And let me take your hand.
I am running away from danger—
   I am flying before I fall ;
I am going because with heart and soul
   I love you—that is all.

There, now, you are white with anger,
   I knew it would be so.
You should not question a man too close
   When he tells you he must go.

POEMS OF PASSION

THROUGH THE VALLEY

[AFTER JAMES THOMSON]

As I came through the Valley of Despair,
  As I came through the valley, on my sight,
  More awful than the darkness of the night,
Shone glimpses of a Past that had been fair,
  And memories of eyes that used to smile,
  And wafts of perfume from a vanished isle,
As I came through the valley.

As I came through the valley I could see,
  As I came through the valley, fair and far,
  As drowning men look up and see a star,
The fading shore of my lost Used-to-be;
  And like an arrow in my heart I heard
  The last sad notes of Hope's expiring bird,
As I came through the valley.

As I came through the valley desolate,
  As I came through the valley, like a beam
  Of lurid lightning I beheld a gleam
Of Love's great eyes that now were full of hate.
  Dear God! dear God! I could bear all but that;
  But I fell down soul-stricken, dead, thereat,
As I came through the valley.

ELLA WHEELER WILCOX

TIRED

I AM tired to-night, and something,
  The wind maybe, or the rain,
Or the cry of a bird in the copse outside,
  Has brought back the past and its pain.
And I feel as I sit here thinking,
  That the hand of a dead old June
Has reached out hold of my heart's loose strings,
  And is drawing them up in tune.

I am tired to-night, and I miss you,
  And long for you, love, through tears;
And it seems but to-day that I saw you go—
  You, who have been gone for years.
And I seem to be newly lonely—
  I, who am so much alone;
And the strings of my heart are well in tune,
  But they have not the same old tone.

I am tired; and that old sorrow
  Sweeps down the bed of my soul,
As a turbulent river might suddenly break
  Away from a dam's control.
It beareth a wreck on its bosom,
  A wreck with a snow-white sail,
And the hand on my heart-strings thrums away,
  But they only respond with a wail.

40

POEMS OF PASSION

SHOW ME THE WAY

SHOW me the way that leads to the true life.
　　I do not care what tempests may assail me,
I shall be given courage for the strife,
　　I know my strength will not desert or fail me;
I know that I shall conquer in the fray:
　　　　　　　　　　　　　Show me the way.

Show me the way up to a higher plane,
　　Where body shall be servant to the soul.
I do not care what tides of woe, or pain,
　　Across my life their angry waves may roll
If I but reach the end I seek some day:
　　　　　　　　　　　　　Show me the way.

Show me the way, and let me bravely climb
　　Above vain grievings for unworthy treasures;
Above all sorrow that finds balm in time—
　　Above small triumphs, or belittling pleasures;
Up to those heights where these things seem child's
　　play:
　　　　　　　　　　　　　Show me the way.

Show me the way to that calm, perfect peace
　　Which springs from an inward consciousness of right;
To where all conflicts with the flesh shall cease,
　　And self shall radiate with the spirit's light.
Though hard the journey and the strife, I pray
　　　　　　　　　　　　　Show me the way.

ELLA WHEELER WILCOX

SOLITUDE

LAUGH, and the world laughs with you ;
  Weep, and you weep alone,
For sad old earth must borrow its mirth,
  But has trouble enough of its own.
Sing, and the hills will answer ;
  Sigh, it is lost on the air,
The echoes bound to a joyful sound,
  But shrink from voicing care.

Rejoice, and men will seek you ;
  Grieve, and they turn and go.
They want full measure of all your pleasure.
  But they do not need your woe.
Be glad, and your friends are many ;
  Be sad, and you lose them all—
There are none to decline your nectar'd wine,
  But alone you must drink life's gall.

Feast, and your halls are crowded ;
  Fast, and the world goes by.
Succeed and give, and it helps you live,
  But no man can help you die.
There is room in the halls of pleasure
  For a large and lordly train,
But one by one we must all file on
  Through the narrow aisles of pain.

The Beautiful Land of Nod.

POEMS OF PASSION

THE BEAUTIFUL LAND OF NOD

COME, cuddle your head on my shoulder, dear,
  Your head like the golden-rod,
And we will go sailing away from here
  To the beautiful Land of Nod.
Away from life's hurry, and flurry, and worry,
  Away from earth's shadows and gloom,
To a world of fair weather we'll float off together
  Where roses are always in bloom.

Just shut up your eyes, and fold your hands,
  Your hands like the leaves of a rose,
And we will go sailing to those fair lands
  That never an atlas shows.
On the North and the West they are bounded by rest,
  On the South and the East, by dreams ;
'Tis the country ideal, where nothing is real,
  But everything only seems.

Just drop down the curtains of your dear eyes,
  Those eyes like a bright blue-bell,
And we will sail out under starlit skies,
  To the land where the fairies dwell.
Down the river of sleep, our barque shall sweep,
  Till it reaches that mystical Isle
Which no man hath seen, but where all have been,
  And there **we** will pause awhile.

43

ELLA WHEELER WILCOX

I will croon you a song as we float along,
  To that shore that is blessed of God,
Then ho! for that fair land, we're off for that rare land,
  That beautiful Land of Nod.

I WILL BE WORTHY OF IT

I MAY not reach the heights I seek,
    My untried strength may fail me;
Or, half-way up the mountain peak
    Fierce tempests may assail me.
But though that place I never gain,
Herein lies comfort for my pain—
    I will be worthy of it.

I may not triumph in success,
    Despite my earnest labour;
I may not grasp results that bless
    The efforts of my neighbour.
But though my goal I never see,
This thought shall always dwell with me—
    I will be worthy of it.

The golden glory of Love's light
    May never fall on my way;
My path may always lead through night,
    Like some deserted byway.
But though life's dearest joy I miss
There lies a nameless strength in this—
    I will be worthy of it.

EARNESTNESS

THE hurry of the times affects us so
    In this swift rushing hour, we crowd, and press
And thrust each other backward, as we go,
    And do not pause to lay sufficient stress
    Upon that good, strong, true word, Earnestness.
In our impetuous haste, could we but know
Its full, deep meaning, its vast import, oh,
    Then might we grasp the secret of success !

In that receding age when men were great,
    The bone, and sinew, of their purpose lay
In this one word. God likes an earnest soul—
Too earnest to be eager. Soon or late
    It leaves the spent horde breathless by the way,
And stands serene, triumphant, at the goal.

A PIN

OH, I know a certain lady who is reckoned with
    the good,
Yet she fills me with more terror than a raging lion
    would.
The little chills run up and down my spine whene'er we
    meet,
Though she seems a gentle creature, and she's very trim
    and neat.

And she has a thousand virtues and not one acknow-
ledged sin,
But she is the sort of person you could liken to a pin.
And she pricks you and she sticks you in a way that
can't be said.
If you seek for what has hurt you—why, you cannot
find the head !

But she fills you with discomfort and exasperating pain.
If anybody asks you why, you really can't explain !
A pin is such a tiny thing, of that there is no doubt,
Yet when it's sticking in your flesh you're wretched
till it's out.

She's wonderfully observing—when she meets a pretty
girl,
She is always sure to tell her if her hair is out of curl ;
And she is so sympathetic to her friend who's much
admired,
She is often heard remarking, " Dear, you look so worn
and tired."

And she is an honest critic, for on yesterday she eyed
The new dress I was airing with a woman's natural
pride,
And she said, " Oh, how becoming ! " and then gently
added, " it
Is really a misfortune that the basque is such a fit."

Then she said, " If you had heard me yester eve, I'm
 sure, my friend,
You would say I was a champion who knows how to
 defend,"
And she left me with the feeling—most unpleasant,
 I aver—
That the whole world would despise me if it hadn't
 been for her.

Whenever I encounter her, in such a nameless way
She gives me the impression I am at my worst that
 day.
And the hat that was imported (and which cost me
 half a sonnet),
With just one glance from her round eyes becomes a
 Bowery bonnet.

She is always bright and smiling, sharp and pointed
 for a thrust ;
Use does not seem to blunt her point, nor does she
 gather rust.
Oh ! I wish some hapless specimen of mankind would
 begin
To tidy up the world for me, by picking up this pin !

ELLA WHEELER WILCOX

ILLOGICAL

SHE stood beside me while I gave an order for a
  bonnet.
She shuddered when I said, " And put a bright bird's
  wing upon it."

A member of the Audubon Society was she ;
And cutting were her comments made on worldly folks
  like me.

She spoke about the helpless birds we wickedly were
  harming ;
She quoted the statistics, and they really were alarming ;

She said God meant His little birds to sing in trees and
  skies ;
And there was pathos in her voice, and tears were in
  her eyes.

" Oh, surely in this beauteous world you can find
  lovely things
Enough to trim your hats," she said, " without the
  dear birds' wings."

I sat beside her that same day, in her own house at
  dinner,
Angelic being that she was, to entertain a sinner !

Her well-appointed table groaned beneath the ample
    spread,
Course followed appetising course, and hunger sated
    fled ;

But still my charming hostess urged, " Do have a reed-
    bird, dear ;
They are so delicate and sweet at this time of the year."

BUT ONE

THE year has but one June, dear friend,
    The year has but one June ;
And when that perfect month doth end,
The robin's song, though loud, though long,
    Seems never quite in tune.

The rose, though still its blushing face
    By bee and bird is seen,
May yet have lost that subtle grace—
That nameless spell the winds know well—
    Which makes it gardens' queen.

Life's perfect June, love's red, red rose,
    Have burned and bloomed for me.
Though still youth's summer sunlight glows ;
Though thou art kind, dear friend, I find
    I have no heart for thee.

ELLA WHEELER WILCOX

THE SPEECH OF SILENCE

THE solemn Sea of Silence lies between us ;
   I know thou livest, and thou lovest me ;
And yet I wish some white ship would come sailing
   Across the ocean, bearing word from thee.

The dead-calm awes me with its awful stillness.
   No anxious doubts or fears disturb my breast ;
I only ask some little wave of language,
   To stir this vast infinitude of rest.

I am oppressed with this great sense of loving ;
   So much I give, so much receive from thee,
Like subtle incense, rising from a censer,
   So floats the fragrance of thy love round me.

All speech is poor, and written words unmeaning ;
   Yet such I ask, blown hither by some wind,
To give relief to this too perfect knowledge,
   The Silence so impresses on my mind.

How poor the love that needeth word or message,
   To banish doubt or nourish tenderness !
I ask them but to temper love's convictions
   The Silence all too fully doth express.

POEMS OF PASSION

Too deep the language which the spirit utters ;
  Too vast the knowledge which my soul hath stirred ;
Send some white ship across the Sea of Silence
  And interrupt its utterance with a word.

THE CREED

WHOEVER was begotten by pure love,
    And came desired and welcomed into life,
Is of immaculate conception. He
Whose heart is full of tenderness and truth,
Who loves mankind more than he loves himself
And cannot find room in his heart for hate,
May be another Christ. We all may be
The Saviours of the world, if we believe
In the Divinity which dwells in us,
And worship it, and nail our grosser selves,
Our tempers, greeds, and our unworthy aims,
Upon the cross. Who giveth love to all
Pays kindness for unkindness, smiles for frowns,
And lends new courage to each fainting heart,
And strengthens hope and scatters joy abroad,
He too is a Redeemer, Son of God.

MY FRIEND

WHEN first I looked upon the face of Pain,
    I shrunk repelled, as one shrinks from a foe
Who stands with dagger poised, as for a blow.
I was in search of Pleasure and of Gain ;

I turned aside to let him pass : in vain ;
    He looked straight in my eyes and would not go.
    " Shake hands," he said, " our paths are one,
        and so
We must be comrades on the way, 'tis plain."

I felt the firm clasp of his hand on mine ;
    Through all my veins it sent a strengthening glow.
    I straightway linked my arm in his, and lo !
He led me forth to joys almost divine ;
    With God's great truths enriched me in the end,
    And now I hold him as my dearest friend.

ART AND HEART

THOUGH critics may bow to art, and I am its own
        true lover,
It is not art, but heart, which wins the wide world
    over.

Though smooth be the heartless prayer, no ear in Heaven
    will mind it,
And the finest phrase falls dead, if there is no feeling
    behind it

Though perfect the player's touch, little if any he
    sways us,
Unless we feel his heart throb through the music he
    plays us.

POEMS OF PASSION

Though the poet may spend his life in skilfully round-
  ing a measure,
Unless he writes from a full warm heart, he gives us
  little pleasure.

So it is not the speech which tells, but the impulse
  which goes with the saying,
And it is not the words of the prayer, but the yearning
  back of the praying.

It is not the artist's skill, which into our soul comes
  stealing
With a joy that is almost pain, but it is the player's
  feeling.

And it is not the poet's song, though sweeter than sweet
  bells chiming,
Which thrills us through and through, but the heart
  which beats under the rhyming.

And therefore I say again, though I am art's own
  true lover,
That it is not art, but heart, which wins the wide world
  over.

AS BY FIRE

SOMETIMES I feel so passionate a yearning
  For spiritual perfection here below,
This vigorous frame with healthful fervour burning,
  Seems my determined foe.

ELLA WHEELER WILCOX

So actively it makes a stern resistance,
  So cruelly sometimes it wages war
Against a wholly spiritual existence
  Which I am striving for.

It interrupts my soul's intense devotions,
  Some hope it strangles of divinest birth,
With a swift rush of violent emotions
  Which link me to the earth.

It is as if two mortal foes contended
  Within my bosom in a deadly strife,
One for the loftier aims for souls intended,
  One for the earthly life.

And yet I know this very war within me,
  Which brings out all my will-power and control,
This very conflict at the last shall win me
  The loved and longed-for goal.

The very fire which seems sometimes so cruel
  Is the white light, that shows me my own strength.
A furnace, fed by the divinest fuel,
  It may become at length.

Ah! when in the immortal ranks enlisted,
  I sometimes wonder if we shall not find
That not by deeds, but by what we've resisted,
  Our places are assigned.

POEMS OF PASSION

RESPONSE

I SAID this morning, as I leaned and threw
    My shutters open to the Spring's surprise,
" Tell me, O Earth, how is it that in you
    Year after year the same fresh feelings rise ?
How do you keep your young exultant glee ?
No more those sweet emotions come to me.

" I note through all your fissures, how the tide
    Of healthful life goes leaping as of old.
Your royal dawns retain their pomp and pride ;
    Your sunsets lose no atom of their gold.
How can this wonder be ? "   My soul's fine ear
Leaned, listening, till a small voice answered near—

" My days lapse never over into night ;
    My nights encroach not on the rights of dawn.
I rush not breathless after some delight ;
    I waste no grief for any pleasure gone.
My July noons burn not the entire year.
Heart, hearken well ! "   Yes, yes ; go on ; I hear.

" I do not strive to make my sunsets' gold
    Pave all the dim and distant realms of space.
I do not bid my crimson dawns unfold
    To lend the midnight a fictitious grace.
I break no law, for all God's laws are good.
Heart, hast thou heard ? "   Yes, yes ; and under-
    stood.

ELLA WHEELER WILCOX

LIFE IS TOO SHORT

LIFE is too short for any vain regretting;
Let dead delight bury its dead, I say,
And let us go upon our way forgetting
The joys, and sorrows, of each yesterday.
Between the swift sun's rising and its setting,
We have no time for useless tears or fretting,
Life is too short.

Life is too short for any bitter feeling;
Time is the best avenger if we wait,
The years speed by, and on their wings bear
healing,
We have no room for anything like hate.
This solemn truth the low mounds seem re-
vealing
That thick and fast about our feet are stealing,
Life is too short.

Life is too short for aught but high endeavour,—
Too short for spite, but long enough for love.
And love lives on for ever and for ever,
It links the worlds that circle on above;
'Tis God's first law, the universe's lever,
In His vast realm the radiant souls sigh never
" Life is too short."

POEMS OF PASSION

A SCULPTOR

AS the ambitious sculptor, tireless, lifts
    Chisel and hammer to the block at hand,
  Before my half-formed character I stand
And ply the shining tools of mental gifts.
  I'll cut away a huge, unsightly side
    Of selfishness, and smooth to curves of grace
The angles of ill-temper.
             And no trace
Shall my sure hammer leave of silly pride.
  Chip after chip must fall from vain desires,
    And the sharp corners of my discontent
Be rounded into symmetry, and lent
Great harmony by faith that never tires.
  Unfinished still, I must toil on and on,
    Till the pale critic, Death, shall say, " 'Tis done."

CREATION

THE impulse of all love is to create.
    God was so full of love, in His embrace
  He clasped the empty nothingness of space,
And lo ! the solar system ! High in state
The mighty sun sat, so supreme and great
    With this same essence, one smile of its face
    Brought myriad forms of life forth ; race on race

57

ELLA WHEELER WILCOX

From insects up to men.

                      Through love, not hate,
All that is grand in nature or in art
   Sprang into being. He who would build sublime
   And lasting works, to stand the test of time,
Must inspiration draw from his full heart.
   And he who loveth widely, well and much,
   The secret holds of the true master touch.

SONNET

METHINKS oft-times my heart is like some bee,
      That goes forth through the summer day
        and sings,
   And gathers honey from all growing things
In garden plot, or on the clover lea.
When the long afternoon grows late, and she
   Would seek her hive, she cannot lift her wings,
   So heavily the too sweet burden clings,
From which she would not, and yet would, fly free.
So with my full fond heart ; for when it tries
   To lift itself to peace-crowned heights, above
   The common way where countless feet have trod
Lo ! then, this burden of dear human ties,
   This growing weight of precious earthly love,
   Binds down the spirit that would soar to God.

MOCKERY

WHY do we grudge our sweets so to the living,
   Who, God knows, find at best too much of gall ;
And then with generous, open hands kneel, giving
   Unto the dead our all ?

Why do we pierce the warm heart's sin or sorrow,
   With idle jests, or scorn, or cruel sneers,
And when it cannot know, on some to-morrow,
   Speak of its woe through tears ?

What do the dead care for the tender token—
   The love, the praise, the floral offerings ?
But palpitating, living hearts are broken
   For want of just these things.

REGRET

THERE is a haunting phantom called Regret,
   A shadowy creature robed somewhat like Woe,
   But fairer in the face, whom all men know
By her sad mien, and eyes for ever wet.
No heart would seek her ; but once having met
   All take her by the hand, and to and fro
   They wander through those paths of long ago—
Those hallowed ways 'twere wiser to forget.

ELLA WHEELER WILCOX

One day she led me to that lost land's gate
  And bade me enter ; but I answered " No !
I will pass on with my bold comrade Fate ;
  I have no tears to waste on thee—no time—
  My strength I hoard for heights I hope to climb ;
No friend art thou, for souls that would be great."

POEMS OF PLEASURE

SURRENDER

LOVE, when we met, 'twas like two planets meeting.
      Strange chaos followed ; body, soul, and heart
Seemed shaken, thrilled, and startled by that greeting,
   Old ties, old dreams, old aims, all torn apart,
And wrenched away, left nothing there the while
But the great shining glory of your smile.

I knew no past ; 'twas all a blurred, bleak waste ;
   I asked no future ; 'twas a blinding glare.
I only saw the present : as men taste
   Some stimulating wine, and lose all care,
I tasted Love's elixir, and I seemed
Dwelling in some strange land, like one who dreamed.

It was a godlike separate existence ;
   Our world was set apart in some fair clime.
I had no will, no purpose, no resistance ;
   I only knew I loved you for all time.
The earth seemed something foreign and afar,
And we two, sovereigns dwelling in a star !

ELLA WHEELER WILCOX

It is so sad, so strange, I almost doubt
  That all those years *could be,* before we met.
Do you not wish that we could blot them out ?
  Obliterate them wholly, and forget
That we had any part in life until
We clasped each other with Love's rapture thrill ?

My being trembled to its very centre
  At that first kiss.   Cold Reason stood aside
With folded arms to let a grand Love enter
  In my Soul's secret chamber to abide.
Its great High Priest, my first Love and my last,
There on its altar I consumed my past.

And all my life I lay upon its shrine
  The best emotions of my heart and brain,
Whatever gifts and graces may be mine ;
  No secret thought, no memory I retain,
But give them all for dear Love's precious sake ;
Complete surrender of the whole I make.

TWO SINNERS

THERE was a man, it was said one time,
    Who went astray in his youthful prime.
Can the brain keep cool and the heart keep quiet
When the blood is a river that's running riot ?
And boys will be boys the old folks say,
And a man is the better who's had his day.

POEMS OF PLEASURE

The sinner reformed ; and the preacher told
Of the prodigal son who came back to the fold.
And Christian people threw open the door,
With a warmer welcome than ever before.
Wealth and honour were his to command,
And a spotless woman gave him her hand.
And the world strewed their pathway with blossoms
    abloom,
Crying " God bless ladye, and God bless groom ! "

There was a maiden who went astray
In the golden dawn of her life's young day.
She had more passion and heart than head,
And she followed blindly where fond Love led.
And Love unchecked is a dangerous guide
To wander at will by a fair girl's side.

The woman repented and turned from sin,
But no door opened to let her in.
The preacher prayed that she might be forgiven,
But told her to look for mercy—in Heaven.
For this is the law of the earth, we know :
That the woman is stoned, while the man may go.

A brave man wedded her after all,
But the world said, frowning, " We shall not call."

ELLA WHEELER WILCOX

SECRET THOUGHTS

I HOLD it true that thoughts are things
   Endowed with bodies, breath, and wings,
And that we send them forth to fill
The world with good results—or ill.

That which we call our secret thought
Speeds to the earth's remotest spot,
And leaves its blessings or its woes
Like tracks behind it as it goes.

It is God's law. Remember it
In your still chamber as you sit
With thoughts you would not dare have known,
And yet made comrades when alone.

These thoughts have life ; and they will fly
And leave their impress by and by,
Like some marsh breeze, whose poisoned breath
Breathes into homes its fevered breath.

And after you have quite forgot
Or all outgrown some vanished thought,
Back to your mind to make its home,
A dove or raven, it will come.

Then let your secret thoughts be fair ;
They have a vital part and share
In shaping worlds and moulding fate—
God's system is so intricate.

POEMS OF PLEASURE

THERE COMES A TIME

THERE comes a time to every mortal being,
  What'er his station or his lot in life,
When his sad soul yearns for the final freeing
  From all this jarring and unceasing strife.

There comes a time, when, having lost its savour,
  The salt of wealth is worthless ; when the mind
Grows wearied with the world's capricious favour,
  And sighs for something that it cannot find.

There comes a time, when, though kind friends are
    thronging,
  About our pathway with sweet acts of grace,
We feel a vast and overwhelming longing
  For something that we cannot name or place.

There comes a time, when, with earth's best love by us,
  To feed the heart's great hunger and desire,
We find not even this can satisfy us ;
  The soul within us cries for something higher.

What greater proof need we that we inherit
  A life immortal in another sphere ?
It is the homesick longing of the spirit
  That cannot find its satisfaction here.

ELLA WHEELER WILCOX

NECESSITY

NECESSITY, whom long I deemed my foe,
   Thou cold, unsmiling, and hard-visaged dame,
Now I no longer see thy face, I know
   Thou wert my friend beyond reproach or blame.

My best achievements and the fairest flights
   Of my winged fancy were inspired by thee ;
Thy stern voice stirred me to the mountain heights ;
   Thy importunings bade me do and be.

But for thy breath, the spark of living fire
   Within me might have smouldered out at length ;
But for thy lash which would not let me tire,
   I never would have measured my own strength.

But for thine oft-times merciless control
   Upon my life, that nerved me past despair,
I never should have dug deep in my soul
   And found the mine of treasures hidden there.

And though we walk divided pathways now,
   And I no more may see thee, to the end,
I weave this little chaplet for thy brow,
   That other hearts may know, and hail thee friend.

THE WAY OF IT

THIS is the way of it, wide world over,
  One is beloved, and one is the lover,
One gives and the other receives.
One lavishes all in a wild emotion,
One offers a smile for a life's devotion,
  One hopes and the other believes,
One lies awake in the night to weep
And the other drifts off in a sweet sound sleep.

One soul is aflame with a godlike passion,
One plays with love in an idler's fashion,
  One speaks and the other hears.
One sobs " I love you," and wet eyes show it,
And one laughs lightly, and says " I know it,"
  With smiles for the other's tears.
One lives for the other and nothing beside,
And the other remembers the world is wide.

This is the way of it, sad earth over,
The heart that breaks is the heart of the lover,
  And the other learns to forget.
" For what is the use of endless sorrow ?
Though the sun goes down, it will rise to-morrow ;
  And life is not over yet."
Oh ! I know this truth, if I know no other,
That passionate Love is Pain's own mother.

ELLA WHEELER WILCOX

ANGEL OR DEMON

YOU call me an angel of love and of light,
    A being of goodness and heavenly fire,
Sent out from God's kingdom to guide you aright,
    In paths where your spirit may mount and aspire.
You say that I glow like a star on its course,
Like a ray from the altar, a spark from the source.

Now list to my answer; let all the world hear it,
    I speak unafraid what I know to be true :—
A pure, faithful love is the creative spirit
    Which makes women angels ! I live but in you.
We are bound soul to soul by life's holiest laws ;
If I am an Angel—why, you are the cause.

As my ship skims the sea, I look up from the deck,
    Fair, firm at the wheel shines Love's beautiful form,
And shall I curse the barque that last night went to
        wreck,
    By the pilot abandoned to darkness and storm ?
My craft is no stauncher, she too had been lost—
Had the wheelman deserted, or slept at his post.

I laid down the wealth of my soul at your feet
    (Some woman does this for some man every day).
No desperate creature who walks in the street
    Has a wickeder heart than I might have, I say,
Had you wantonly misused the treasures you won,
As so many men with heart riches have done.

POEMS OF PLEASURE

This fire from God's altar, this holy love-flame
    That burns like sweet incense for ever for you,
Might now be a wild conflagration of shame,
    Had you tortured my heart, or been base or untrue.
For angels and devils are cast in one mould,
Till love guides them upward, or downward, I hold.

I tell you the women who make fervent wives
    And sweet tender mothers, had Fate been less fair,
Are the women who might have abandoned their lives
    To the madness that springs from and ends in despair.
As the fire on the hearth which sheds brightness around,
Neglected, may level the walls to the ground.

The world makes grave errors in judging these things,
    Great good and great evil are born in one breast.
Love horns us and hoofs us—or gives us our wings,
    And the best could be worst, as the worst could be best.
You must thank your own worth for what I grew to be,
For the demon lurked under the angel in me.

BLASÉ

THE world has outlived all its passion,
    Its men are inane and blasé,
Its women mere puppets of fashion :
    Life now is a comedy play.
Our Abélard sighs for a season,
    Then yields with decorum to fate,
Our Héloïse listens to reason,
    And seeks a new mate.

ELLA WHEELER WILCOX

Our Romeo's flippant emotion
  Grows pale as the summer grows old ;
Our Juliet proves her devotion
  By clasping—a cup filled with gold.
Vain Antony boasts of his favours
  From fair Cleopatra the frail,
And the death of the sorceress savours
  Less of asps than of ale.

With the march of bold civilisation
  Great loves and great faiths are down-trod,
They belonged to an era and nation
  All fresh with the imprint of God.
High culture emasculates feeling,
  The over-taught brain robs the heart,
And the shrine now where mortals are kneeling
  Is a commonplace mart.

Our effeminate fathers and brothers
  Keep carefully out of life's storm,
From the lady-like minds of our mothers
  We are taught that to feel is " bad form,"
Our worshippers now and our lovers
  Are calmly devout with their brains,
And we laugh at the man who discovers
  Warm blood in his veins.

But you, O twin souls, passion-mated,
  Who love as the gods loved of old,

POEMS OF PLEASURE

What blundering destiny fated
    Your lives to be cast in this mould ?
Like a lurid volcanic upheaval,
    In pastures prosaic and grey,
You seem with your fervours primeval,
    Among us to-day.

You dropped from some planet of splendour,
    Perhaps as it circled afar,
And your constancy, swerveless and tender,
    You learned from the course of that star.
Fly back to its bosom, I warn you—
    As back to the ark flew the dove—
The minions of earth will but scorn you,
    Because you can love.

THREE AND ONE

SOMETIMES she seems so helpless and so mild,
        So full of sweet unreason and so weak,
    So prone to some capricious whim or freak ;
Now gay, now tearful, and now anger-wild,
By her strange moods of waywardness beguiled
    And entertained, I stroke her pretty cheek,
    And soothing words of peace and comfort speak ;
And love her as a father loves a child.

ELLA WHEELER WILCOX

Sometimes when I am troubled and sore pressed
  On every side by fast-advancing care,
  She rises up with such majestic air,
I deem her some Olympian goddess-guest,
Who brings my heart new courage, hope, and rest ;
  In her brave eyes dwells balm for my despair,
  And then I seem, while fondly gazing there,
A loving child upon my mother's breast.

Again, when her warm veins are full of life,
  And youth's volcanic tidal wave of fire
  Sends the swift mercury of her pulses higher,
Her beauty stirs my heart to maddening strife,
And all the tiger in my blood is rife ;
  I love her with a lover's fierce desire,
  And find in her my dream, complete, entire,
Child, Mother, Mistress—all in one word—Wife.

INBORN

AS long as men have eyes wherewith to gaze,
    As long as men have eyes,
The sight of beauty to their sense shall be
As mighty winds are to a sleeping sea
    When stormy billows rise.
And beauty's smile shall stir youth's ardent blood
As rays of sunlight burst the swelling bud ;
    As long as men have eyes wherewith to gaze.

72

POEMS OF PLEASURE

As long as men have words wherewith to praise,
    As long as men have words,
They shall describe the softly-moulded breast,
Where Love and Pleasure make their downy nest,
    Like little singing birds ;
And lovely limbs, and lips of luscious fire,
Shall be the theme of many a poet's lyre,
    As long as men have words wherewith to praise.

As long as men have hearts that long for homes,
    As long as men have hearts,
Hid often like the acorn in the earth,
Their inborn love of noble woman's worth,
    Beyond all beauty's arts,
Shall stem the sensuous current of desire,
And urge the world's best thought to something higher,
    As long as men have hearts that long for homes.

TWO PRAYERS

HIS

DEAR, when you lift your gentle heart in prayer,
    Ask God to send his angel Death to me
Long ere he comes to you, if that may be.
I would dwell with you in that new life there,
But having, manlike, sinned, I must prepare,
    By sad probation, ere I hope to see
    Those upper realms which are at once thrown free

73

ELLA WHEELER WILCOX

To sweet, white souls like yours, unstained and fair.
Time is so brief on earth, I well might spare
   A few short years, if so I could atone
   For my marred past, ere you are called above.
My soul would glory in its own despair,
   Till purified I met you at God's throne,
   And entered on Eternities of Love.

HERS

Nay, Love, not so I frame my prayer to God;
   I want you close beside me to the end;
   If it could be, I would have Him send
A simultaneous death, and let one sod
Cover our two hushed hearts. If you have trod
   Paths strange to me on earth, oh, let me wend
   My way with yours hereafter; let me blend
My tears with yours beneath the chastening rod.
If you must pay the penalty for sin,
   In vales of darkness, ere you pass on higher,
   I will petition God to let me go.
I would not wait on earth, nor enter in
   To any joys before you. I desire
   No glory greater than to share your woe.

LOVE MUCH

LOVE much.   Earth has enough of bitter in it;
      Cast sweets into its cup whene'er you can.
No heart so hard, but love at last may win it;
   Love is the grand primeval cause of man;
   All hate is foreign to the first great plan.

Love much.   Your heart will be led out to slaughter,
   On altars built of envy and deceit.
Love on, love on! 'tis bread upon the water;
   It shall be cast in loaves yet at your feet,
   Unleavened manna, most divinely sweet.

Love much.   Your faith will be dethroned and shaken,
   Your trust betrayed by many a fair, false lure.
Remount your faith, and let new trusts awaken.
   Though clouds obscure them, yet the stars are pure;
   Love is a vital force and must endure.

Love much.   Men's souls contract with cold suspicion,
   Shine on them with warm love, and they expand.
'Tis love, not creeds, that from a low condition
   Lead mankind up to heights supreme and grand.
   Oh, that the world could see and understand!

ELLA WHEELER WILCOX

Love much.   There is no waste in freely giving ;
  More blessed is it, even, than to receive.
He who loves much, alone finds life worth living ;
  Love on, through doubt and darkness ; and believe
  There is no thing which Love may not achieve.

ONE OF US TWO

THE day will dawn when one of us shall hearken
  In vain to hear a voice that has grown dumb.
And morns will fade, noons pale, and shadows darken,
  While sad eyes watch for feet that never come.

One of us two must sometime face existence
  Alone with memories that but sharpen pain.
And these sweet days shall shine back in the distance,
  Like dreams of summer dawns, in nights of rain.

One of us two, with tortured heart half broken,
  Shall read long-treasured letters through salt tears,
Shall kiss with anguished lips each cherished token
  That speaks of these love-crowned, delicious years.

One of us two shall find all light, all beauty,
  All joy on earth, a tale for ever done ;
Shall know henceforth that life means only duty.
  Oh, God ! Oh, God ! have pity on that one.

POEMS OF PLEASURE

DESIRE

NO joy for which thy hungering heart has panted,
  No hope it cherishes through waiting years,
But, if thou dost deserve it, shall be granted—
  For with each passionate wish the blessing nears.

Tune up the fine, strong instrument of thy being
  To chord with thy dear hope, and do not tire.
When both in key and rhythm are agreeing,
  Lo ! thou shalt kiss the lips of thy desire.

The thing thou cravest so waits in the distance,
  Wrapt in the silences, unseen and dumb :
Essential to thy soul and thy existence—
  Live worthy of it—call, and it shall come.

DEATHLESS

THERE lies in the centre of each man's heart
  A longing and love for the good and pure ;
And if but an atom, or larger part,
  I tell you this shall endure—endure—
After the body has gone to decay—
Yea, after the world has passed away.

ELLA WHEELER WILCOX

The longer I live and the more I see
    Of the struggle of souls toward the heights above,
The stronger this truth comes home to me :
    That the Universe rests on the shoulders of love ;
A love so limitless, deep, and broad,
That men have renamed it and called it—God.

And nothing that ever was born or evolved,
    Nothing created by light or force,
But deep in its system there lies dissolved
    A shining drop from the Great Love Source ;
A shining drop that shall live for aye—
Though kingdoms may perish and stars decay.

THE FAULT OF THE AGE

THE fault of the age is a mad endeavour
    To leap to heights that were made to climb :
By a burst of strength, of a thought most clever,
    We plan to forestall and outwit Time.

We scorn to wait for the thing worth having ;
    We want high noon at the day's dim dawn ;
We find no pleasure in toiling and saving,
    As our forefathers did in the old times gone.

We force our roses, before their season,
    To bloom and blossom for us to wear ;
And then we wonder and ask the reason
    Why perfect buds are so few and *rare*.

POEMS OF PLEASURE

We crave the gain, but despise the getting ;
   We want wealth—not as reward but dower ;
And the strength that is wasted in useless fretting
   Would fell a forest or build a tower.

To covet the prize, yet to shrink from the winning ;
   To thirst for glory, yet fear to fight ;
Why, what can it lead to at last, but sinning,
   To mental languor and moral blight ?

Better the old slow way of striving,
   And counting small gains when the year is done,
Than to use our force and our strength in contriving,
   And to grasp for pleasure we have not won.

ARTIST AND MAN

MAKE thy life better than thy work. Too oft
   Our artists spend their skill in rounding soft,
Fair curves upon their statues, while the rough
And ragged edges of the unhewn stuff
In their own natures startle and offend
The eye of critic and the heart of friend.

If in thy too brief day thou must neglect
Thy labour or thy life, let men detect
Flaws in thy work ! while their most searching gaze
Can fall on nothing which they may not praise
In thy well-chiselled character. The Man
Should not be shadowed by the Artisan !

ELLA WHEELER WILCOX

WHATEVER IS—IS BEST

I KNOW as my life grows older
  And mine eyes have clearer sight—
That under each rank wrong, somewhere
  There lies the root of Right ;
That each sorrow has its purpose,
  By the sorrowing oft unguessed,
But as sure as the sun brings morning,
  Whatever is—is best.

I know that each sinful action
  As sure as the night brings shade,
Is somewhere, some time punished,
  Tho' the hour be long delayed.
I know that the soul is aided
  Sometimes by the heart's unrest,
And to grow means often to suffer—
  But whatever is—is best.

I know there are no errors
  In the great Eternal plan,
And all things work together
  For the final good of man.
And I know when my soul speeds onward
  In its grand Eternal quest,
I shall say as I look back earthward
  Whatever is—is best.

PEACE OF THE GOAL

FROM the soul of a man who was homeless
    Came the deathless song of home ;
And the praises of rest are chanted best
   By those who are forced to roam.

In a time of fast and hunger
   We can talk over feasts divine ;
But the banquet done, why, where is the one
   Who can tell you the taste of the wine ?

We think of the mountain's grandeur
   As we walk in the heat afar—
But when we sit in the shadows of it
   We think how at rest we are.

With the voice of the craving passions
   We can picture a love to come.
But the heart once filled, lo ! the voice is stilled,
   And we stand in the silence—dumb.

ELLA WHEELER WILCOX

ACHIEVEMENT

TRUST in thine own untried capacity
    As thou wouldst trust in God Himself. Thy soul
Is but an emanation from the whole.
Thou dost not dream what forces lie in thee,
Vast and unfathomed as the grandest sea.
    Thy silent mind o'er diamond caves may roll,
    Go seek them—but let pilot will control
Those passions which thy favouring winds can be.
No man shall place a limit in thy strength ;
    Such triumphs as no mortal ever gained
    May yet be thine if thou wilt but believe
In thy Creator and thyself. At length
    Some feet will tread all heights now unattained—
    Why not thine own ? Press on ! achieve ! achieve !

BELIEF

THE pain we have to suffer seems so broad,
    Set side-by-side with this life's narrow span,
We need no greater evidence that God
    Has some diviner destiny for man.

He would not deem it worth His while to send
    Such crushing sorrows as pursue us here,
Unless beyond this fleeting journey's end
    Our chastened spirits found another sphere

Babyland

POEMS OF PLEASURE

So small this world ! So vast its agonies !
 A future life is needed to adjust
These ill-proportioned, wide discrepancies
 Between the spirit and its frame of dust.

So when my soul writhes with some aching grief,
 And all my heart-strings tremble at the strain,
My Reason lends new courage to Belief,
 And all God's hidden purposes seem plain.

BABYLAND

HAVE you heard of the Valley of Babyland,
 The realm where the dear little darlings stay,
Till the kind storks go, as all men know,
 And oh ! so tenderly bring them away ?
The paths are winding and past all finding,
 By all save the storks who understand
The gates and the highways and the intricate byways
      That lead to Babyland.

All over the Valley of Babyland
 Sweet flowers bloom in the soft green moss ;
And under the ferns fair, and under the plants there,
 Lie little heads like spools of floss.
With a soothing number the river of slumber
 Flows o'er a bedway of silver sand ;
And angels are keeping watch o'er the sleeping
      Babes of Babyland.

ELLA WHEELER WILCOX

The path to the Valley of Babyland
　　Only the kingly, kind storks know ;
If they fly over mountains, or wade through fountains,
　　No man sees them come or go.
But an angel maybe, who guards some baby,
　　Or a fairy perhaps, with her magic wand,
Brings them straightway to the wonderful gateway
　　　　　　　　　　　That leads to Babyland.

And there in the Valley of Babyland,
　　Under the mosses and leaves and ferns,
Like an unfledged starling they find the darling,
　　For whom the heart of a mother yearns ;
And they lift him lightly, and snug him tightly
　　In feathers soft as a lady's hand ;
And off with a rockaway step they walk away
　　　　　　　　　　　Out of Babyland.

As they go from the Valley of Babyland,
　　Forth into the world of great unrest,
Sometimes in weeping he wakes from sleeping
　　Before he reaches his mother's breast.
Ah ! how she blesses him, how she caresses him,
　　Bonniest bird in the bright home band
That o'er land and water, the kind stork brought her
　　　　　　　　　　　From far-off Babyland.

WHAT LOVE IS

LOVE is the centre and circumference ;
  The cause and aim of all things—'tis the key
To joy and sorrow, and the recompense
  For all the ills that have been, or may be.

Love is as bitter as the dregs of sin,
  As sweet as clover-honey in its cell ;
Love is the password whereby souls get in
  To Heaven—the gate that leads, sometimes, to Hell.

Love is the crown that glorifies ; the curse
  That brands and burdens ; it is life and death ;
It is the great law of the universe ;
  And nothing can exist without its breath.

Love is the impulse which directs the world,
  And all things know it and obey its power.
Man, in the maelstrom of his passions whirled ;
  The bee that takes the pollen to the flower ;

The earth, uplifting her bare, pulsing breast
  To fervent kisses of the amorous sun ;—
Each but obeys creative Love's behest,
  Which everywhere instinctively is done.

ELLA WHEELER WILCOX

Love is the only thing that pays for birth,
   Or makes death welcome. Oh, dear God above,
This beautiful but sad, perplexing earth,
   Pity the hearts that know—or know not—Love!

CONSTANCY

I WILL be true.   Mad stars forsake their courses,
   And, led by reckless meteors, turn away
From paths appointed by Eternal Forces ;
   But my fixed heart shall never go astray
Like those calm worlds whose sun-directed motion
   Is undisturbed by strife of wind or sea,
So shall my swerveless and serene devotion
   Sweep on for ever, loyal unto thee.

I will be true.   The fickle tide, divided
   Between two wooing shores, in wild unrest
May to and fro shift always undecided ;
   Not so the tide of Passion in my breast.
With the grand surge of some resistless river,
   That hurries on, past mountain, vale, and sea,
Unto the main, its waters to deliver,
   So my full heart keeps all its wealth for thee.

I will be true.   Light barques may be belated,
   Or turned aside by every breeze at play,
While sturdy ships, well-manned and richly freighted,
   With fair sails flying, anchor safe in bay.

POEMS OF PLEASURE

Like some firm rock, that, steadfast and unshaken,
  Stands all unmoved when ebbing billows flee,
So would my heart stand, faithful if forsaken—
  I will be true, though thou art false to me.

RESOLVE

AS the dead year is clasped by a dead December,
    So let your dead sins with your dead days lie.
A new life is yours, and a new hope. Remember,
  We build our own ladders to climb to the sky.
Stand out in the sunlight of Promise, forgetting
  Whatever the Past held of sorrow or wrong.
We waste half our strength in a useless regretting ;
  We sit by old tombs in the dark too long.

Have you missed in your aim ? Well, the mark is still
    shining.
  Did you faint in the race ? Well, take breath for the
    next.
Did the clouds drive you back ? But see yonder their
    lining.
  Were you tempted and fell ? Let it serve for a text.
As each year hurries by let it join that procession
  Of skeleton shapes that march down to the Past,
While you take your place in the line of Progression,
  With your eyes on the heavens, your face to the
    blast.

ELLA WHEELER WILCOX

I tell you the future can hold no terrors
  For any sad soul while the stars revolve,
If he will stand firm on the grave of his errors,
  And instead of regretting, resolve, resolve.
It is never too late to begin rebuilding,
  Though all into ruins your life seems hurled,
For see how the light of the New Year is gilding
  The wan, worn face of the bruised old world.

OPTIMISM

I'M no reformer ; for I see more light
    Than darkness in the world ; mine eyes are quick
To catch the first dim radiance of the dawn,
And slow to note the cloud that threatens storm.
The fragrance and the beauty of the rose
Delight me so, slight thought I give its thorn ;
And the sweet music of the lark's clear song
Stays longer with me than the night hawk's cry.
And e'en in this great throe of pain called Life,
I find a rapture linked with each despair,
Well worth the price of Anguish. I detect
More good than evil in humanity.
Love lights more fires than hate extinguishes,
And men grow better as the world grows old.

The Lady of Tears.

POEMS OF PLEASURE

ANSWERED PRAYERS

I PRAYED for riches, and achieved success;
　　All that I touched turned into gold.　Alas!
My cares were greater and my peace was less,
　　When that wish came to pass.

I prayed for glory, and I heard my name
　　Sung by sweet children and by hoary men.
But ah! the hurts—the hurts that come with fame!
　　I was not happy then.

I prayed for Love, and had my heart's desire.
　　Through quivering heart and body, and through brain
There swept the flame of its devouring fire,
　　And but the scars remain.

I prayed for a contented mind.　At length
　　Great light upon my darkened spirit burst.
Great peace fell on me also, and great strength—
　　Oh, had that prayer been first!

THE LADY OF TEARS

THROUGH valley and hamlet and city,
　　Wherever humanity dwells,
With a heart full of infinite pity,
　　A breast that with sympathy swells,

ELLA WHEELER WILCOX

She walks in her beauty immortal.
  Each household grows sad as she nears,
But she crosses at length every portal,
  The mystical Lady of Tears.

If never this vision of sorrow
  Has shadowed your life in the past,
You will meet her, I know, some to-morrow—
  She visits all hearthstones at last.
To hovel, and cottage, and palace,
  To servant and king she appears,
And offers the gall of her chalice—
  The unwelcome Lady of Tears.

To the eyes that have smiled but in gladness,
  To the souls that have basked in the sun,
She seems, in her garments of sadness,
  A creature to dread and to shun.
And lips that have drunk but of pleasure
  Grow pallid and tremble with fears,
As she portions the gall from her measure,
  The merciless Lady of Tears.

But in midnight, lone hearts that are quaking,
  With the agonised numbness of grief,
Are saved from the torture of breaking,
  By her bitter-sweet draught of relief.
Oh, then do all graces enfold her ;
  Like the goddess she looks and appears,
And the eyes overflow that behold her—
  The beautiful Lady of Tears.

POEMS OF PLEASURE

Though she turns to lamenting all laughter,
　Though she gives us despair for delight,
Life holds a new meaning thereafter
　For those who will greet her aright.
They stretch out their hands to each other,
　For Sorrow unites and endears,
The children of one tender mother—
　The sweet, blessed Lady of Tears.

THE ROOM BENEATH THE RAFTERS

SOMETIMES when I have dropped to sleep,
　Draped in a soft luxurious gloom,
Across my drowsing mind will creep
　The memory of another room,
Where resinous knots in roof-boards made
A frescoing of light and shade,
And sighing poplars brushed their leaves
Against the humbly sloping eaves.

Again I fancy, in my dreams,
　I'm lying in my trundle bed;
I seem to see the bare old beams
　And unhewn rafters overhead.
The mud-wasp's shrill falsetto hum
I hear again, and see him come
Forth from his dark-walled hanging house,
Dressed in his black and yellow blouse.

ELLA WHEELER WILCOX

There, summer dawns, in sleep I stirred,
  And wove into my fair dream's woof
The chattering of a martin bird,
  Or rain-drops pattering on the roof.
Or, half awake, and half in fear,
I saw the spider spinning near
His pretty castle, where the fly
Should come to ruin by and by.

And there I fashioned from my brain
  Youth's shining structures in the air.
I did not wholly build in vain,
  For some were lasting, firm and fair,
And I am one who lives to say
My life has held more gold than grey,
And that the splendour of the real
Surpassed my early dream's ideal.

But still I love to wander back
  To that old time, and that old place ;
To thread my way o'er Memory's track,
  And catch the early morning grace,
In that quaint room beneath the rafter,
That echoed to my childish laughter ;
To dream again the dreams that grew
More beautiful as they came true.

POEMS OF PLEASURE

ENTRE-ACTE REVERIES

BETWEEN the acts while the orchestra played
    That sweet old waltz with the lilting measure,
I drifted away to a dear dead day,
    When the dance, for me, was the sum of all pleasure;
When my veins were rife with the fever of life,
    When hope ran high as an inswept ocean,
And my heart's great gladness was almost madness,
    As I floated off to the music's motion.

How little I cared for the world outside!
    How little I cared for the dull day after!
The thought of trouble went up like a bubble,
    And burst in a sparkle of mirthful laughter,
Oh! and the beat of it, oh! and the sweet of it—
    Melody, motion, and young blood melted;
The dancers swaying, the players playing,
    The air song-deluged and music-pelted.

I knew no weariness, no, not I—
    My step was as light as the waving grasses
That flutter with ease on the strong-armed breeze,
    As it waltzes over the wild morasses.
Life was all sound and swing; youth was a perfect
    thing;
    Night was the goddess of satisfaction.
Oh, how I tripped away, right to the edge of day!
    Joy lay in motion, and rest lay in action.

ELLA WHEELER WILCOX

I dance no more on the music's wave,
  I yield no more to its wildering power,
That time has flown like a rose that is blown,
  Yet life is a garden for ever in flower,
Though storms of tears have watered the years,
  Between to-day and the day departed,
Though trials have met me, and grief's waves wet me,
  And I have been tired and trouble-hearted.

Though under the sod of a wee green grave,
  A great, sweet hope in darkness perished,
Yet life, to my thinking, is a cup worth drinking,
  A gift to be glad of, and loved, and cherished.
There is deeper pleasure in the slower measure
  That Time's grand orchestra now is playing.
Its mellowed minor is sadder but finer,
  And life grows daily more worth the living.

A PLEA

COLUMBIA, large-hearted and tender,
  Too long for the good of your kin
You have shared your home's comfort and splendour
  With all who have asked to come in.
The smile of your true eyes has lighted
  The way to your wide-open door,
You have held out full hands, and invited
  The beggar to take from your store.

POEMS OF PLEASURE

Your overrun proud sister nations,
  Whose offspring you help them to keep,
Are sending their poorest relations,
  Their unruly vicious black sheep ;
Unwashed and unlettered you take them,
  And lo ! we are pushed from your knee ;
We are governed by laws as they make them,
  We are slaves in the land of the free.

Columbia, you know the devotion
  Of those who have sprung from your soil ;
Shall aliens, born over the ocean,
  Dispute us the fruits of our toil ?
Most noble and gracious of mothers,
  Your children rise up and demand
That you bring us no more foster-brothers,
  To breed discontent in the land.

Be prudent before you are zealous,
  Not generous only—but just.
Our hearts are grown wrathful and jealous
  Toward those who have outraged your trust.
They jostle and crowd in our places,
  They sneer at the comforts you gave.
We say, shut the door in their faces—
  Until they have learned to behave !

In hearts that are greedy and hateful,
  They harbour ill-will and deceit ;
They ask for more favours, ungrateful
  For those you have poured at their feet.

ELLA WHEELER WILCOX

Rise up in your grandeur, and straightway
  Bar out the bold clamouring mass ;
Let sentinels stand at your gateway
  To see who is worthy to pass.

Give first to your own faithful toilers
  The freedom our birthright should claim,
And take from these ruthless despoilers
  The power which they use to our shame.
Columbia, too long you have dallied
  With foes whom you feed from your store ;
It is time that your wardens were rallied
  And stationed outside the locked door.

AN OLD FAN

(TO KITTY. HER REVERIE)

IT is soiled, and quite passé,
  Broken too, and out of fashion,
But it stirs my heart some way,
As I hold it here to-day,
  With a dead year's grace and passion.
    Oh, my pretty fan !

Precious dream and thrilling strain,
  Rise up from that vanished season ;
Back to heart and nerve and brain

Sweeps the joy as keen as pain,
  Joy that asks no cause or reason.
    Oh, my dainty fan !

Hopes that perished in a night
  Gaze at me like spectral faces ;
Grim despair and lost delight,
Sorrow long since gone from sight—
  All are hiding in these laces.
    Oh, my broken fan !

Let us lay the thing away—
  I am sadder now, and older ;
Fled the ball-room and the play—
You have had your foolish day,
  And the night and life are colder.
    Exit—little fan !

A FACE

BETWEEN the curtains of snowy lace,
  Over the way is a baby's face ;
It peeps forth, smiling in merry glee,
  And waves its pink little hand at me.

My heart responds with a lonely cry—
  But in the wonderful By-and-By—
Out from the window of God's " To Be,"
  That other baby shall beckon to me.

ELLA WHEELER WILCOX

That ever-haunting and longed-for face,
  That perfect vision of infant grace,
Shall shine on me in a splendour of light,
  Never to fade from my eager sight.

All that was taken shall be made good;
  All that puzzles me understood;
And the wee white hand that I lost, one day,
  Shall lead me into the Better Way.

NO CLASSES!

NO classes here! Why, that is idle talk,
  The village beau sneers at the country boor;
The importuning mendicants who walk
  Our cities' streets despise the parish poor.

The daily toiler at some noisy loom
  Holds back her garments from the kitchen aid.
Meanwhile the latter leans upon her broom,
  Unconscious of the bow the laundress made.

The grocer's daughter eyes the farmer's lass
  With haughty glances; and the lawyer's wife
Would pay no visits to the trading class,
  If policy were not her creed in life.

"The Grocer's
daughter
eyes the Farmer's
son
With haughty glances'
No Classes!

POEMS OF PLEASURE

The merchant's son nods coldly at the clerk ;
  The proud possessor of a pedigree
Ignores the youth whose father rose by work ;
  The title-seeking maiden scorns all three.

The aristocracy of blood looks down
  Upon the " nouveau riche " ; and in disdain,
The lovers of the intellectual frown
  On both, and worship at the shrine of brain.

" No classes here," the clergyman has said ;
  " We are one family." Yet see his rage
And horror when his favourite son would wed
  Some pure and pretty player on the stage.

It is the vain but natural human way
  Of vaunting our weak selves, our pride, our worth !
Not till the long-delayed millennial day
  Shall we behold " no classes " on God's earth.

A GREY MOOD

AS we hurry away to the end, my friend,
    Of this sad little farce called existence,
We are sure that the future will bring one thing,
  And that is the grave in the distance.

ELLA WHEELER WILCOX

And so when our lives run along all wrong,
    And nothing seems real or certain,
We can comfort ourselves with the thought (or not)
    Of that spectre behind the curtain.

But we haven't much time to repine or whine,
    Or to wound or jostle each other;
And the hour for us each is to-day, I say,
    If we mean to assist a brother.
And there is no pleasure that earth gives birth,
    But the worry it brings is double;
And all that repays for the strife of life
    Is helping some soul in trouble.

I tell you, if I could go back the track
    To my life's morning hour,
I would not set forth seeking name or fame,
    Or that poor bauble called power.
I would be like the sunlight, and live to give;
    I would lend, but I would not borrow;
Nor would I be blind and complain of pain,
    Forgetting the meaning of sorrow.

This world is a vaporous jest at best,
    Tossed off by the gods in laughter;
And a cruel attempt at wit were it,
    If nothing better came after.
It is reeking with hearts that ache and break,
    Which we ought to comfort and strengthen,
As we hurry away to the end, my friend,
    And the shadows behind us lengthen.

THE LOST LAND

THERE is a story of a beauteous land,
    Where fields were fertile and where flowers were
      bright ;
Where tall towers glistened in the morning light,
Where happy children wandered hand in hand,
Where lovers wrote their names upon the sand.
They say it vanished from all human sight,
The hungry sea devoured it in a night.

You doubt the tale ? ah, you will understand ;
For, as men muse upon that fable old,
They give sad credence always at the last,
However they have cavilled at its truth,
When with a tear-dimmed vision they behold,
Swift sinking in the ocean of the Past,
The lovely lost Atlantis of their Youth.

AT AN OLD DRAWER

BEFORE this scarf was faded,
    What hours of mirth it knew !
How gaily it paraded
    For smiling eyes to view !

ELLA WHEELER WILCOX

The days were tinged with glory,
  The nights too quickly sped,
And life was like a story
  Where all the people wed.

Before this rosebud wilted,
  How passionately sweet
The wild waltz swelled and lilted
  In time for flying feet !
How loud the bassoons muttered !
  The horns grew madly shrill ;
And, oh ! the vows lips uttered
  That hearts could not fulfil.

Before this fan was broken,
  Behind its lace and pearl
What whispered words were spoken—
  What hearts were in a whirl !
What homesteads were selected
  In Fancy's realm of Spain !
What castles were erected,
  Without a room for pain !

When this odd glove was mated,
  How thrilling seemed the play !
Maybe our hearts are sated—
  They tire so soon to-day.
Oh, shut away those treasures,
  They speak the dreary truth—
We have outgrown the pleasures
  And keen delights of youth.

The City.

POEMS OF PLEASURE

THE CITY

I OWN the charms of lovely Nature ; still,
    In human nature more delight I find.
Though sweet the murmuring voices of the rill,
    I much prefer the voices of my kind.

I like the roar of cities.   In the mart,
    Where busy toilers strive for place and gain,
I seem to read humanity's great heart,
    And share its hopes, its pleasures, and its pain.

The rush of hurrying trains that cannot wait,
    The tread of myriad feet, all say to me :
" You are the architect of your own fate ;
    Toil on, hope on, and dare to do and be."

I like the jangled music of the loud
    Bold bells ; the whistle's sudden shrill reply ;
And there is inspiration in a crowd—
    A magnetism flashed from eye to eye.

My sorrows all seem lightened, and my joys
    Augmented, when the comrade world walks near ;
Close to mankind my soul best keeps its poise.
Give me the great town's bustle, strife, and noise,
    And let who will, hold Nature's calm more dear.

ELLA WHEELER WILCOX

WOMAN

GIVE us that grand word " woman " once again,
    And let's have done with " lady " : one's a term
Full of fine force, strong, beautiful, and firm,
Fit for the noblest use of tongue or pen ;
And one's a word for lackeys.   One suggests
The Mother, Wife, and Sister !   One the dame
Whose costly robe, mayhap, gives her the name.
One word upon its own strength leans and rests ;
The other minces tiptoe.   Who would be
The perfect woman must grow brave of heart
And broad of soul to play her troubled part
Well in life's drama.   While each day we see
The " perfect lady " skilled in what to do
And what to say, grace in each tone and act
('Tis taught in schools, but needs some native tact),
Yet narrow in her mind as in her shoe.
Give the first place then to the nobler phrase,
And leave the lesser word for lesser praise.

LIFE'S JOURNEY

AS we speed out of youth's sunny station
    The track seems to shine in the light,
But it suddenly shoots over chasms
  Or sinks into tunnels of night.

POEMS OF PLEASURE

And the hearts that were brave in the morning
  Are filled with repining and fears,
As they pause at the City of Sorrow
  Or pass through the Valley of Tears.

But the road of this perilous journey
  The hand of the Master has made ;
With all its discomforts and dangers,
  We need not be sad or afraid.
Paths leading from light into darkness,
  Ways plunging from gloom to despair,
Wind out through the tunnels of midnight
  To fields that are blooming and fair.

Though the rocks and the shadows surround us,
  Though we catch not one gleam of the day,
Above us fair cities are laughing,
  And dipping white feet in some bay.
And always, eternal, for ever,
  Down over the hills in the west,
The last final end of our journey,
  There lies the great Station of Rest.

'Tis the Grand Central point of all railways,
  All roads unite here when they end ;
'Tis the final resort of all tourists,
  All rival lines meet here and blend.
All tickets, all seasons, all passes,
  If stolen or begged for or bought,
On whatever road or division,
  Will bring you at last to this spot.

ELLA WHEELER WILCOX

If you pause at the City of Trouble,
  Or wait in the Valley of Tears,
Be patient, the train will move onward,
  And rush down the track of the years.
Whatever the place is you seek for,
  Whatever your game or your quest,
You shall come at the last with rejoicing
  To the beautiful City of Rest.

You shall store all your baggage of worries,
  You shall feel perfect peace in this realm,
You shall sail with old friends on fair waters,
  With joy and delight at the helm.
You shall wander in cool, fragrant gardens
  With those who have loved you the best,
And the hopes that were lost in life's journey
  You shall find in the City of Rest.

THE ACTOR

OH, man, with your wonderful dower,
  Oh, woman, with genius and grace,
You can teach the whole world with your power,
  If you are but worthy the place.
The stage is a force and a factor
  In moulding the thought of the day,
If only the heart of the actor
  Is high as the theme of the play.

POEMS OF PLEASURE

No discourse or sermon can reach us
  Through feeling to reason like you ;
No author can stir us and teach us
  With lessons as subtle and true.
Your words and your gestures obeying,
  We weep or rejoice with your part,
And the player, behind all his playing,
  He ought to be great as his art.

No matter what rôle you are giving,
  No matter what skill you betray,
The everyday life you are living,
  Is certain to colour the play.
The thoughts we call secret and hidden
  Are creatures of malice, in fact ;
They steal forth unseen and unbidden,
  And permeate motive and act.

The genius that shines like a comet
  Fills only one part of God's plan,
If the lesson the world derives from it
  Is marred by the life of the man.
Be worthy your work if you love it ;
  The king should be fit for the crown ;
Stand high as your art, or above it,
  And make us look up and not down.

ELLA WHEELER WILCOX

NEW YEAR

AS the old year sinks down in Time's ocean,
  Stand ready to launch with the new,
And waste no regrets, no emotion,
  As the masts and the spars pass from view.
Weep not if some treasures go under,
  And sink in the rotten ship's hold,
That blithe bonny barque sailing yonder
  May bring you more wealth than the old.

For the world is for ever improving,
  All the past is not worth one to-day,
And whatever deserves our true loving,
  Is stronger than death or decay.
Old love, was it wasted devotion ?
  Old friends, were they weak or untrue ?
Well, let them sink there in mid-ocean,
  And gaily sail on to the new.

Throw overboard toil misdirected,
  Throw overboard ill-advised hope,
With aims which, your soul has detected,
  Have self as their centre and scope.
Throw overboard useless regretting
  For deeds which you cannot undo,
And learn the great art of forgetting
  Old things which embitter the new.

POEMS OF PLEASURE

Sing who will of dead years departed,
 I shroud them and bid them adieu,
And the song that I sing, happy-hearted,
 Is a song of the glorious new.

NOW

ONE looks behind him to some vanished time
 And says, " Ah, I was happy then, alack !
I did not know it was my life's best prime—
 Oh, if I could go back ! "

Another looks, with eager eyes aglow,
 To some glad day of joy that yet will dawn,
And sighs, " I shall be happy then, I know.
 Oh, let me hurry on."

But I—I look out on my fair To-day ;
 I clasp it close and kiss its radiant brow,
Here with the perfect present let me stay,
 For I am happy now !

PEACE AND LOVE

THERE are two angels, messengers of light,
 Both born of God, who yet are bitterest foes.
No human breast their dual presence knows.

109

ELLA WHEELER WILCOX

As violently opposed as wrong and right,
When one draws near, the other takes swift flight,
    And when one enters, thence the other goes.
    Till mortal life in the immortal flows,
So must these two avoid each other's sight.
Despair and hope may meet within one heart,
The vulture may be comrade to the dove !
Pleasure and Pain swear friendship leal and true :
But till the grave unites them, still apart
Must dwell these angels known as Peace and Love,
For only Death can reconcile the two.

THE INSTRUCTOR

NOT till we meet with Love in all his beauty,
    In all his solemn majesty and worth,
Can we translate the meaning of life's duty,
    Which God oft writes in cipher at our birth.

Not till Love comes in all his strength and terror
    Can we read others' hearts ; not till then know
A wide compassion for all human error,
    Or sound the quivering depths of mortal woe.

Not till we sail with him o'er stormy oceans,
    Have we seen tempests ; hidden in his hand
He holds the keys to all the great emotions ;
    Till he unlocks them, none can understand.

POEMS OF PLEASURE

Not till we walk with him on lofty mountains
  Can we quite measure heights.   And, O sad truth !
When once we drink from his immortal fountains,
  We bid farewell to the light heart of youth.

Thereafter our most perfect day will borrow
  A dimming shadow from some dreaded night ;
So great grows joy it merges into sorrow,
  And evermore pain tinctures our delight.

IMMORTALITY

IMMORTAL life is something to be earned,
    By slow self-conquest, comradeship with Pain,
And patient seeking after higher truths.
We cannot follow our own wayward wills,
And feed our baser appetites, and give
Loose rein to foolish tempers year on year,
And then cry, " Lord, forgive me, I believe ! "
And straightway bathe in glory.   Men must learn
God's system is too grand a thing for that.
The spark divine dwells in our souls, and we
Can fan it to a steady flame of light,
Whose lustre gilds the pathway to the tomb,
And shines on through Eternity, or else,
Neglect it till it glimmers down to Death,
And leaves us but the darkness of the grave.
Each conquered passion feeds the living flame ;
Each well-borne sorrow is a step towards God ;

ELLA WHEELER WILCOX

Faith cannot rescue, and no blood redeem
The soul that will not reason and resolve.
Lean on thyself, yet prop thyself with prayer
(All hope is prayer ; who calls it hope no more,
Sends prayer footsore forth over weary wastes,
While he who calls it prayer gives wings to hope),
And there are spirits, messengers of Love,
Who come at call and fortify our strength.
Make friends with them, and with thine inner self ;
Cast out all envy, bitterness, and hate ;
And keep the mind's fair tabernacle pure.
Shake hands with Pain, give greeting unto Grief,
Those angels in disguise, and thy glad soul
From height to height, from star to shining star,
Shall climb and claim blest immortality.

THE WORLD

WITH noiseless steps good goes its way ;
  The earth shakes under evil's tread.
We hear the uproar, and 'tis said,
The world grows wicked every day.

It is not true. With quiet feet,
  In silence, Virtue sows her seeds ;
  While Sin goes shouting out his deeds,
And echoes listen and repeat.

But surely as the old world moves,
    And circles round the shining sun,
    So surely does God's purpose run,
And all the human race improves.

Despite bold evil's noise and stir,
    Truth's golden harvests ripen fast ;
    The Present far outshines the Past ;
Men's thoughts are higher than they were.

Who runs may read this truth, I say :
    Sin travels in a rumbling car,
    While Virtue soars on like a star—
The world grows better every day.

KEEP OUT OF THE PAST

KEEP out of the Past ! for its highways
    Are damp with malarial gloom ;
Its gardens are sere and its forests are drear,
    And everywhere moulders a tomb.
Who seeks to regain its lost pleasures
    Finds only a rose turned to dust ;
And its storehouse of wonderful treasures
    Are covered and coated with rust.

Keep out of the Past.   It is haunted :
    He who in its avenues gropes
Shall find there the ghost of a joy prized the most,
    And a skeleton throng of dead hopes.

In place of its beautiful rivers,
  Are pools that are stagnant with slime ;
And these graves gleaming white in a phosphoric light, _
  Hide dreams that were slain in their prime.

Keep out of the Past. It is lonely,
  And barren and bleak to the view ;
Its fires have grown cold, and its stories are old—
  Turn, turn to the Present—the New ;
To-day leads you up to the hill-tops
  That are kissed by the radiant sun,
To-day shows no tomb, life's hopes are in bloom,
  And to-day holds a prize to be won.

DISTRUST

DISTRUST that man who tells you to distrust ;
  He takes the measure of his own small soul,
And thinks the world no larger. He who prates
Of human nature's baseness and deceit
Looks in the mirror of his heart, and sees
His kind therein reflected. Or perchance
The honeyed wine of life was turned to gall
By sorrow's hand, which brimmed his cup with tears,
And made all things seem bitter to his taste.
Give him compassion ! But be not afraid
Of nectared Love, or Friendship's strengthening draught,
Nor think a poison underlies their sweets.
Look through true eyes—you will discover truth ;
Suspect suspicion, and doubt only doubt.

THE SOUL'S FAREWELL TO
THE BODY

SO we must part for ever ; and although
    I long have beat my wings and cried to go,
Free from your narrow limiting control,
Forth into space, the true home of the soul.

' Yet now, yet now that hour is drawing near,
I pause reluctant, finding you so dear.
All joys await me in the realm of God—
Must you, my comrade, moulder in the sod ?

I was your captive, yet you were my slave :
Your prisoner, yet obedience you gave
To all my earnest wishes and commands.
Now to the worm I leave those willing hands

That toiled for me or held the books I read,
Those feet that trod where'er I wished to tread,
Those arms that clasped my dear ones, and the breast
On which one loved and loving heart found rest,

Those lips through which my prayers to God have risen,
Those eyes that were the windows to my prison.
From these, all these, Death's Angel bids me sever ;
Dear Comrade Body, fare thee well for ever !

ELLA WHEELER WILCOX

I go to my inheritance, and go
With joy that only the freed soul can know ;
Yet in my spirit wanderings I trust
I may sometimes pause near your sacred dust.

REFUTED

" Anticipation is sweeter than realisation "

IT may be, yet I have not found it so.
　In those first golden dreams of future fame
　I did not find such happiness as came
When toil was crowned with triumph.　Now I know
My words have recognition, and will go
　Straight to some listening heart, my early aim,
　To win the idle glory of a name,
Pales like a candle in the noonday's glow.

So with the deeper joys of which I dreamed :
　Life yields more rapture than did childhood's fancies,
　And each year brings more pleasure than I waited.
Friendship proves truer than of old it seemed,
　And, all beyond youth's passion-hued romances,
　Love is more perfect than anticipated.

POEMS OF LIFE

LIFE

I FEEL the great immensity of life.
  All little aims slip from me, and I reach
My yearning soul toward the Infinite.

As when a mighty forest, whose green leaves
Have shut it in, and made it seem a bower
For lovers'-secrets, or for children's sports,
Casts all its clustering foliage to the winds,
And lets the eye behold it, limitless,
And full of winding mysteries of ways :
So now with life that reaches out before,
And borders on the unexplained Beyond
I see the stars above me, world on world :
I hear the awful language of all Space ;
I feel the distant surging of great seas,
That hide the secrets of the Universe
In their eternal bosoms ; and I know
That I am but an atom of the Whole.

ELLA WHEELER WILCOX

A SONG OF LIFE

IN the rapture of life and of living,
  I lift up my heart and rejoice,
And I thank the great Giver for giving
  The soul of my gladness a voice.
In the glow of the glorious weather,
  In the sweet-scented sensuous air,
My burdens seem light as a feather—
  They are nothing to bear.

In the strength and the glory of power,
  In the pride and the pleasure of wealth,
(For who dares dispute me my dower
  Of talents and youth-time and health ?)
I can laugh at the world and its sages—
  I am greater than seers who are sad,
For he is most wise in all ages
  Who knows how to be glad.

I lift up my eyes to Apollo,
  The god of the beautiful days,
And my spirit soars off like a swallow
  And is lost in the light of its rays.
Are you troubled and sad ? I beseech you
  Come out of the shadows of strife—
Come out in the sun while I teach you
  The secret of life.

POEMS OF LIFE

Come out of the world—come above it—
    Up over its crosses and graves.
Though the green earth is fair and I love it,
    We must love it as masters, not slaves.
Come up where the dust never rises—
    But only the perfume of flowers—
And your life shall be glad with surprises
    Of beautiful hours.

Come up where the rare golden wine is
    Apollo distils in my sight,
And your life shall be happy as mine is
    And as full of delight.

CONVERSION

WHEN this world's pleasures for my soul sufficed,
    Ere my heart's plummet sounded depths of pain,
I called on reason to control my brain,
And scoffed at that old story of the Christ.

But when o'er burning wastes my feet had trod,
    And all my life was desolate with loss,
    With bleeding hands I clung about the cross,
And cried aloud, " Man needs a suffering God ! "

LIFE AND I

LIFE and I are lovers, straying
    Arm in arm along :
Often like two children Maying,
    Full of mirth and song.

ELLA WHEELER WILCOX

Life plucks all the blooming hours
  Growing by the way ;
Binds them on my brow like flowers ;
  Calls me Queen of May.

Then again, in rainy weather,
  We sit vis-à-vis,
Planning work we'll do together
  In the years to be.

Sometimes Life denies me blisses,
  And I frown or pout ;
But we make it up with kisses
  Ere the day is out.

Woman-like, I sometimes grieve him,
  Try his trust and faith,
Saying I shall one day leave him
  For his rival Death.

Then he always grows more zealous,
  Tender, and more true ;
Loves the more for being jealous,
  As all lovers do.

Though I swear by stars above him,
  And by worlds beyond,
That I love him—love him—love him ;
  Though my heart is fond ;

POEMS OF LIFE

Though he gives me, doth my lover,
Kisses with each breath—
I shall one day throw him over
And plight troth with Death.

LIMITLESS

THERE is nothing, I hold, in the way of work
That a human being may not achieve
If he does not falter, or shrink or shirk,
And more than all, if he will *believe*.

Believe in himself and the power behind
That stands like an aid on a dual ground,
With hope for the spirit and oil for the wound,
Ready to strengthen the arm or mind.

When the motive is right and the will is strong
There are no limits to human power ;
For that great force back of us moves along
And takes us with it, in trial's hour.

And whatever the height you yearn to climb,
Tho' it never was trod by the foot of man,
And no matter how steep—I say you *can*,
If you will be patient—and use your time.

121

ELLA WHEELER WILCOX

TWO SUNSETS

IN the fair morning of his life,
   When his pure heart lay in his breast,
   Panting, with all that wild unrest
To plunge into the great world's strife

That fills young hearts with mad desire,
   He saw a sunset. Red and gold
   The burning billows surged and rolled,
And upward tossed their caps of fire.

He looked. And as he looked, the sight
   Sent from his soul, through breast and brain,
   Such intense joy, it hurt like pain.
His heart seemed bursting with delight.

So near the Unknown seemed, so close
   He might have grasped it with his hand.
   He felt his inmost soul expand,
As sunlight will expand a rose.

One day he heard a singing strain—
   A human voice, in bird-like trills.
   He paused, and little rapture-rills
Went trickling downward through each vein.

And in his heart the whole day long,
   As in a temple veiled and dim,
   He kept and bore about with him
The beauty of that singer's song.

POEMS OF LIFE

And then ? But why relate what then ?
　His smouldering heart flamed into fire—
　He had his one supreme desire,
And plunged into the world of men.

For years queen Folly held her sway
　With pleasures of the grosser kind.
　She fed his flesh and drugged his mind,
Till, shamed, he sated turned away.

He sought his boyhood's home. That hour
　Triumphant should have been, in sooth,
　Since he went forth an unknown youth,
. And came back crowned with wealth and power.

The clouds made day a gorgeous bed ;
　He saw the splendour of the sky
　With unmoved heart and stolid eye ;
He only knew the West was red.

Then suddenly a fresh young voice
　Rose, bird-like, from some hidden place,
　He did not even turn his face ;
It struck him simply as a noise.

He trod the old paths up and down.
　Their rich-hued leaves by Fall winds whirled—
　How dull they were—how dull the world—
Dull even in the pulsing town.

ELLA WHEELER WILCOX

O ! worst of punishments, that brings
  A blunting of all finer sense,
  A loss of feelings keen, intense,
And dulls us to the higher things.

O ! penalty most dire, most sure,
  Swift following after gross delights,
  That we no more see beauteous sights,
Or hear as hear the good and pure.

O ! shape more hideous and more dread
  Than Vengeance takes in creed-taught minds,
  This certain doom that blunts and blinds,
And strikes the holiest feelings dead.

UNREST

IN the youth of the year, when the birds were build-
  ing,
  When the green was showing on tree and hedge,
And the tenderest light of all lights was gilding
  The world from zenith to outermost edge,
My soul grew sad and longingly lonely !
  I sighed for the season of sun and rose,
And I said, " In the Summer and that time only
  Lies sweet contentment and blest repose."

With bee and bird for her maids of honour
  Came Princess Summer in robes of green.
And the King of day smiled down upon her
  And wooed her, and won her, and made her queen.

124

POEMS OF LIFE

Fruit of their union and true love's pledges,
  Beautiful roses bloomed day by day,
And rambled in gardens and hid in hedges
  Like royal children in sportive play.

My restless soul for a little season
  Revelled in rapture of glow and bloom,
And then, like a subject who harbours treason,
  Grew full of rebellion and grey with gloom.
And I said, " I am sick of the Summer's blisses,
  Of warmth and beauty, and nothing more.
The full fruition my sad soul misses
  That beauteous Fall time holds in store ! "

But now when the colours are almost blinding,
  Burning and blending on bush and tree,
And the rarest fruits are mine for the finding,
  And the year is ripe as a year can be,
My soul complains in the same old fashion ;
  Crying aloud in my troubled breast
Is the same old longing, the same old passion.
  O where is the treasure which men call rest ?

" ARTIST'S LIFE "

OF all the waltzes the great Strauss wrote,
    Mad with melody, rhythm—rife
From the very first to the final note,
  Give me his " Artist's Life " !

ELLA WHEELER WILCOX

It stirs my blood to my finger ends,
  Thrills me and fills me with vague unrest,
And all that is sweetest and saddest blends
  Together within my breast.

It brings back that night in the dim arcade,
  In love's sweet morning and life's best prime,
When the great brass orchestra played and played,
  And set our thoughts to rhyme.

It brings back that Winter of mad delights,
  Of leaping pulses and tripping feet,
And those languid moon-washed Summer nights
  When we heard the band in the street.

It brings back rapture and glee and glow,
  It brings back passion and pain and strife,
And so of all the waltzes I know,
  Give me the " Artist's Life."

For it is so full of the dear old time—
  So full of the dear old friends I knew.
And under its rhythm, and lilt, and rhyme,
  I am always finding—*you*.

NOTHING BUT STONES

I THINK I never passed so sad an hour,
  Dear friend, as that one at the church to-night.
The edifice from basement to the tower
  Was one resplendent blaze of coloured light.

POEMS OF LIFE

Up through broad aisles the stylish crowd was thronging,
  Each richly robed like some king's bidden guest.
" Here will I bring my sorrow and my longing,"
  I said, " and here find rest."

I heard the heavenly organ's voice of thunder,
  It seemed to give me infinite relief.
I wept. Strange eyes looked on in well-bred wonder
  I dried my tears : their gaze profaned my grief.
Wrapt in the costly furs, and silks and laces
  Beat alien hearts, that had no part with me.
I could not read, in all those proud cold faces,
  One thought of sympathy.

I watched them bowing and devoutly kneeling,
  Heard their responses like sweet waters roll.
But only the glorious organ's sacred pealing
  Seemed gushing from a full and fervent soul.
I listened to the man of holy calling,
  He spoke of creeds, and hailed his own as best ;
Of man's corruption and of Adam's falling,
  But naught that gave me rest.

Nothing that helped me bear the daily grinding
  Of soul with body, heart with heated brain.
Nothing to show the purpose of this blinding
  And sometimes overwhelming sense of pain.
And then, dear friend, I thought of thee, so lowly,
  So unassuming, and so gently kind,
And lo ! a peace, a calm serene and holy,
  Settled upon my mind.

127

ELLA WHEELER WILCOX

Ah, friend, my friend ! one true heart, fond and tender,
   That understands our troubles and our needs,
Brings us more near to God than all the splendour
   And pomp of seeming worship and vain creeds.
One glance of thy dear eyes so full of feeling,
   Doth bring me closer to the Infinite,
Than all that throng of worldly people kneeling
   In blaze of gorgeous light.

SECRETS

THINK not some knowledge rests with thee alone.
   Why, even God's stupendous secret, Death,
  We one by one, with our expiring breath,
Do, pale with wonder, seize and make our own ;
The bosomed treasures of the Earth are shown,
   Despite her careful hiding ; and the air
   Yields its mysterious marvels in despair
To swell the mighty storehouse of things known.
In vain the sea expostulates and raves ;
   It cannot cover from the keen world's sight
   The curious wonders of its coral caves.
And so, despite thy caution or thy tears,
The prying fingers of detective years
   Shall drag *thy* secret out into the light.

POEMS OF LIFE

USELESSNESS

LET mine not be the saddest fate of all,
    To live beyond my greater self ; to see
  My faculties decaying, as the tree
Stands stark and helpless while its green leaves fall
Let me hear rather the imperious call,
    Which all men dread, in my glad morning time,
    And follow death ere I have reached my prime,
Or drunk the strengthening cordial of life's gall.
The lightning's stroke or the fierce tempest blast
    Which fells the green tree to the earth to-day
Is kinder than the calm that lets it last,
    Unhappy witness of its own decay.
    May no man ever look on me and say,
" She lives, but all her usefulness is past."

WILL

THERE is no chance, no destiny, no fate,
    Can circumvent or hinder or control
  The firm resolve of a determined soul.
Gifts count for nothing ; will alone is great ;
All things give way before it, soon or late.
    What obstacle can stay the mighty force
    Of the sea-seeking river in its course,
Or cause the ascending orb of day to wait ?

ELLA WHEELER WILCOX

Each well-born soul must win what it deserves.
Let the fool prate of luck.   The fortunate
  Is he whose earnest purpose never swerves,
  Whose slightest action or inaction serves
The one great aim.   Why, even Death stands still,
And waits an hour sometimes for such a will.

WINTER RAIN

FALLING upon the frozen world last night
    I heard the slow beat of the winter rain—
  Poor foolish drops, down-dripping all in vain ;
The ice-bound Earth but mocked their puny might ;
Far better had the fixedness of white
And uncomplaining snows—which make no sign,
But coldly smile, when pitying moonbeams shine—
Concealed its sorrow from all human sight.
Long, long ago, in blurred and burdened years,
  I learned the uselessness of uttered woe.
  Though sinewy Fate deals her most skilful blow,
I do not waste the gall now of my tears,
  But feed my pride upon its bitter, while
  I look straight in the world's bold eyes, and smile.

INEVITABLE

TO-DAY I was so weary, and I lay
    In that delicious state of semi-waking,
When baby, sitting with his nurse at play,
  Cried loud for " mamma," all his toys forsaking.

POEMS OF LIFE

I was so weary and I needed rest,
 And signed to nurse to bear him from the room,
Then, sudden, rose and caught him to my breast,
 And kissed the grieving mouth and cheeks of bloom.

For swift as lightning came the thought to me,
 With pulsing heart-throes and a mist of tears,
Of days inevitable, that are to be,
 If my fair darling grows to manhood's years ;

Days when he will not call for " mamma," when
 The world with many a pleasure and bright joy,
Shall tempt him forth into the haunts of men
 And I shall lose the first place with my boy ;

When other homes and loves shall give delight,
 When younger smiles and voices will seem best.
And so I held him to my heart to-night,
 Forgetting all my need of peace and rest.

THE OCEAN OF SONG

IN a land beyond sight or conceiving,
 In a land where no blight is, no wrong,
No darkness, no graves, and no grieving,
 There lies the great ocean of song.
And its waves, oh, its waves unbeholden
 By any save gods, and their kind,
Are not blue, are not green, but are golden,
 Like moonlight and sunlight combined.

ELLA WHEELER WILCOX

It was whispered to me that their waters
   Were made from the gathered-up tears
That were wept by the sons and the daughters
   Of long-vanished eras and spheres.
Like white sands of heaven the spray is
   That falls all the happy day long,
And whoever it touches straightway is
   Made glad with the spirit of song.

Up, up to the clouds where their hoary
   Crowned heads melt away in the skies,
The beautiful mountains of glory
   Each side of the song-ocean rise.
Here day is one splendour of sky light,
   Of God's light with beauty replete ;
Here night is not night, but is twilight,
   Pervading, enfolding, and sweet.

Bright birds from all climes and all regions
   That sing the whole glad summer long,
Are dumb, till they flock here in legions
   And lave in the ocean of song.
It is here that the four winds of heaven,
   The winds that do sing and rejoice,
It is here they first came and were given
   The secret of sound and a voice.

Far down along beautiful beeches,
   By night and by glorious day,
The throng of the gifted ones reaches,
   Their foreheads made white with the spray.

And a few of the sons and the daughters
　　Of this kingdom, cloud-hidden from sight,
Go down in the wonderful waters,
　　And bathe in those billows of light.

And their souls evermore are like fountains,
　　And liquid and lucent and strong,
High over the tops of the mountains
　　Gush up the sweet billows of song.
No drouth-time of waters can dry them.
　　Whoever has bathed in that sea,
All dangers, all deaths, they defy them,
　　And are gladder than gods are, with glee.

GETHSEMANE

IN golden youth when seems the earth
　　A Summer-land of singing mirth,
When souls are glad and hearts are light,
And not a shadow lurks in sight,
We do not know it, but there lies
Somewhere veiled under evening skies
A garden which we all must see—
The garden of Gethsemane.

With joyous steps we go our ways,
Love lends a halo to our days;
Light sorrows sail like clouds afar,
We laugh and say how strong we are.

ELLA WHEELER WILCOX

We hurry on ; and hurrying, go
Close to the border-land of woe,
That waits for you, and waits for me—
For ever waits Gethsemane.

Down shadowy lanes, across strange streams,
Bridged over by our broken dreams ;
Behind the misty caps of years,
Beyond the great salt fount of tears,
The garden lies.   Strive as you may,
You cannot miss it in your way.
All paths that have been, or shall be,
Pass somewhere through Gethsemane.

All those who journey, soon or late,
Must pass within the garden's gate ;
Must kneel alone in darkness there,
And battle with some fierce despair.
God pity those who cannot say,
" Not mine but thine," who only pray,
" Let this cup pass," and cannot see
The *purpose* in Gethsemane.

DUST-SEALED

I KNOW not wherefore, but mine eyes
   See bloom, where other eyes see blight.
They find a rainbow, a sunrise,
   Where others but discern deep night.

POEMS OF LIFE

Men call me an enthusiast,
  And say I look through gilded haze,
Because where'er my gaze is cast,
  I see something that calls for praise.

I say, " Behold those lovely eyes—
  That tinted cheek of flowerlike grace."
They answer in amused surprise :
  " We thought it such a common face."

I say, " Was ever scene more fair ?
  I seem to walk in Eden's bowers."
They answer, with a pitying air,
  " The weeds are choking out the flowers."

I know not wherefore, but God lent
  A deeper vision to my sight.
On whatsoe'er my gaze is bent,
  I catch the beauty Infinite ;

That underlying, hidden half
  That all things hold of Deity.
So let the dull crowd sneer and laugh—
  Their eyes are blind, they cannot see.

" ADVICE "

I MUST do as you do ?   Your own way I own
  Is a very good way.   And still,
There are sometimes two straight roads to a town,
  One over, one under the hill.

ELLA WHEELER WILCOX

You are treading the safe and the well-worn way
  That the prudent choose each time ;
And you think me reckless and rash to-day
  Because I prefer to climb.

Your path is the right one, and so is mine.
  We are not like peas in a pod,
Compelled to lie in a certain line,
  Or else be scattered abroad.

'Twere a dull old world, methinks, my friend,
  If we all went just one way ;
Yet our paths will meet no doubt at the end,
  Though they lead apart to-day.

You like the shade, and I like the sun ;
  You like an even pace,
I like to mix with the crowd and run,
  And then rest after the race.

I like danger, and storm and strife,
  You like a peaceful time ;
I like the passion and surge of life,
  You like its gentle rhyme,

You like buttercups, dewy sweet,
  And crocuses, framed in snow ;
I like roses, born of the heat,
  And the red carnation's glow.

POEMS OF LIFE

I must live my life, not yours, my friend,
　For so it was written down ;
We must follow our given paths to the end—
　But I trust we shall meet—in town.

OVER THE BANISTERS

OVER the banisters bends a face,
　　Daringly sweet and beguiling.
Somebody stands in careless grace,
　And watches the picture, smiling.

The light burns dim in the hall below,
　Nobody sees her standing,
Saying good-night again, soft and slow,
　Half way up to the landing.

Nobody only the eyes of brown,
　Tender and full of meaning,
That smile on the fairest face in town,
　Over the banisters leaning.

Tired and sleepy, with dropping head,
　I wonder why she lingers ;
Now, when the good-nights all are said,
　Why somebody holds her fingers.

He holds her fingers and draws her down
　Suddenly growing bolder,
Till the loose hair drops its masses brown
　Like a mantle over his shoulder.

ELLA WHEELER WILCOX

Over the banisters soft hands, fair,
  Brush his cheeks like a feather,
And bright brown tresses and dusky hair
  Meet and mingle together.

There's a question asked, there's a swift caress,
  She has flown like a bird from the hall-way,
But over the banisters drops a " yes "
  That shall brighten the world for him alway.

MOMUS, GOD OF LAUGHTER

THOUGH with the gods the world is cumbered,
  Gods unnamed, and gods unnumbered,
Never god was known to be
Who had not his devotee.
So I dedicate to mine,
Here in verse, my temple-shrine.

'Tis not Ares—mighty Mars,
Who can give success in wars ;
'Tis not Morpheus, who doth keep
Guard above us while we sleep ;
'Tis not Venus, she whose duty
'Tis to give us love and beauty.
Hail to these, and others, after
Momus, gleesome god of laughter.

POEMS OF LIFE

Quirinus would guard my health,
Plutus would insure me wealth ;
Mercury looks after trade,
Hera smiles on youth and maid.
All are kind, I own their worth,
After Momus, god of mirth.

Though Apollo, out of spite,
Hides away his face of light,
Though Minerva looks askance,
Deigning me no smiling glance,
Kings and queens may envy me
While I claim the god of glee.

Wisdom wearies, Love has wings—
Wealth makes burdens, Pleasure stings,
Glory proves a thorny crown—
So all gifts the gods throw down
Bring their pains and troubles after ;
All save Momus, god of laughter.
He alone gives constant joy,
Hail to Momus, happy boy.

THE FAREWELL

'TIS not the untried soldier new to danger
    Who fears to enter into active strife.
Amidst the roll of drums, the cannon's rattle,
    He craves adventure, and thinks not of life.

But the scarred veteran knows the price of glory,
  He does not court the conflict or the fray.
He has no longing to rehearse that gory
  And most dramatic act, of war's dark play.

He who to love has always been a stranger,
  All unafraid may linger in your spell.
My heart has known the warfare, and its danger.
  It craves no repetition—so farewell.

THE PAST

I FLING my past behind me, like a robe
  Worn theadbare in the seams, and out of date.
I have outgrown it. Wherefore should I weep
And dwell upon its beauty, and its dyes
Of Oriental splendour, or complain
That I must needs discard it ? I can weave
Upon the shuttles of the future years
A fabric far more durable. Subdued,
It may be, in the blending of its hues,
Where sombre shades commingle, yet the gleam
Of golden warp shall shoot it through and through
While over all a fadeless lustre lies,
And starred with gems made out of crystalled tears
My new robe shall be richer than the old.

POEMS OF LIFE

" IT MIGHT HAVE BEEN "

WE will be what we could be. Do not say,
 " It might have been, had not or that, or this."
No fate can keep us from the chosen way ;
 He only might who *is*.

We will do what we could do. Do not dream
 Chance leaves a hero, all uncrowned to grieve.
I hold, all men are greatly what they seem ;
 He does who could achieve.

We will climb where we could climb. Tell me not
 Of adverse storms that kept thee from the height.
What eagle ever missed the peak he sought ?
 He always climbs who might.

I do not like the phrase, " It might have been ! "
 It lacks all force, and life's best truths perverts :
For I believe we have, and reach, and win,
 Whatever our deserts.

THE SONNET

ALONE it stands in Poesy's fair land,
 A temple by the muses set apart ;
A perfect structure of consummate art,
By artists builded and by genius planned.

ELLA WHEELER WILCOX

Beyond the reach of the apprentice hand,
  Beyond the ken of the untutored heart,
  Like a fine carving in a common mart,
Only the favoured few will understand.
A *chef-d'œuvre* toiled over with great care,
  Yet which the unseeing careless crowd goes by.
A plainly set, but well-cut soltaire,
An ancient bit of pottery, too rare
  To please or hold aught save the special eye—
These only with the sonnet can compare.

NOTHING NEW

FROM the dawn of spring till the year grows hoary,
    Nothing is new that is done or said,
The leaves are telling the same old story—
  " Budding, bursting, dying, dead."
And ever and always the wild birds' chorus
  Is " coming, building, flying, fled."

Never the round Earth roams or ranges
  Out of her circuit, so old, so old,
And the smile o' the sun knows but these changes—
  Beaming, burning, tender, cold,
As spring-time softens or winter estranges
  The mighty heart of this orb of gold.

From our great sire's birth to the last morn's breaking
  There were tempest, sunshine, fruit, and frost.

POEMS OF LIFE

And the sea was calm or the sea was shaking
   His mighty mane like a lion crossed,
And ever this cry the heart was making—
   Longing, loving, losing, lost.

For ever the wild wind wanders, crying,
   Southerly, easterly, north and west,
And one worn song the fields are sighing,
   " Sowing, growing, harvest, rest,"
And the tired thought of the world, replying
   Like an echo to what is last and best,
                  Murmurs—" Rest."

HELENA

LAST night I saw Helena.   She whose praise
   Of late all men have sounded.   She for whom
   Young Angus rashly sought a silent tomb
Rather than live without her all his days.

Wise men go mad who look upon her long,
   She is so ripe with dangers.   Yet meanwhile
   I find no fascination in her smile,
Although I make her theme of this poor song.

" Her golden tresses ? " yes, they may be fair,
   And yet to me each shining silken tress
   Seems robbed of beauty and all lustreless—
Too many hands have stroked Helena's hair.

ELLA WHEELER WILCOX

(I know a little maiden so demure
  She will not let her one true lover's hands
  In playful fondness touch her soft brown bands
So dainty minded is she and so pure.)

" Her great dark eyes that flash like gems at night ?
  Large, long-lashed eyes and lustrous ? " that may be
  And yet they are not beautiful to me.
Too many hearts have sunned in their delight.

(I mind me of two tender blue eyes, hid
  So underneath white curtains, and so veiled
  That I have sometimes pled for hours, and failed
To see more than the shyly-lifted lid.)

" Her perfect mouth, so like a carved kiss ? "
  " Her honeyed mouth, where hearts do, fly-like,
      drown ? "
  I would not taste its sweetness for a crown ;
Too many lips have drunk its nectared bliss.

(I know a mouth whose virgin dew, undried,
  Lies like a young grape's bloom, untouched and sweet,
  And though I plead in passion at her feet,
She would not let me brush if it I died.)

In vain, Helena ! though wise men may vie
  For thy rare smile or die from loss of it,
  Armoured by my sweet lady's trust, I sit,
And know thou art not worth her faintest sigh.

POEMS OF LIFE

NOTHING REMAINS

NOTHING remains of unrecorded ages
  That lie in the silent cemetery of time;
Their wisdom may have shamed our wisest sages,
  Their glory may have been indeed sublime.
How weak do seem our strivings after power,
  How poor the grandest efforts of our brains,
If out of all we are, in one short hour,
    Nothing remains.

Nothing remains but the Eternal Spaces,
  Time and decay uproot the forest trees.
Even the mighty mountains leave their places,
  And sink their haughty heads beneath strange seas;
The great earth writhes in some convulsive spasm
  And turns the proudest cities into plains.
The level sea becomes a yawning chasm—
    Nothing remains.

Nothing remains but the Eternal Forces,
  The sad seas cease complaining and grow dry.
Rivers are drained and altered in their courses,
  Great stars pass out and vanish from the sky.
Ideas die, and old religions perish,
  Our rarest pleasures and our keenest pains
Are swept away with all we hate or cherish—
    Nothing remains.

ELLA WHEELER WILCOX

Nothing remains but the Eternal Nameless
  And all-creative spirit of the Law,
Uncomprehended, comprehensive, blameless,
  Invincible, resistless, with no flaw ;
So full of love it must create for ever,
  Destroying that it may create again—
Persistent and perfecting in endeavour,
  It yet must bring forth angels, after men—
    This, this remains.

FINIS

AN idle rhyme of the summer time,
    Sweet, and solemn, and tender ;
Fair with the haze of the moon's pale rays,
  Bright with the sunset's splendour.

Summer and beauty over the lands—
  Careless hours of pleasure ;
A meeting of eyes and a touching of hands—
  A change in the floating measure.

A deeper hue in the skies of blue,
  Winds from the tropics blowing ;
A softer grace on the fair moon's face,
  And the summer going, going.

The leaves drift down, the green grows brown,
  And tears with smiles are blended ;
A twilight hour and a treasured flower,—
  And now the poem is ended.

APPLAUSE

I HOLD it one of the sad certain laws
   Which make our failures sometimes seem more kind
   Than that success which brings sure loss behind—
True greatness dies, when sounds the world's applause.
Fame blights the object it would bless, because
   Weighed down with men's expectancy, the mind
   Can no more soar to those far heights, and find
That freedom which its inspiration was.
When once we listen to its noisy cheers
   Or hear the populace' approval, then
We catch no more the music of the spheres,
Or walk with gods and angels, but with men.
Till, impotent from our self-conscious fears,
The plaudits of the world turn into sneers.

LIFE

LIFE, like a romping schoolboy, full of glee,
   Doth bear us on his shoulders for a time.
There is no path too steep for him to climb,
With strong, lithe limbs, as agile and as free
As some young roe, he speeds by vale and sea,
By flowery mead, by mountain peak sublime,
And all the world seems motion set to rhyme,
Till, tired out, he cries, " Now carry me ! "

ELLA WHEELER WILCOX

In vain we murmur. " Come," Life says, " fair play !"
And seizes on us. God ! he goads us so !
   He does not let us sit down all the day.
At each new step we feel the burden grow,
Till our bent backs seem breaking as we go,
   Watching for Death to meet us on the way.

THE STORY

THEY met each other in the glade—
   She lifted up her eyes ;
Alack the day ! Alack the maid !
   She blushed in swift surprise.
Alas ! alas ! the woe that comes from lifting up the
   eyes.

The pail was full, the path was steep—
   He reached to her his hand ;
She felt her warm young pulses leap,
   But did not understand.
Alas ! alas ! the woe that comes from clasping hand
   with hand.

She sat beside him in the wood—
   He wooed with words and sighs ;
Ah ! love in spring seems sweet and good,
   And maidens are not wise.
Alas ! alas ! the woe that comes from listing lovers'
   sighs.

POEMS OF LIFE

The summer sun shone fairly down,
 The wind blew from the south ;
As blue eyes gazed in eyes of brown,
 His kiss fell on her mouth.
Alas ! alas ! the woe that comes from kisses on the
 mouth.

And now the autumn time is near,
 The lover roves away,
With breaking heart and falling tear,
 She sits the livelong day.
Alas ! alas ! for breaking hearts when lovers rove away.

LET THEM GO

LET the dream go. Are there not other dreams
 In vastness of clouds hid from thy sight
That yet shall gild with beautiful gold gleams,
 And shoot the shadows through and through with
  light ?
 What matters one lost vision of the night ?
         Let the dream go !

Let the hope set. Are there not other hopes
 That yet shall rise like new stars in thy sky ?
Not long a soul in sullen darkness gropes
 Before some light is lent it from on high.
 What folly to think happiness gone by !
         Let the hope set !

ELLA WHEELER WILCOX

Let the joy fade.   Are there not other joys,
   Like the frost-bound bulbs, that yet shall start and
     bloom ?
Severe must be the winter that destroys
   The hardy roots locked in their silent tomb.
   What cares the Earth for her brief time of gloom ?
                     Let the joy fade !

Let the love die.   Are there not other loves
   As beautiful and full of sweet unrest,
Flying through space like snowy-pinioned doves ?
   They yet shall come and nestle in thy breast,
  And thou shalt say of each, " Lo, this is best ! "
                     Let the love die !

THE ENGINE

INTO the gloom of the deep, dark night,
   With panting breath and a startled scream ;
Swift as a bird in sudden flight,
  Darts this creature of steel and steam.

Awful dangers are lurking nigh,
   Rocks and chasms are near the track,
But straight by the light of its great white eye,
   It speeds through the shadows, dense and black.

Terrible thoughts and fierce desires
   Trouble its mad heart many an hour,
Where burn and smoulder the hidden fires,
   Coupled ever with might and power.

POEMS OF LIFE

It hates, as a wild horse hates the rein,
  The narrow track by vale and hill :
And shrieks with a cry of startled pain ;
  And longs to follow its own wild will.

O, what am I but an engine, shod
  With muscle and flesh, by the hand of God,
Speeding on through the dense, dark night,
  Guided alone by the soul's white light.

Often and often my mad heart tires,
  And hates its way with a bitter hate,
And longs to follow its own desires,
  And leave the end in the hands of fate.

O mighty engine of steel and steam ;
  O human engine of blood and bone,
Follow the white light's certain beam—
  There lies safety, and there alone.

The narrow track of fearless truth,
  Lit by the soul's great eye of light,
O passionate heart of restless youth,
  Alone will carry you through the night.

IN THE LONG RUN

IN the long run fame finds the deserving man.
  The lucky wight may prosper for a day,
But in good time true merit leads the van,
  And vain pretence, unnoticed, goes its way.

ELLA WHEELER WILCOX

There is no Chance, no Destiny, no Fate,
But Fortune smiles on those who work and wait,
    In the long run.

In the long run all goodly sorrows pay,
  There is no better thing than righteous pain !
The sleepless nights, the awful thorn-crowned days,
  Bring sure reward to tortured soul and brain.
Unmeaning joys enervate in the end,
But sorrow yields a glorious dividend—
    In the long run.

In the long run all hidden things are known ;
  The eye of truth will penetrate the night,
And good or ill, thy secret shall be known,
  However well 'tis guarded from the light.
All the unspoken motives of the breast
Are fathomed by the years, and stand confest—
    In the long run.

In the long run all love is paid by love,
  Though undervalued by the hosts of earth ;
The great eternal Government above
  Keeps strict account and will redeem its worth.
Give thy love freely ; do not count the cost ;
So beautiful a thing was never lost
    In the long run.

A SONG

IS anyone sad in the world, I wonder ?
  Does anyone weep on a day like this
With the sun above, and the green earth under ?
  Why, what is life but a dream of bliss ?

With the sun, and the skies, and the birds above me,
  Birds that sing as they wheel and fly—
With the winds to follow and say they love me—
  Who could be lonely ?   O no, not I !

Somebody said, in the street this morning,
  As I opened my window to let in the light,
That the darkest day of the world was dawning ;
  But I looked, and the East was a gorgeous sight.

One who claims that he knows about it
  Tells me the Earth is a vale of sin ;
But I and the bees and the birds—we doubt it,
  And think it a world worth living in.

Some one says that hearts are fickle,
  That love is sorrow, that life is care,
And the reaper Death, with his shining sickle,
  Gathers whatever is bright and fair.

ELLA WHEELER WILCOX

I told the thrush, and we laughed together,
  Laughed till the woods were all a-ring;
And he said to me, as he plumed each feather,
  " Well, people must croak, if they cannot sing."

Up he flew, but his song, remaining,
  Rang like a bell in my heart all day,
And silenced the voices of weak complaining,
  That pipe like insects along the way.

O world of light, and O world of beauty!
  Where are there pleasures so sweet as thine?
Yes, life is love, and love is duty;
  And what heart sorrows? O no, not mine!

THE TWO GLASSES

THERE sat two glasses filled to the brim,
  On a rich man's table, rim to rim.
One was ruddy and red as blood,
And one was clear as the crystal flood.
Said the glass of wine to his paler brother:
" Let us tell tales of the past to each other;
I can tell of banquet, and revel, and mirth,
Where I was king, for I ruled in might;
For the proudest and grandest souls on earth
Fell under my touch, as though struck with blight.
From the heads of kings I have torn the crown;
From the heights of fame I have hurled men down.

I have blasted many an honoured name ;
I have taken virtue and given shame ;
I have tempted the youth with a sip, a taste,
That has made his future a barren waste.
Far greater than any king am I,
Or than any army beneath the sky.
I have made the arm of the driver fail,
And sent the train from the iron rail.
I have made good ships go down at sea,
And the shrieks of the lost were sweet to me.
Fame, strength, wealth, genius before me fall,
And my might and power are over all !
Ho, ho ! pale brother," said the wine,
" Can you boast of deeds as great as mine ? "
Said the water-glass : " I cannot boast
Of a king dethroned, or a murdered host,
But I can tell of hearts that were sad
By my crystal drops made bright and glad ;
Of thirsts I have quenched, and brows I have laved ;
Of hands I have cooled, and souls I have saved.
I have leaped through the valley, dashed down the
   mountain,
Slept in the sunshine, and dripped from the fountain.
I have burst my cloud-fetters and dropped from the sky,
And everywhere gladdened the prospect and eye ;
I have eased the hot forehead of fever and pain ;
I have made the parched meadows grow fertile with
   grain.
I can tell of the powerful wheel of the mill,
That ground out the flour and turned at my will.

ELLA WHEELER WILCOX

I can tell of manhood debased by you,
That I have uplifted and crowned anew ;
I cheer, I help, I strengthen and aid ;
I gladden the heart of man and maid ;
I set the wine-chained captive free,
And all are better for knowing me."

These are the tales they told each other,
The glass of wine and its paler brother,
As they sat together, filled to the brim,
On a rich man's table, rim to rim.

WHAT WE NEED

WHAT does our country need ? Not armies standing
    With sabres gleaming ready for the fight.
Not increased navies, skilful and commanding,
    To bound the waters with an iron might.
Not haughty men with glutted purses trying
    To purchase souls, and keep the power of place.
Not jewelled dolls with one another vying
    For palms of beauty, elegance, and grace.

But we want women, strong of soul, yet lowly,
    With that rare meekness, born of gentleness,
Women whose lives are pure and clean and holy,
    The women whom all little children bless.
Brave, earnest women, helpful to each other,
    With finest scorn for all things low and mean ;
Women who hold the names of wife and mother
    Far nobler than the title of a Queen.

Is it done?

POEMS OF LIFE

Oh, these are they who mould the men of story,
   These mothers, ofttimes shorn of grace and youth,
Who, worn and weary, ask no greater glory
   Than making some young soul the home of truth;
Who sow in hearts all fallow for the sowing
   The seeds of virtue and of scorn for sin,
And, patient, watch the beauteous harvest growing
   And weed out tares which crafty hands cast in.

Women who do not hold the gift of beauty
   As some rare treasure to be bought and sold,
But guard it as a precious aid to duty—
   The outer framing of the inner gold;
Women who, low above their cradles bending,
   Let flattery's voice go by, and give no heed,
While their pure prayers like incense are ascending;
   These are our country's pride, our country's need.

IS IT DONE?

IT is done! in the fire's fitful flashes,
   The last line has withered and curled.
In a tiny white heap of dead ashes
   Lie buried the hopes of your world.
There were mad foolish vows in each letter,
   It is well they have shrivelled and burned,
And the ring! oh, the ring was a fetter
   It was removed and returned.

ELLA WHEELER WILCOX

But, ah, is it done ? in the embers,
   Where letters and tokens were cast,
Have you burned up the heart that remembers,
   And treasures its beautiful past ?
Do you think in this swift reckless fashion
   To ruthlessly burn and destroy
The months that were freighted with passion,
   The dreams that were drunken with joy ?

Can you burn up the rapture of kisses
   That flashed from the lips to the soul ?
Or the heart that grows sick for lost blisses
   In spite of its strength of control ?
Have you burned up the touch of warm fingers
   That thrilled through each pulse and each vein,
Or the sound of a voice that still lingers
   And hurts with a haunting refrain ?

Is it done ? is the life drama ended ?
   You have put all the lights out, and yet,
Though the curtain, rung down, has descended,
   Can the actors go home and forget ?
Ah, no ! they will turn in their sleeping
   With a strange restless pain in their hearts,
And in darkness, and anguish and weeping,
   Will dream they are playing their parts.

BURDENED

DEAR God ! there is no sadder fate in life,
    Than to be burdened so that you cannot
Sit down contented with the common lot
Of happy mother and devoted wife.
To feel your brain wild and your bosom rife
    With all the sea's commotion ; to be fraught
    With fires and frenzies which you have not sought,
And weighed down with the wide world's weary strife.

To feel a fever always in your breast,
    To lean and hear half in affright, half shame,
    A loud-voiced public boldly mouth your name,
To reap your hard-sown harvest in unrest,
    And know, however great your meed of fame,
You are but a weak woman at the best.

TO MARRY OR NOT TO MARRY ?
A GIRL'S REVERIE

MOTHER says, " Be in no hurry,
    Marriage oft means care and worry."

Auntie says, with manner grave,
" Wife is synonym for slave."

Father asks, in tones commanding,
" How does Bradstreet rate his standing ? "

ELLA WHEELER WILCOX

Sister, crooning to her twins,
Sighs, " With marriage care begins."

Grandma, near life's closing days,
Murmurs, " Sweet are girlhood's ways."

Maud, twice widowed (" sod and grass ")
Looks at me and moans " Alas ! "

They are six, and I am one,
Life for me has just begun.

They are older, calmer, wiser :
Age should aye be youth's adviser.

They must know—and yet, dear me,
When in Harry's eyes I see

All the world of love there burning—
On my six advisers turning,

I make answer, " Oh, but Harry,
Is not like most men who marry.

" Fate has offered me a prize,
Life with love means Paradise.

" Life without it is not worth
All the foolish joys of earth."

So, in spite of all they say,
I shall name the wedding-day.

THE KINGDOM
of LOVE

POEMS OF LOVE

THE KINGDOM OF LOVE

IN the dawn of the day, when the sea and the earth
  Reflected the sunrise above,
I set forth, with a heart full of courage and mirth,
  To seek for the Kingdom of Love.
I asked of a Poet I met on the way,
  Which cross-road would lead me aright,
And he said : " Follow me, and ere long you will see
  Its glistening turrets of Light."

And soon in the distance a city shone fair ;
  " Look yonder," he said, " there it gleams ! "
But alas ! for the hopes that were doomed to despair,
  It was only the Kingdom of Dreams.
Then the next man I asked was a gay cavalier,
  And he said : " Follow me, follow me."
And with laughter and song we went speeding along
  By the shores of life's beautiful sea,

Till we came to a valley more tropical far
  Than the wonderful Vale of Cashmere,
And I saw from a bower a face like a flower
  Smile out on the gay cavalier,

ELLA WHEELER WILCOX

And he said : " We have come to humanity's goal—
  Here love and delight are intense."
But alas ! and alas ! for the hope of my soul—
  It was only the Kingdom of Sense.

As I journeyed more slowly, I met on the road
  A coach with retainers behind,
And they said : " Follow us, for our lady's abode
  Belongs in the realm you would find."
'Twas a grand dame of fashion, a newly-wed bride ;
  I followed, encouraged and bold.
But my hope died away, like the last gleams of day,
  For we came to the Kingdom of Gold.

At the door of a cottage I asked a fair maid.
  " I have heard of that Realm," she replied,
" But my feet never roam from the Kingdom of Home,
  So I know not the way," and she sighed.
I looked on the cottage, how restful it seemed !
  And the maid was as fair as a dove.
Great light glorified my soul as I cried,
  " Why, *home* is the Kingdom of Love ! "

LOVE

THE day is drawing near, my dear,
    When you and I must sever ;
Yet whether near or far we are,
Our hearts will love forever,
Our hearts will love forever.

POEMS OF LOVE

O sweet, I will be true, and you
Must never fail or falter ;
I hold a love like mine divine,
And yours—it must not alter,
O, swear it will not alter.

A FATAL IMPRESS

A LITTLE leaf just in the forest's edge,
    All summer long, had listened to the wooing
Of amorous birds that flew across the hedge,
Singing their blithe sweet songs for her undoing.
So many were the flattering things they told her,
The parent tree seemed quite too small to hold her.

At last one lonesome day she saw them fly
Across the fields behind the coquette summer,
They passed her with a laughing light good-bye,
When from the north, there strode a strange new comer ;
Bold was his mien, as he gazed on her, crying,
" How comes it, then, that thou art left here sighing !

" Now by my faith thou art a lovely leaf—
May I not kiss that cheek so fair and tender ? "
Her slighted heart welled full of bitter grief,
The rudeness of his words did not offend her,
She felt so sad, so desolate, so deserted,
Oh, if her lonely fate might be averted.

ELLA WHEELER WILCOX

" One little kiss," he sighed, " I ask no more—"
His face was cold, his lips too pale for passion.
She smiled assent ; and then bold Frost leaned lower,
And clasped her close, and kissed in lover's fashion.
Her smooth cheek flushed to sudden guilty splendour,
Another kiss, and then complete surrender.

Just for a day she was a beauteous sight,
The world looked on to pity and admire
This modest little leaf, that in a night
Had seemed to set the forest all on fire.
And then—this victim of a broken trust,
A withered thing, was trodden in the dust.

LOVE WILL WANE

WHEN your love begins to wane,
 Spare me from the cruel pain
Of all speech that tells me so—
 Spare me words, for I shall know,

By the half-averted eyes,
 By the breast that no more sighs,
By the rapture I shall miss
 From your strangely-altered kiss ;

By the arms that still enfold
 But have lost their clinging hold,
And, too willing, let me go,
 I shall know, love, I shall know.

POEMS OF LOVE

Bitter will the knowledge be,
   Bitterer than death to me.
Yet, 'twill come to me some day,
   For it is the sad world's way.

Make no vows—vows cannot bind
   Changing hearts or wayward mind.
Men grow weary of a bliss
   Passionate and fond as this.

Love will wane. But I shall know,
   If you do not tell me so.
Know it, tho' you smile and say,
   That you love me more each day.

Know it by the inner sight
   That forever sees aright.
Words could but increase my woe,
   And without them, I shall know.

THREE-FOLD

SOMEWHERE I've read a thoughtful mind's reflec-
   tion :
" All perfect things are three-fold " ; and I know
Our love has this rare symbol of perfection ;
   The brain's response, the warm blood's rapturous glow
The soul's sweet language, silent and unspoken.
   All these unite us with a deathless tie.
For when our frail, clay tenement is broken,
   Our spirits will be lovers still, on high.

ELLA WHEELER WILCOX

My dearest wish, you speak before I word it.
  You understand the workings of my heart.
My soul's thought, breathed where only God has heard it,
  You fathom with your strange divining art.
And like a fire, that cheers, and lights, and blesses,
  And floods a mansion full of happy heat,
So does the subtle warmth of your caresses,
  Pervade me with rapture, keen as sweet.

And so sometimes, as you and I together
  Exult in all dear love's three-fold delights,
I cannot help but vaguely wonder whether
  When our freed souls attain their spirit heights,
E'en if we reach that upper realm where God is,
  And find the tales of heavenly glory true,
I wonder if we shall not miss our bodies,
  And long, at times, for hours on earth we knew.

As now, we sometimes pray to leave our prison
  And soar beyond all physical demands,
So may we not sigh, when we have arisen,
  For just one old-time touch of lips and hands ?
I know, dear heart, a thought like this seems daring
  Concerning God's vast Government above,
Yet, even *There*, I shrink from wholly sparing
  One element, from this, our Three-fold Love.

A MAIDEN'S SECRET

I HAVE written this day down in my heart
　　As the sweetest day in the season;
From all of the others I've set it apart—
　　But I will not tell you the reason,
That is my secret—I must not tell;
　　But the skies are soft and tender,
And never before, I know full well,
　　Was the earth so full of splendour.

I sing at my labour the whole day long,
　　And my heart is as light as a feather;
And there is a reason for my glad song
　　Besides the beautiful weather.
But I will not tell it to you; and though
　　That thrush in the maple heard it,
And would shout it aloud if he could, I know
　　He hasn't the power to word it.

Up, where I was sewing, this morn came one
　　Who told me the sweetest stories,
He said I had stolen my hair from the sun,
　　And my eyes from the morning glories.
Grandmother says that I must not believe
　　A word men say, for they flatter;
But I'm sure *he* would never try to deceive,
　　For he told me—but there—no matter!

ELLA WHEELER WILCOX

Last night I was sad, and the world to me
  Seemed a lonely and dreary dwelling,
But some one then had not asked me to be—
  There now! I am almost telling.
Not another word shall my two lips say,
  I will shut them fast together,
And never a mortal shall know to-day
  Why my heart is as light as a feather.

ART AND LOVE

FOR many long uninterrupted years
    She was the friend and confidant of Art;
They walked together, heart communed with heart
In that sweet comradeship that so endears.
Her fondest hopes, her sorrows and her fears
She told her mate; who would in turn impart
Important truths and secrets. But a dart,

Shot by that unskilled, mischievous boy, who peers
From ambush on us, struck one day her breast,
And Love sprang forth to kiss away her tears.
She thought his brow shone with a wondrous grace;
But, when she turned to introduce her guest
To Art, behold, she found an empty place,
The goddess fled, with sad, averted face.

POEMS OF LOVE

RIVER AND SEA

UNDER the light of the silver moon
   We two sat, when our hearts were young;
The night was warm with the breath of June,
   And loud from the meadow the cricket sung,
And darker and deeper, oh, love, than the sea,
Were your dear eyes, as they beamed on me.

The moon hung clear, and the night was still:
   The waters reflected the glittering skies:
The nightingale sang on the distant hill;
   But sweeter than all was the light in your eyes—
Your dear, dark eyes, your eyes like the sea—
And up from the depths shone love for me.

My heart, like a river, was mad and wild—
   And a river is not deep, like the sea;
But I said your love was the love of a child,
   Compared with the love that was felt by me;
A river leaps noisily, kissing the land,
But the sea is fathomless, deep and grand.

I vowed to love you, for ever and ever!
   I called you cold, on that night in June,
But my fierce love, like a reckless river,
   Dashed on, and away, and was spent too soon;
While yours—ah, yours was deep like the sea;
I cheated you, love, but you died for me!

ELLA WHEELER WILCOX

WHEN YOU GO AWAY

WHEN you go away, my friend,
  When you say your last good-bye,
Then the summer time will end,
  And the winter will be nigh.

Though the green grass decks the heather,
  And the birds sing all the day,
There will be no summer weather
  After you have gone away.

When I look into your eyes,
  I shall thrill with deepest pain,
Thinking that beneath the skies
  I may never look again.

You will feel a moment's sorrow,
  I shall feel a lasting grief;
You forgetting on the morrow,
  I to mourn with no relief.

When we say the last sad word,
  And you are no longer near,
And the winds and all the birds
  Cannot keep the summer here,

Life will lose its full completeness—
  Lose it not for you, but me;
All the beauty and the sweetness
  Each can hold, I shall not see.

A BABY IN THE HOUSE

I KNEW that a baby was hid in that house,
  Though I saw no cradle and heard no cry ;
But the husband was tip-toeing 'round like a mouse
  And the good wife was humming a soft lullaby ;
And there was a look on the face of the mother,
That I knew could mean only one thing, and no other.

The mother, I said to myself, for I knew
  That the woman before me was certainly that ;
And there lay in a corner a tiny cloth shoe,
  And I saw on a stand such a wee little hat ;
And the beard of the husband said, plain as could be,
" Two fat chubby hands have been tugging at me."

And he took from his pocket a gay picture-book,
  And a dog that could bark, if you pulled on a string ;
And the wife laid them up, with such a pleased look ;
  And I said to myself, " There is no other thing
But a babe that could bring about all this, and so
That one is in hiding here somewhere, I know."

I stayed but a moment, and saw nothing more,
  And heard not a sound, yet I know I was right ;
What else could the shoe mean that lay on the floor,
  The book and the toy, and the faces so bright ;
And what made the husband as still as a mouse ?
I am sure, very sure, there's a babe in that house.

ELLA WHEELER WILCOX

IN FAITH

WHEN the soft sweet wind o' the south went by,
  I dwelt in the light of a dark brown eye;
And out where the robin sang his song,
We lived and loved, while the days were long.

In the sweet, sweet eves, when the moon swung high,
We wandered under the starry sky;
Or sat in the porch, and the moon looked through
The latticed wall, where the roses grew.

My lips, that had known no lover's kiss,
You taught the art, till they thrilled in bliss;
And the moon, and the stars, and the roses knew
That the heart you won was pure and true.

But true hearts weary men, maybe,
For you grew weary of love, and me.
Over the porch the dead vines hang,
And a mourning dove sobs where the robin sang.

In a warmer clime does another sigh
Under the light of your dark brown eye?
Did you follow the soft sweet wind o' the south,
And are you kissing a redder mouth?

Lips may be redder, and eyes more bright;
The face may be fairer you see to-night;
But never, love, while the stars shall shine,
Will you find a heart that is truer than mine.

POEMS OF LOVE

Sometime, perhaps, when south winds blow,
You will think of a love you used to know;
Sometime, perhaps, when a robin sings,
Your heart will go back to olden things.

Sometime you will weary of this world's arts,
Of deceit and change and hollow hearts,
And, wearying, sigh for the "used to be,"
And your feet will turn to the porch, and me.

I shall watch for you here when days grow long;
I shall list for your step through the robin's song;
I shall sit in the porch where the moon looks through,
And a vacant chair will wait—for you.

You may stray, and forget, and rove afar,
But my changeless love, like the polar star,
Will draw you at length o'er land and sea—
And I know you will yet come back to me.

The years may come, and the years may go,
But sometime again, when south winds blow,
When roses bloom, and the moon swings high,
I shall live in the light of your dark brown eye.

ELLA WHEELER WILCOX

I TOLD YOU

I TOLD you the winter would go, love,
  I told you the winter would go,
That he'd flee in shame when the south wind came,
  And you smiled when I told you so.
You said the blustering fellow
  Would never yield to a breeze,
That his cold, icy breath had frozen to death
  The flowers, and birds, and trees.

And I told you the snow would melt, love,
  In the passionate glance o' the sun ;
And the leaves o' the trees, and the flowers and bees,
  Would come back again, one by one.
That the great, gray clouds would vanish,
  And the sky turn tender and blue ;
And the sweet birds would sing, and talk of the spring,
  And, love, it has all come true.

I told you that sorrow would fade, love,
  And you would forget half your pain ;
That the sweet bird of song would waken ere long,
  And sing in your bosom again.
That hope would creep out of the shadows,
  And back to its nest in your heart,
And gladness would come, and find its old home,
  And that sorrow at length would depart.

POEMS OF LOVE

I told you that grief seldom killed, love,
   Though the heart might *seem* dead for awhile.
But the world is so bright, and so full of warm light
   That 'twould waken at length, in its smile.
Ah, love! was I not a true prophet?
   There's a sweet happy smile on your face;
Your sadness has flown—the snow-drift is gone,
   And the buttercups bloom in its place.

IN THE GARDEN

ONE moment alone in the garden,
   Under the August skies;
The moon had gone, but the stars shone on,—
   Shone like your beautiful eyes.
Away from the glitter and gaslight,
   Alone in the garden there,
While the mirth of the throng, in laugh and song,
   Floated out on the air.

You looked down through the starlight,
   And I looked up at you;
And a feeling came that I could not name,—
   Something strange and new.
Friends of a few weeks only,—
   Why should it give me pain
To know you would go on the morrow,
   And would not come again?

ELLA WHEELER WILCOX

Formal friends of a season.
  What matter that we must part ?
But under the skies, with a swift surprise,
  Each read the other's heart.
We did not speak, but your breath on my cheek
  Was like a breeze of the south :
And your dark hair brushed my forehead
  . And your kiss fell on my mouth.

Some one was searching for me,—
  Some one to say good-night ;
And we went in from the garden,
  Out of the sweet starlight,
Back to the glitter and music,
  And we said " Good-bye " in the hall,
When a dozen heard and echoed the word,
  And then—well, that was all.

The river that rolls between us
  Can never be crossed, I know,
For the waters are deep and the shores are steep,
  And a maelstrom whirls below ;
But I think we shall always remember,
  Though we both may strive to forget,
How you looked in my eyes, 'neath the August skies,
  After the moon had set ;—

How you kissed my lips in the garden,
  And we stood in a trance of bliss,
And our hearts seemed speaking together
  In that one thrilling kiss.

POEMS OF LOVE

LOST

YOU left me with the autumn time;
　　When winter stripped the forest bare,
Then dressed it in his spotless rime;
　　When frosts were lurking in the air
You left me here and went away.
The winds were cold; you could not stay.

You sought a warmer clime, until
　　The south wind, artful maid, should break
The winter's trumpets, and should fill
　　The air with songs of birds; and wake
The sleeping blossoms on the plain
And make the brooks to flow again.

I thought the winter desolate,
　　And all times felt a sense of loss.
I taught my longing heart to wait,
　　And said, " When Spring shall come across
The hills, with blossoms in her track,
Then she, our loved one, will come back."

And now the hills with grass and moss
　　The spring with cunning hands has spread,
And yet I feel my grievous loss.
　　My heart will not be comforted,
But crieth daily, " Where is she
You promised should come back to me ? "

ELLA WHEELER WILCOX

Oh, love! where are you? day by day
  I seek to find you, but in vain.
Men point me to a grave, and say:
  " There is her bed upon the plain."
But though I see no trace of you,
I cannot think their words are true.

You were too sweet to wholly pass
  Away from earth, and leave no trace;
You were too fair to let the grass
  Grow rank and tall above your face.
Your voice, that mocked the robin's trill,
I cannot think is hushed and still.

I thought I saw your golden hair
  One day, and reached to touch a strand;
I found but yellow sunbeams there—
  The bright rays fell aslant my hand,
And seemed to mock, with lights and shades,
The silken meshes of your braids.

Again, I thought I saw your hand
  Wave, as if beckoning to me;
I found 'twas but a lily, fanned
  By the cool zephyrs from the sea.
Oh, love! I find no trace of you—
I wonder if their words *were* true?

One day I heard a singing voice;
  A burst of music, trill on trill.

It made my very soul rejoice ;
  My heart gave an exultant thrill.
I cried, " Oh, heart, we've found her—hush ! "
But no—'twas the silver-throated thrush.

And once I thought I saw your face,
  And wild with joy I ran to you ;
But found, when I had reached the place,
  'Twas but a blush rose, bathed in dew.
Ah, love ! I think you *must* be dead ;
And I believe the words they said.

" THE OLD MOON IN THE NEW MOON'S ARMS "

THE beautiful and slender young New Moon,
  In trailing robes of pink and palest blue,
Swept close to Venus, and breathed low : " A boon,
  A precious boon, I ask, dear friend, of you.

" O queen of light and beauty, you have known
  The pangs of love—its passions and alarms ;
Then grant me this one favour, let my own—
  My lost Old Moon be once more in my arms."

Swift thro' the vapours and the golden mist—
  The Full Moon's shadowy shape shone on the night,
The New Moon reached out clasping arms and kissed
  Her phantom lover in the whole world's sight.

ELLA WHEELER WILCOX

THE WILD BLUE BELLS

CAME a bouquet from the city,
  Fragrant, rich and debonair—
Sweet carnation and geranium,
  Heliotrope and roses rare.

Down beside the crystal river,
  Where the moss-grown rocks are high,
And the ferns, from niche and crevice,
  Stretch to greet the azure sky;

In the chaste October sunlight,
  High above the path below,
Grew a tuft of lovely blue-bells,
  Softly wind-swung to and fro.

Reached a dainty hand to grasp them,
  Bore them home with loving care,
Tenderly and proudly placed them
  'Mid the flowers so sweet and fair.

But my timid little blue-bells,
  Children of the leafy wild,
Dazzled by their city sisters,
  Turned away and, tearful, smiled.

POEMS OF LOVE

When, alone, I bent to kiss them,
  Pleadingly they sighed to me,
" Take us, when we die, we pray thee,
  Back beneath the dear old tree

" We would sleep where first the sunshine
  Kissed us in the dewy morn ;
Where, while soft, warm zephyrs fanned us,
  Leaf and bud and flower were born."

So I bore them, when they faded,
  Back to where love sighed for them ;
Laid them near the ferns and mosses,
  'Neath the dear old parent stem ;—

Deeply grieved that all things lovely
  Must so soon forever die,—
That upon the gentle blue-bells
  Winter's cold, deep snow must lie.

And I half arraigned the goodness
  That made Death king everywhere—
Stretching forth his cruel sceptre—
  Lord of sea, and earth, and air.

———

Summer came, and all the hillsides
  Wore a shim'ring robe of green ;
And with rifts of sky and cloudlet
  Flashed the river's golden sheen.

ELLA WHEELER WILCOX

I was walking the old pathway,
  When a tiny shout I heard;
Harken! was it elfin fairy,
  Or some truant mocking bird?

No! a family of blue-bells
  Waved their slender arms on high,
Clapped their tiny arms in triumph,
  Crying, " See! we did not die.

" Never more distrust the Master,
  Love and Truth His ways attend;
Death is but a darkened portal
  Of a life that ne'er shall end.

" Loved ones, parted from in anguish,
  Your glad eyes again shall see,—
Brighter than the hopes you cherished
  Shall the glad fruition be."

A WAIF

MY soul is like a poor caged bird to-night,
  Beating its wings against the prison bars,
Longing to reach the outer world of light,
  And, all untrammelled, soar among the stars.
Wild, mighty thoughts struggle within my soul
For utterance. Great waves of passion roll

POEMS OF LOVE

Through all my being.   As the lightnings play
Through thunder clouds, so beams of blinding light
Flash for a moment on my darkened brain—
Quick, sudden, glaring beams, that fade away
And leave me in a darker, deeper night.

Oh, poet souls ! that struggle all in vain
 To live in peace and harmony with earth,
It cannot be !   They must endure the pain
 Of conscience and of unacknowledged worth,
Moving and dwelling with the common herd,
 Whose highest thought has never strayed as far,
 Or never strayed beyond the horizon's bar ;
Whose narrow hearts and souls are never stirred
 With keenest pleasures, or with sharpest pain ;
 Who rise and eat and sleep, and rise again,
Nor question why or wherefore.   Men whose minds
Are never shaken by wild passion winds ;

Women whose broadest, deepest realm of thought
The bridal veil will cover.
                                        Who see not
God's mighty work lying undone to-day,—
Work that a woman's hands can do as well,
Oh, soul of mine ; better to live alway
In this tumultuous inward pain and strife,
 Doing the work that in thy reach doth fall,
 Weeping because thou canst not do it all ;
Oh, better, my soul, in this unrest to dwell,
Than grovel as *they* grovel on through life.

ELLA WHEELER WILCOX

SEARCHING

THESE quiet Autumn days,
  My soul, like Noah's dove, on airy wings
Goes out and searches for the hidden things
Beyond the hills of haze.

With mournful, pleading cries,
  Above the waters of the voiceless sea
  That laps the shore of broad Eternity,
Day after day, it flies,

Searching, but all in vain,
  For some stray leaf that it may light upon,
  And read the future, as the days agone—
Its pleasures, and its pain.

Listening patiently
  For some voice speaking from the mighty deep
  Revealing all the things that it doth keep
In secret there for me.

Come back and wait, my soul!
  Day after day thy search has been in vain.
  Voiceless and silent o'er the future's plain
Its mystic waters roll.

God, seeing, knoweth best,
  And in His time the waters shall subside,
  And thou shalt know what lies beneath the tide,
Then wait, my soul, and rest,

OUR BLESSINGS

SITTING to-day in the sunshine,
    That touched me with fingers of love,
I thought of the manifold blessings
    God scatters on earth, from above ;
And they seemed, as I numbered them over,
    Far more than we merit, or need,
And all that we lack is the angels
    To make earth a heaven indeed.

The winter brings long, pleasant evenings,
    The spring brings a promise of flowers
That summer breathes into fruition,
    And autumn brings glad, golden hours.
The woodlands re-echo with music,
    The moonbeams ensilver the sea ;
There is sunlight and beauty about us,
    And the world is as fair as can be.

But mortals are always complaining,
    Each one thinks his own a sad lot ;
And forgetting the good things about him,
    Goes mourning for those he has not.

ELLA WHEELER WILCOX

Instead of the star-spangled heavens,
  We look on the dust at our feet ;
We drain out the cup that is bitter,
  Forgetting the one that is sweet.

We mourn o'er the thorn in the flower,
  Forgetting its odour and bloom ;
We pass by a garden of blossoms,
  To weep o'er the dust of the tomb.
There are blessings unnumbered about us,—
  Like the leaves of the forest they grow ;
And the fault is our own—not the Giver's—
  That we have not an Eden below.

GOING AWAY

WALKING to-day on the Common,
    I heard a stranger say
To a friend who was standing near him,
  " Do you know I am going away ? "
I had never seen their faces,
  May never see them again ;
Yet the words the stranger uttered,
  Stirred me with nameless pain.

For I knew some heart would miss him,
  Would ache at his going away !
And the earth would seem all cheerless
  For many and many a day.

POEMS OF LOVE

No matter how light my spirits,
  No matter how glad my heart,
If I hear those two words spoken,
  The teardrops always start.

They are so sad and solemn,
  So full of a lonely sound ;
Like dead leaves rustling downward,
  And dropping upon the ground,
Oh, I pity the naked branches,
  When the skies are dull and gray,
And the last leaf whispers softly,
  " Good-bye, I am going away."

In the dreary, dripping autumn,
  The wings of the flying birds,
As they soar away to the south land,
  Seem always to say those words.
Wherever they may be spoken,
  They fall with a sob and sigh ;
And heartaches follow the sentence,
  " I am going away, Good-bye."

O God, in Thy blessed kingdom,
  No lips shall ever say,
No ears shall ever hearken
  To the words " I am going away."
For no soul ever wearies
  Of the dear, bright angel land,
And no saint ever wanders
  From the sunny golden land.

ELLA WHEELER WILCOX

BE NOT WEARY

SOMETIMES, when I am toil-worn and aweary,
  And tired out with working long and well,
And earth is dark, and skies above are dreary,
  And heart and soul are all too sick to tell,
These words have come to me like angel fingers
  Pressing the spirit's eyelids down in sleep,
" Oh let us not be weary in well doing,
  For in due season we shall surely reap."

Oh, blessed promise !   When I seem to hear it,
  Whispered by angel voices on the air,
It breathes new life and courage to my spirit,
  And gives me strength to suffer and forbear.
And I can wait most patiently for harvest,
  And cast my seeds, nor ever faint, nor weep,
If I know surely that my work availeth,
  And in God's season, I at last shall reap.

When mind and body were borne down completely,
  And I have thought my efforts were all in vain,
These words have come to me so softly, sweetly,
  And whispered hope, and urged me on again.
And though my labour seems all unavailing,
  And all my striving fruitless, yet the Lord
Doth treasure up each little seed I scatter,
  And sometime, *sometime*, I shall reap reward.

THE SUMMONS

SOME day, when the golden glory
  Of June is over the earth,
And the birds are singing together
  In a wild, mad strain of mirth;
When the skies are as clear and cloudless
  As the skies of June can be,
I would like to have the summons
  Sent down from God to me.

Some glowing, golden morning
  In the heart of the summer time,
As I stand in the perfect vigour
  And strength of my youth's glad prime;
When my heart is light and happy,
  And the world seems bright to me,
I would like to drop from this earth life,
  As a green leaf drops from the tree.

I would not wait for the furrows—
  For the faded eyes and hair;
But pass out swift and sudden,
  Ere I grow heart-sick with care;
I would break some morn in my singing—
  Or fall in my springing walk
As a full-blown flower will sometimes
  Drop, all a-bloom, from the stalk.

ELLA WHEELER WILCOX

I think the leaf would sooner
  Be the first to break away,
Than to hang alone in the orchard
  In the bleak November day.
And I think the fate of the flower
  That falls in the midst of bloom
Is sweeter than if it lingered
  To die in the autumn's gloom.

And so, in my youth's glad morning,
  While the summer walks abroad,
I would like to hear the summons,
  That must come, sometime, from God.
I would pass from the earth's perfection
  To the endless June above :
From the fullness of living and loving,
  To the noon of Immortal Love.

DENIED

THE winds came out of the west one day,
  And hurried the clouds before them ;
And drove the shadows and mists away,
  And over the mountains bore them.
And I wept, " Oh, wind, blow into my mind,
  Blow into my soul and heart,
And scatter the clouds that hang like shrouds,
  And make the shadows depart."

POEMS OF LOVE

The rain came out of the leaden skies
　　And beat on the earth's cold bosom.
It said to the sleeping grass, " Arise,"
　　And the young buds sprang in blossom.
And I wept in pain, " Oh, blessèd rain,
　　Beat into my heart to-day ;
Thaw out the snows that are chilling it so,
　　Till it blossoms in hope, I pray."

The sunshine fell on the bare-armed trees,
　　In a wonderful sheen of glory ;
And the young leaves rustled and sang to the breeze,
　　And whispered a love-fraught story.
And " Sun, oh, shine on this heart of mine,
　　And woo it to life," I cried ;
But the wind, and sun, and rain, each one
　　The coveted boon denied.

OVER THE ALLEY

HERE in my office I sit and write
　　Hour on hour, and day on day,
With no one to speak to from morn till night,
　　Though I have a neighbour just over the way.
Across the alley that yawns between
　　A maiden sits sewing the whole day long ;
A face more lovely is seldom seen
　　In hall or castle or country throng.

ELLA WHEELER WILCOX

Her curling tresses are golden brown ;
  Her eyes, I think, are violet blue,
Though her long, thick lashes are always down,
  Jealously hiding the orbs from view ;
Her neck is slender, and round, and white,
  And this way and that way her soft hair blows,
As there in the window, from morn till night,
  She sits in her beauty, and sings and sews.

And I, in my office chair, lounge and dream,
  In an idle way, of a sweet " might be,"
While the maid at her window sews her seam,
  With never a glance or a thought for me.
Perhaps she is angry because I look
  So long and often across the way,
Over the top of my ledger book ;
  But those stolen glances brighten the day.

And I am blameless of any wrong ;—
  She the transgressor, by sitting there
And making my eyes turn oft and long
  To a face so delicate, pure and fair.
Work is forgotten ; the page lies clean,
  Untouched by the pen, while hours go by.
Oh, maid of the pensive air and mien !
  Give me one glance of your violet eye.

Drop your thimble or spool of thread
  Down in the alley, I pray, my sweet,
Or the comb or ribbon from that fair head,
  That I may follow with nimble feet ;

For how can I tell you my heart has gone
   Across the alley, and lingers there,
Till I know your name, my beautiful one ?
   How could I venture, and how could I dare ?

Just one day longer I'll wait and dream,
   And then, if you grant me no other way,
I shall write you a letter : " Maid of the seam,
   You have stolen my property ; now give pay,
Beautiful robber and charming thief !
   Give but a glance for the deed you've done."
Thus shall I tell you my loss and grief,
   Over the alley, my beautiful one.

AT THE WINDOW

EVERY morning, as I walk down
   From my dreary lodgings, toward the town,
I see at a window, near the street,
The face of a woman, fair and sweet,
With soft brown eyes and chestnut hair,
And red lips, warm with the kiss left there.
And she stands there as long as she can see
The man who walks just ahead of me.

At night, when I come from my office down town,
There stands the woman with eyes of brown,
Smiling out through the window blind
At the man who is walking just behind.

ELLA WHEELER WILCOX

This fellow and I resemble each other—
At least so I'm told by one and another,
(Though I think I'm the handsomer far, of the two,)
I don't know him at all, save to " how d'ye do,"
Or nod when I meet him.   I think he's at work
In a dry-goods store, as a salaried clerk.
And I am a lawyer of high renown,
Have a snug bank account and an office down town,—
Yet I feel for that fellow an envious spite,
(It has no other name, so I speak it outright.)
There were symptoms before ; but it's grown, I believe,
Alarmingly fast, since one cloudy eve,
When passing the little house close by the street,
I heard the patter of two little feet,
And a figure in pink fluttered down to the gate,
And a sweet voice exclaimed, " Oh, Will, you are late !
And, darling, I've watched at the window until——
Sir, I beg pardon !   I thought it was Will ! "

I passed on my way, with such a strange feeling
Down in my heart.   My brain seemed to be reeling ;
For, as it happens, my name, too, is Will,
And that voice, crying " darling," sent such an odd thrill
Throughout my whole being !   " How nice it would be,"
Thought I, " if it were in reality me
That she's watched and longed for, instead of that lout ! "
(It was envy that made me use that word, no doubt,)
For he's a fine fellow, and handsome !—(ahem !)
But then it's absurd that this rare little gem
Of a woman should stand there and look out for him

Till she brings on a headache, and makes her eyes dim,
While I go to lodgings, dull, dreary and bare,
With no one to welcome me, no one to care
If I'm early or late.   No soft eyes of brown
To watch when I go to, or come from the town.

This bleak, wretched, bachelor life is about
(If I may be allowed the expression) played out.
Somewhere there must be, in the wide world, I think,
Another fair woman who dresses in pink,
And I know of a cottage, for sale, just below,
And it has a French window in front, and—heigho !
I wonder how long, at the longest, 'twill be
Before, coming home from the office, I'll see
A nice little woman there, watching for me.

MY SHIP

IF all the ships I have at sea
   Should come a-sailing home to me,
Laden with precious gems and gold,
Ah, well ! the harbour could not hold
So many sails as there would be,
If all my ships came in from sea.

If half my ships came home from sea,
And brought their precious freight to me,
Ah, well ! I should have wealth as great
As any king who rules in state,
So rich the treasures that would be
If half my ships now out at sea.

ELLA WHEELER WILCOX

If just one ship I have at sea
Should come a-sailing home to me,
Ah, well ! the storm clouds then might frown ;
For if the others all went down,
Still rich, and proud, and glad, I'd be
If that one ship came back to me.

If that one ship went down at sea,
And all the others came to me,
Weighed down with gems and wealth untold,
With glory, honour, riches, gold—
The poorest soul on earth I'd be
If that one ship came not to me.

O skies, be calm ! O winds, blow free !
Blow all my ships safe home to me ;
But if thou sendest some a-wrack
To never more come sailing back,
Send any—all that skim the sea,
But bring my love-ship home to me.

INDEPENDENCE ODE

COLUMBIA, fair queen in your glory !
Columbia, the pride of the earth !
We crown you with song-wreath and story ;
We honour the day of your birth !

POEMS OF LOVE

The wrath of a king and his minions
    You braved, to be free, on that day ;
And the eagle sailed up on strong pinions,
    And frightened the lion at bay.

Since the chains and the shackles are broken,
    And citizens now replace slaves,
Since the hearts of your heroes have spoken
    How dear they held freedom—by graves.

Your beautiful banner is blotless
    As it floats to the breezes unfurled,
And but for one blemish, all spotless
    Is the record you show to the world.

Like a scar on the features of beauty,
    Lies Utah, sin-cursed, in the west.
Columbia ! Columbia ! your duty
    Is to wipe out that stain with the rest !

Not only in freedom, and science,
    And letters, should you lead the earth ;
But let the earth learn your reliance
    In honour and true moral worth.

When Liberty's torch shall be lighted,
    Let her brightest most far-reaching rays
Discover no wrong that's unrighted—
    Go challenge the jealous world's gaze !

ELLA WHEELER WILCOX

Columbia, your star is ascending !
Columbia, all lands own your sway !
May your reign be as proud and unending
As your glory is brilliant to-day.

" SWEET DANGER "

THE danger of war, with its havoc of life,
The danger of ocean, when storms are rife,
The danger of jungles, where wild beasts hide,
The danger that lies in the mountain slide—
Why, what are they but all mere child's play,
Or the idle sport of a summer day,
Beside those battles that stir and vex
The world forever, of sex with sex ?

The warrior returns from the captured fort,
The mariner sails to a peaceful port ;
The wild beast quails 'neath the strong man's eye,
The avalanche passes the traveller by—
But who can rescue from passion's pyre
The hearts that were offered to feed its fire ?
Ah ! he who emerges from that fierce flame
Is scarred with sorrow or blackened with shame.

Battle and billow, and beast of prey,
They only threaten the mortal clay ;
The soul unfettered can take to wing,
But the danger of love is another thing.

POEMS OF LOVE

Once under the tyrant Passion's control,
He crushes body, and heart, and soul.
An hour of rapture, an age of despair,
Ah! these are the trophies of love's warfare.

And yet forever, since time began,
Has man dared woman and woman lured man
To that sweet danger that lurks and lies
In the bloodless battle of eyes with eyes;
That reckless danger, as vast as sweet,
Whose bitter ending is joy's defeat.
Ah! thus forever, while time shall last,
On passion's altar must hearts be cast!

ONE WOMAN'S PLEA

NOW God be with the men who stand
    In legislative halls, to-day.
Those chosen princes of our land—
    May God be with them all, I say,
And may His wisdom guide and shield them,
For mighty is the trust we yield them.

Oh, men! who hold a people's fate,
    There in the hollow of your hand,
Each word you utter, soon or late,
    Shall leave its impress on our land—
Forth from the halls of legislation,
Shall speed its way through all our nation.

ELLA WHEELER WILCOX

Then, may the Source of Truth, and Light,
  Be ever o'er them, ever near,
And may He guide each word aright ;
  May no false precept greet the ear,
No selfish love, for purse, or faction,
Stay Justice's hand, or guide one action.

And may no one among these men
  Lift to his lips the damning glass,
Let no man say, with truth, again,
  What has been said, in truth, alas !
" Men drink, in halls of legislation—
Why shouldn't we, of lower station ? "

And may God's lasting curses fall
  On those who hint, or boldly say,
That men have need of alcohol,
  Or that wine helps them, anyway.
These imps of hell—for all who aid them
May God's eternal curse upbraid them.

Oh, men ! you see, you hear this beast,
  This fiend that pillages the earth,
Whose work is death—whose hourly feast,
  Is noble souls, and minds of worth—
You see—and if you will not chain him,
Nor reach one hand forth, to detain him,

For God's sake, do not give him aid,
  Nor urge him onward. Oh, to me

POEMS OF LOVE

It seems so strange that laws are made
  To crush all other crimes, while he
Who bears down through Hell's gaping portals
The countless souls of rum-wrecked mortals

Is left to wander, to and fro,
  In perfect freedom through the land,
And those who ought to see, and know,
  Will lift no warning voice or hand.
Oh, men in halls of legislation,
Rise to the combat, save the nation!

IF

IF I were sent to represent
    A portion of a nation
I would not chat, on this and that,
  In the halls of legislation.
To show my power, I'd waste no hour
  In aimless talk and bother,
Nor fritter away a precious day
  On this and that and the other.

Whether the food a dog consumes
  Wouldn't make a porker fatter,
And about a thousand useless things
  Of no import or matter—

ELLA WHEELER WILCOX

Whether each day a man should pray
  For our welfare, or shouldn't.
Now I do not say men do this way;
  I merely say I wouldn't!

No! were I sent to represent
  A state, or town, or county,
I'd do some good, and all I could,
  To earn the people's bounty.
Instead of a dog, or a fattening hog,
  I'd talk about men's drinking!
And, with words of fire, I would inspire
  The stolid and unthinking.

And the time that I might idly waste,
  (I don't say men do waste it),
I'd spend in pleading for my cause,
  And, with tongue and pen, I'd haste it
Through all the land, till a mighty band,
  With laws and legislation,
Should cleanse the stain and cut the chain
  That binds our helpless nation.

And little need would there be then,
  When that bright sun had risen,
Of asylum wings or building sites—
  Of county or State prison.
The need is made by the liquor trade!
  Oh, ye wise, sage law-makers,
'Tis the friend you smile upon that makes
  Our madmen and law-breakers.

POEMS OF REFLECTION

BOHEMIA

BOHEMIA, o'er thy unatlased borders
   How many cross, with half-reluctant feet,
And unformed fears of dangers and disorders,
   To find delights, more wholesome and more sweet
   Than ever yet were known to the " *élite*."

Herein can dwell no pretence and no seeming;
   No stilted pride thrives in this atmosphere,
Which stimulates a tendency to dreaming.
   The shores of the ideal world, from here,
   Seem sometimes to be tangible and near.

We have no use for formal codes of fashion;
   No " Etiquette of Courts " we emulate;
We know it needs sincerity and passion
   To carry out the plans of God, or fate;
   We do not strive to seem inanimate.

We call no time lost that we give to pleasure;
   Life's hurrying river speeds to Death's great sea;
We cast out no vain plummet-line to measure
   Imagined depths of that unknown To Be,
   But grasp the *Now*, and fill it full of glee.

ELLA WHEELER WILCOX

All creeds have room here, and we all together
  Devoutly worship at Art's sacred shrine ;
But he who dwells once in thy golden weather,
  Bohemia—sweet, lovely land of mine—
  Can find no joy outside thy border-line.

·

PENALTY

BECAUSE of the fullness of what I had,
  All that I have seems poor and vain.
If I had not been happy, I were not sad—
  Tho' my salt is savourless, why complain ?

From the ripe perfection of what was mine,
  All that is mine seems worse than naught ;
Yet I know, as I sit in the dark and pine,
  No cup could be drained which had not been fraught.

From the throb and thrill of a day that was,
  The day that now is seems dull with gloom ;
Yet I bear the dullness and darkness, because
  'Tis but the reaction of glow and bloom.

From the royal feast that of old was spread
  I am starved on the diet that now is mine ;
Yet, I could not turn hungry from water and bread
  If I had not been sated on fruit and wine.

POEMS OF REFLECTION

ONLY DREAMS

A MAIDEN sat in the sunset glow
　　Of the shadowy, beautiful Long Ago,
　That we see through a mist of tears.
She sat and dreamed, with lips apart,
With thoughtful eyes and a beating heart,
　Of the mystical future years ;
And brighter far than the sunset skies
Was the vision seen by the maiden's eyes.

There were castles built of the summer air,
And beautiful voices were singing there,
　In a soft and floating strain.
There were skies of azure and fields of green,
With never a cloud to come between,
　And never a thought of pain ;
There was music, sweet as the silvery notes
That flow from a score of thrushes' throats.

There were hands to clasp with a loving hold ;
There were lips to kiss, and eyes that told
　More than the lips could say.
And all the faces she loved were there,
With their snowy brows untouched by care,
　And locks that were never grey.
And Love was the melody each heart beat,
And the beautiful vision was all complete.

ELLA WHEELER WILCOX

But the castles built of the summer wind
I have vainly sought. I only find
   Shadows, all grim and cold ;—
For I was the maiden who thought to see
Into the future years,—Ah, me !
   And I am grey and old.
My dream of earth was as fair and bright
As my hope of heaven is to-night.

Dreams are but dreams at the very best,
And the friends I loved lay down to rest
   With their faces hid away.
They had furrowed brows and snowy hair,
And they willingly laid their burdens where
   Mine shall be laid one day.
A shadow came over my vision scene
As the clouds of sorrow came in between.

The hands that I thought to clasp are crossed,
The lips and the beautiful eyes are lost,
   And I seek them all in vain.
The gushes of melody, sweet and clear,
And the floating voices, I do not hear,
   But only a sob of pain ;
And the beating hearts have paused to rest.
Ah ! dreams are but dreams at the very best.

POEMS OF REFLECTION

WHEN

I DWELL in the western inland,
　Afar from the sounding sea,
But I seem to hear it sobbing
　And calling aloud to me,
And my heart cries out for the ocean
　As a child for its mother's breast,
And I long to lie on its waters
　And be lulled in its arms to rest.

I can close my eyes and fancy
　That I hear its mighty roar,
And I see its blue waves splashing
　And plunging against the shore ;
And the white foam caps the billow,
　And the sea-gulls wheel and cry,
And the cool wild wind is blowing,
　And the ships go sailing by.

Oh, wonderful, mighty ocean !
　When shall I ever stand,
Where my heart has gone already,
　There on thy gleaming strand !
When shall I ever wander
　Away from this inland west,
And stand by thy side, dear ocean,
　And rock on thy heaving breast ?

ELLA WHEELER WILCOX

CONTENTMENT

IF any line that I ever penned,
  Or any word I have spoken,
Has comforted heart of foe or friend—
  In any way, why my life, I'll say,
Has reaped the reward of labour,
  If aught I have said, or written, has made
Gladder the heart o' my neighbour.

If any deed that I ever did
  Lightened a sad heart's sorrow,
If I have lifted a drooping lid
  Up to the bright to-morrow,
Though the world knows not, nor gives me a thought,
  Nor ever can know, nor praise me,
Yet still I shall say, to my heart alway,
  That my life and labour repay me.

If in any way I have helped a soul,
  Or given a spirit pleasure,
Then my cup of joy, I shall think, is full
  With an overflowing measure.
Though never an eye but the one on high
  Looks on my kindly action,
Yet, O my heart, we shall think of our part
  In the drama, with satisfaction.

MOTHER'S LOSS

IF I could clasp my little babe
  Upon my breast to-night,
I would not mind the blowing wind
  That shrieketh in affright.
Oh, my lost babe ! my little babe,
  My babe with dreamful eyes ;
Thy bed is cold ; and night wind bold
  · Shrieks woeful lullabies.

My breast is softer than the sod ;
  This room, with lighter hearth,
Is better place for thy sweet face
  Than frozen mother earth.
Oh, my babe ! oh, my lost babe !
  Oh, babe with waxen hands,
I want thee so, I need thee so—
  Come from thy mystic lands !

No love that, like a mother's, fills
  Each corner of the heart ;
No loss like hers, that rends, and chills,
  And tears the soul apart.
Oh, babe—my babe, my helpless babe !
  I miss thy little form.
Would I might creep where thou dost sleep,
  And clasp thee through the storm.

ELLA WHEELER WILCOX

I hold thy pillow to my breast,
　To bring a vague relief ;
I sing the songs that soothed thy rest—
　Ah me ! no cheating grief.
My breathing babe ! my sobbing babe !
　I miss thy plaintive moan,
I cannot hear—thou art not near—
　My little one, my own.

Thy father sleeps.　He mourns thy loss,
　But little fathers know
The pain that makes a mother toss
　Through sleepless nights of woe.
My clinging babe ! my nursing babe !
　What knows thy father—man—
How my breasts miss thy lips' soft kiss—
　None but a mother can.

Worn out, I sleep ; I wake—I weep—
　I sleep—hush, hush, my dear ;
Sweet lamb, fear not—Oh, God ! I thought—
　I thought my babe was here.

THE LITTLE BIRD

THE father sits in his lonely room,
　Outside sings a little bird.
But the shadows are laden with death and gloom,
　And the song is all unheard.

POEMS OF REFLECTION

The father's heart is the home of sorrow ;
  His breast is the seat of grief !
Who will hunt the paper for him on the morrow—
  Who will bring him sweet relief
From wearing thought with innocent chat ?
Who will find his slippers and bring his hat ?
   Still the little bird sings
   And flutters her wings ;
The refrain of her song is, " God knows best !
He giveth His little children rest."
What can she know of these sorrowful things ?

The mother sits by the desolate hearth,
  And weeps o'er a vacant chair.
Sorrow has taken the place of mirth—
  Joy has resigned to despair.
Bitter the cup the mother is drinking,
  So bitter the tear-drops start.
Sad are the thoughts the mother is thinking—
  Oh, they will break her heart.
Who will run on errands, and romp and play,
And mimic the robins the livelong day ?
   Still the little bird sings
   And flutters her wings ;
" God reigns in heaven, and He will keep
The dear little children that fall asleep."
What can she know of these sorrowful things ?

Grandmother sits by the open door,
  And her tears fall down like rain.

ELLA WHEELER WILCOX

Was there ever a household so sad before,
   Will it ever be glad again ?
Many unwelcome thoughts come flitting
   Into the granddame's mind.
Who will take up the stitches she drops in knitting ?
   Who will her snuff-box find ?
Who'll bring her glasses, and wheel her chair,
And tie her kerchief, and comb her hair ?
     Still the little bird sings
     And flutters her wings ;
" God above doeth all things well,
I sang it the same when my nestlings fell."
Ah ! this knows the bird of these sorrowful things.

THE KING AND SIREN

THE harsh King—Winter—sat upon the hills,
   And reigned and ruled the earth right royally.
He locked the rivers, lakes, and all the rills—
   " I am no puny, maudlin king," quoth he,
" But a stern monarch, born to rule, and reign ;
   And I'll show my power to the end.
The Summer's flowery retinue I've slain,
   And taken the bold free North Wind for my friend.

" Spring, Summer, Autumn—feeble queens they were,
   With their vast troops of flowers, birds and bees,
Soft winds, that made the long green grasses stir—
   They lost their own identity in things like these !

I scorn them all ! nay, I defy them all !
   And none can wrest the sceptre from my hand.
The trusty North Wind answers to my call,
   And breathes his icy breath upon the land."

The Siren—South Wind—listening the while,
   Now floated airily across the lea.
" O King ! " she cried, with tender tone and smile,
   " I come to do all homage unto thee.
In all the sunny region, whence I came,
   I find none like thee, King, so brave and grand !
Thine is a well-deserved, unrivalled fame ;
   I kiss, in awe, dear King, thy cold white hand."

Her words were pleasing, and most fair her face,
   He listened rapt to her soft-whispered praise.
She nestled nearer, in her Siren grace.
   " Dear King," she said, " henceforth my voice shall
   raise
But songs of thy unrivalled splendour ! Lo !
   How white thy brow is ! How thy garments shine !
I tremble 'neath thy beaming glance, for oh,
   Thy wondrous beauty makes thee seem divine."

The vain King listened, in a trance of bliss,
   To this most sweet-voiced Siren from the South.
She nestled close, and pressed a lingering kiss
   Upon the stern white pallor of his mouth.
She hung upon his breast, she pressed his cheek,
   And he was nothing loath to hold her there,
While she such tender, loving words did speak,
   And combed his white locks with her fingers fair.

ELLA WHEELER WILCOX

And so she bound him, in her Siren wiles,
  And stole his strength, with every kiss she gave,
And stabbed him through and through, with tender
    smiles,
  And with her loving words, she dug his grave ;
And then she left him, old, and weak, and blind,
  And unlocked all the rivers, lakes, and rills,
While the queen Spring, with her whole troop, behind,
  Of flowers, and birds, and bees, came o'er the hills.

SUNSHINE AND SHADOW

LIFE has its shadows, as well as its sun ;
  Its lights and its shades, all twined together.
I tried to single them out, one by one,
  Single and count them, determining whether
There was less blue than there was grey,
And more of the deep night than of the day.
But dear me, dear me, my task's but begun,
And I am not half way into the sun.

For the longer I look on the bright side of earth,
  The more of the beautiful do I discover ;
And really, I never knew what life was worth
  Till I searched the wide storehouse of happiness over.
It is filled from the cellar well up to the skies,
With things meant to gladden the heart and the eyes.
The doors are unlocked, you can enter each room,
That lies like a beautiful garden in bloom.

POEMS OF REFLECTION

Yet life has its shadow, as well as its sun ;
  Earth has its storehouse of joy and of sorrow.
But the first is so wide—and my task's but begun—
  That the last must be left for a far-distant morrow.
I will count up the blessings God gave in a row,
But dear me ! when I get through them, I know
I shall have little time left for the rest,
For life is a swift-flowing river at best.

WORLDLY WISDOM

IF it were in my dead Past's power
    To let my Present bask
In some lost pleasure for an hour,
  This is the boon I'd ask :

Re-pedestal from out the dust
  Where long ago 'twas hurled,
My beautiful incautious trust
  In this unworthy world.

The symbol of my own soul's truth—
  I saw it go with tears—
The sweet unwisdom of my youth—
  That vanished with the years.

Since knowledge brings us only grief,
  I would return again
To happy ignorance and belief
  In motives and in men.

215

ELLA WHEELER WILCOX

For worldly wisdom learned in pain
    Is in itself a cross,
Significant mayhap of gain,
    Yet sign of saddest loss.

SO LONG IN COMING

WHEN shall I hear the thrushes sing,
    And see their graceful, round throats swelling ?
When shall I watch the bluebirds bring
    The straws and twiglets for their dwelling ?
When shall I hear among the trees
    The little martial partridge drumming ?
Oh ! hasten ! sights and sounds that please—
    The summer is so long in coming.

The winds are talking with the sun ;
    I hope they will combine together
And melt the snow-drifts, one by one,
    And bring again the golden weather.
Oh, haste, make haste, dear sun and wind,
    I long to hear the brown bee humming ;
I seek for blooms I cannot find,
    The summer is so long in coming.

The winter has been cold, so cold ;
    Its winds are harsh, and bleak, and dreary,
And all its sports are stale and old ;
    We wait for something now more cheery.

POEMS OF REFLECTION

Come up, O summer, from the south,
   And bring the harps your hands are thrumming.
We pine for kisses from your mouth!
   Oh! do not be so long in coming.

LAY IT AWAY

WE will lay our summer away, my friend,
   So tenderly lay it away.
It was bright and sweet to the very end,
   Like one long, golden day.
Nothing sweeter could come to me,
   Nothing sweeter to you.
We will lay it away, and let it be,
   Hid from the whole world's view.

We will lay it away like a dear, dead thing—
   Dead, yet for ever fair;
And the fresh green robes of a deathless spring,
   Though dead, it shall always wear.
We will not hide it in grave or tomb,
   But lay it away to sleep,
Guarded by beauty, and light, and bloom,
   Wrapped in a slumber deep.

We were willing to let the summer go—
   Willing to go our ways;
But never on earth again I know
   Will either find such days.

ELLA WHEELER WILCOX

You are my friend, and it may seem strange,
  But I would not see you again ;
I would think of you, though all things change,
  Just as I knew you then.

If we should go back to the olden place,
  And the summer time went too,
It would be like looking a ghost in the face,
  So much would be changed and new.
We cannot live it over again,
  Not even a single day ;
And as something sweet, and free from pain,
  We had better lay it away.

PERISHED

I CALLED to the summer sun,
  " Come over the hills to-day !
Unlock the rivers, and tell them to run,
And kiss the snow-drifts and melt them away."
  And the sun came over—a tardy lover—
  And unlocked the river, and told it to glide,
  And kissed the snow-drift till it fainted and died.

I called to the robin, " Come back !
Come up from the south and sing ! "
  And robin sailed up on an airy track,
And smoothed down his feathers and oiled his wing.
  And the notes came gushing, gurgling, rushing,
  In trills and quavers, clear, mellow, and strong,
  Till the glad air quivered and rang with song.

POEMS OF REFLECTION

I said to the orchard, " Blow ! "
I said to the meadow, " Bloom ! "
And the trees stood white, like brides in a
row,
And the breeze was laden with rare perfume.
And over the meadows, in lights and shadows,
The daisies white and violets blue,
And yellow-haired buttercups blossomed and
grew.

I called to a hope, that died
With the death of the flowers and grass,
" Come back ! for the river is free to glide—
The robin sings, and the daisies bloom." Alas !
For the hope I cherished too rudely perished
To ever awaken and live again,
Though a hundred summers creep over the plain.

THE BELLE'S SOLILOQUY

HEIGH ho ! well, the season's over !
    Once again we've come to Lent !
Programme's changed from balls and parties—
    Now we're ordered to repent.
Forty days of self-denial !
    Tell you what, I think it pays—
Know't'l freshen my complexion
    Going slow for forty days.

ELLA WHEELER WILCOX

No more savoury French suppers—
　Such as Madame R— can give.
Well, I need a little *thinning*—
　Just a trifle—sure's you live.
Sometimes been afraid my plumpness
　Might grow into downright fat.
Rector urges need of fasting—
　Think there's lot of truth in that.

We must meditate, he tells us,
　On our several acts of sin,
And repent them.　Let me see now—
　Whereabouts shall I begin !
Flirting—yes, they say 'tis wicked ;
　Well, I'm awful penitent.
(Wonder if my handsome major
　Goes to early Mass through Lent ?)

Love of dress ! I'm guilty there too—
　Guess it's my besetting sin.
Still I'm somewhat like the lilies,
　For I neither toil nor spin.
Forty days I'll wear my plainest—
　Could repentance be more true ?
What a saving on my dresses !
　They'll make over just like new.

Pride, and worldliness and all that,
　Rector bade us pray about
Every day through Lenten season,
　And I mean to be devout !

My Vision

Papa always talks retrenchment—
  Lent is just the very thing.
Hope he'll get enough in pocket
  So we'll move up town next spring.

MY VISION

WHEREVER my feet may wander,
  Wherever I chance to be,
There comes with the coming of even-time
  A vision sweet to me.
I see my mother sitting
  In the old familiar place,
And she rocks to the tune her needles sing,
  And thinks of an absent face.

I can hear the roar of the city
  About me now as I write ;
But over an hundred miles of snow
  , My thought-steeds fly to-night,
To the dear little cosy cottage,
  And the room where mother sits,
And slowly rocks in her easy-chair
  And thinks of me as she knits.

Sometimes with the merry dancers
  When my feet are keeping time,
And my heart beats high, as young hearts will
  To the music's rhythmic chime,

ELLA WHEELER WILCOX

My spirit slips over the distance,
  Over the glitter and whirl,
To my mother who sits, and rocks, and knits,
  And thinks of her " little girl."

When I listen to voices that flatter,
  And smile, as women do,
To whispered words that may be sweet,
  But are not always true ;
I think of the sweet, quaint picture
  Afar in quiet ways,
And I know one smile of my mother's eyes
  Is better than all their praise.

And I know I can never wander
  Far from the path of right,
Though snares are set for a woman's feet
  In places that seem most bright.
For the vision is with me always,
  Wherever I chance to be,
Of mother sitting, rocking and knitting,
  Thinking and praying for me.

SING TO ME

SING to me ! something of sunlight and bloom,
  I am so compassed with sorrow and gloom,
I am so sick with the world's noise and strife,—
Sing of the beauty and brightness of life—
  Sing to me, sing to me !

POEMS OF REFLECTION

Sing to me! something that's jubilant, glad!
I am so weary, my soul is so sad.
All my earth riches are covered with rust,
All my bright dreams are but ashes and dust.
    Sing to me, sing to me!

Sing of the blossoms that open in spring,
How the sweet flowers blow, and the long lichens cling,
Say, though the winter is round about me,
There are bright summers and springs yet to be.
    Sing to me, sing to me!

Sing me a song full of hope and of truth,
Brimming with all the sweet fancies of youth!
Say, though my sorrow I may not forget,
I have not quite done with happiness yet.
    Sing to me, sing to me!

Lay your soft fingers just here, on my cheek;
Turn the light lower—there—no, do not speak,
But sing! My heart thrills at your beautiful voice;
  Sing till I turn from my grief and rejoice.
    Sing to me, sing to me!

SUMMER SONG

THE meadow lark's trill and the brown thrush's
    whistle
From morning to evening fill all the sweet air,
And my heart is as light as the down of a thistle—
  The world is so bright and the earth is so fair.

ELLA WHEELER WILCOX

There is life in the wood, there is bloom on the meadow ;—
    The air drips with songs that the merry birds sing.
The sunshine has won, in the battle with shadow,
    And she's dressed the glad earth with robes of the
        spring.

The bee leaves his hive for the field of red clover
    And the vale where the daisies bloom white as the snow,
And a mantle of warm yellow sunshine hangs over
    The calm little pond, where the pale lilies grow.
In the woodland beyond it, a thousand gay voices
    Are singing in chorus some jubilant air.
The bird and the bee and all nature rejoices,
    The world is so bright, and the earth is so fair.

I am glad as a child, in this beautiful weather ;
    I have tossed all my burdens and trials away ;
My heart is as light—yes, as light as a feather ;—
    I am care-free, and careless, and happy to-day.
Can it be there approaches a dark, dreary to-morrow ?
    Can shadows e'er fall on this beautiful earth ?
Ah ! to-day is my own ! no forebodings of sorrow
    Shall darken my skies, or shall dampen my mirth.

JOY

MY heart is like a little bird
    That sits and sings for very gladness.
Sorrow is some forgotten word,
    And so, except in rhyme, is sadness.

POEMS OF REFLECTION

The world is very fair to me—
  Such azure skies, such golden weather,
I'm like a long caged bird set free,
  My heart is lighter than a feather.

I rise rejoicing in my life ;
  I live with love for God and neighbour ;
My days flow on unmarred by strife,
  And sweetened by my pleasant labour.

O youth ! O spring ! O happy days,
  Ye are so passing sweet, and tender,
And while the fleeting season stays,
  I revel care-free, in its splendour.

BIRD OF HOPE

SOAR not too high, O bird of Hope !
  Because the skies are fair ;
The tempest may come on apace
  And overcome thee there.

When far above the mountain tops
  Thou soarest, over all—
If, then, the storm should press thee back,
  How great would be thy fall !

And thou wouldst lie here at my feet,
  A poor and lifeless thing,—
A torn and bleeding birdling,
  With a limp and broken wing.

ELLA WHEELER WILCOX

Sing not too loud, O bird of Hope !
  Because the day is bright ;
The sunshine cannot always last—
  The morn precedes the night.

And if thy song is of the day,
  Then when the day grows dim,
Forlorn and voiceless thou wouldst sit
  Among the shadows grim.

Oh ! I would have thee soar and sing,
  But not too high, or loud,
Remembering that day meets night—
  The brilliant sun the cloud.

A GOLDEN DAY

THE subtle beauty of this day
  Hangs o'er me like a fairy spell,
And care and grief have flown away,
  And every breeze sings, " All is well."
I ask, " Holds earth of sin, or woe ? "
  My heart replies, " I do not know."

Nay ! all we know, or feel, my heart,
  To-day is joy undimmed, complete ;
In tears or pain we have no part ;
  The act of breathing is so sweet,
We care no higher joy to name.
  What reck we now of wealth or fame ?

POEMS OF REFLECTION

The past—what matters it to me ?
   The pain it gave has passed away.
The future—that I cannot see !
   I care for nothing save to-day—
This is a respite from all care,
   And trouble flies—I know not where.

Go on, oh, noisy, restless life !
   Pass by, oh, feet that seek for heights !
I have no part in aught of strife ;
   I do not want your vain delights.
The day wraps round me like a spell,
   And every breeze sings, " All is well."

FADING

ALL in the beautiful Autumn weather
   One thought lingers with me and stays ;
Death and winter are coming together,
   Though both are veiled by the amber haze.
I look on the forest of royal splendour !
   I look on the face in my quiet room ;
A face all beautiful, sad and tender,
   And both are stamped with the seal of doom.

All through the days of Indian summer,
   Minute by minute and hour by hour,
I feel the approach of a dreaded Comer—
   A ghastly presence of awful power.

ELLA WHEELER WILCOX

I hear the birds in the early morning,
  As they fly from the fields that are turning brown,
And at noon and at night my heart takes warning,
  For the maple leaves fall down and down.

The sumac bushes are all a-flaming !
  The world is scarlet, and gold, and green,
And my darling's beautiful cheeks are shaming
  The painted bloom of the ball-room queen.
Why talk of winter, amid such glory ?
  Why speak of death of a thing so fair ?
Oh, but the forest king white and hoary
  Is weaving a mantle for both to wear.

God ! if I could by the soft deceiving
  Of forests of splendour and cheeks of bloom
Lull my heart into sweet believing
  Just for a moment and drown my gloom ;
If I could forget for a second only
  And rest from the pain of this awful dread
Of days that are coming long and lonely
  When the Autumn goes and she is dead.

But all the while the sun gilds wood and meadow
  And the fair cheeks, hectic glows and cheats,
I know grim death sits veiled in shadow
  Weaving for both their winding sheets.
I cannot help, and I cannot save her.
  My hands are as weak as a babe's, new-born ;
I must yield her up to One who gave her
  And wait for the resurrection morn.

THE CHANGE

SHE leaned out into the soft June weather,
   With her long loose tresses the night breeze played;
Her eyes were as blue as the bells on the heather:
   Oh, what is so fair as a fair young maid!

She folded her hands, like the leaves of a lily,
   " My life," she said, " is a night in June,
Fair and quiet, and calm and stilly;
   Bring me a change, O changeful moon!

" Who would drift on a lake for ever?
   Young hearts weary—it is not strange,
And sigh for the beautiful bounding river;
   New moon, true moon, bring me a change!"

The rose that rivalled her maiden blushes
   Dropped from her breast, at a stranger's feet;
Only a glance; but the hot blood rushes
   To mantle a fair face, shy and sweet.

To and fro, while the moon is waning,
   They walk, and the stars shine on above;
And one is in earnest, and one is feigning—
   Oh, what is so sweet as a sweet young love?

ELLA WHEELER WILCOX

A young life crushed, and a young heart broken, —
  A bleak wind blows through the lovely bower,
And all that remains of the love vows spoken—
  Is the trampled leaf of a faded flower.

The night is dark, for the moon is failing—
  And what is so pale as a pale old moon !
Cold is the wind through the tree-tops wailing—
  Woe that the change should come so soon.

THE MUSICIANS

THE strings of my heart were strung by Pleasure,
  And I laughed when the music fell on my ear,
For he and Mirth played a joyful measure,
  And they played so loud that I could not hear
The wailing and mourning of souls a-weary—
  The strains of sorrow that floated around,
For my heart's notes rang out loud and cheery,
  And I heard no other sound.

Mirth and Pleasure, the music brothers,
  Played louder and louder in joyful glee ;
But sometimes a discord was heard by others—
  Though only the rhythm was heard by me.
Louder and louder, and faster and faster
  The hands of the brothers played strain on strain,
When all of a sudden a Mighty Master
  Swept them aside ; and Pain,

POEMS OF REFLECTION

Pain, the musician, the soul-refiner,
  Restrung the strings of my quivering heart,
And the air that he played was a plaintive minor,
  So sad that the tear-drops were forced to start;
Each note was an echo of awful anguish,
  As shrill as solemn, as sharp as slow,
And my soul for a season seemed to languish
  And faint with its weight of woe.

With skilful hands that were never weary,
  This Master of Music played strain on strain,
And between the bars of the miserere,
  He drew up the strings of my heart again,
And I was filled with a vague, strange wonder,
  To see that they did not snap in two.
" They are drawn so tight, they will break asunder,"
  I thought, but instead, they grew,

In the hands of the Master, firmer and stronger;
  And I could hear on the stilly air—
Now my ears were deafened by Mirth no longer—
  The sound of sorrow, and grief, and despair;
And my soul grew kinder and tender to others,
  My nature grew sweeter, my mind grew broad,
And I held all men to be my brothers,
  Linked by the chastening rod.

My soul was lifted to God and heaven,
  And when on my heart-strings fell again
The hands of Mirth, and Pleasure, even,
  There was never a discord to mar the strain.

ELLA WHEELER WILCOX

For Pain, the musician, and soul-refiner,
  Attuned the strings with a master hand,
And whether the music be major or minor,
  It is always sweet and grand.

PRESUMPTION

WHENEVER I am prone to doubt or wonder—
  I check myself, and say, " That mighty One
Who made the solar system cannot blunder—
  And for the best all things are being done."
Who set the stars on their eternal courses
  Has fashioned this strange earth by some sure plan.
Bow low, bow low to those majestic forces,
  Nor dare to doubt their wisdom—puny man.

You cannot put one little star in motion,
  You cannot shape one single forest leaf,
Nor fling a mountain up, nor sink an ocean,
  Presumptuous pigmy, large with unbelief.
You cannot bring one dawn of regal splendour,
  Nor bid the day to shadowy twilight fall,
Nor send the pale moon forth with radiance tender,
  And dare you doubt the One who has done all ?

" So much is wrong, there is such pain—such sinning."
  Yet look again—behold how much is right !
And He who formed the world from its beginning
  Knows how to guide it upward to the light.

POEMS OF REFLECTION

Your task, O man, is not to carp and cavil
  At God's achievements, but with purpose strong
To cling to good, and turn away from evil—
  That is the way to help the world along.

LISTEN !

WHOEVER you are as you read this,
  Whatever your trouble or grief,
I want you to know and to heed this:
  The day draweth near with relief.

No sorrow, no woe is unending,
  Though heaven seems voiceless and dumb;
So sure as your cry is ascending,
  So surely an answer will come.

Whatever temptation is near you,
  Whose eyes on this simple verse fall;
Remember good angels will hear you
  And help you to stand, if you call.

Though stunned with despair, I beseech you,
  Whatever your losses, your need,
Believe, when these printed words reach you,
  Believe you were born to succeed.

You are stronger, I tell you, this minute,
  Than any unfortunate fate !
And the coveted prize—you can win it ;
  While life lasts 'tis never too late !

233

ELLA WHEELER WILCOX

DAFT

IN the warm yellow smile of the morning,
  She stands at the lattice pane,
And watches the strong young binders
  Stride down to the fields of grain.
And she counts them over and over
  As they pass her cottage door :
Are they six, she counts them seven ;
  Are they seven, she counts one more.

When the sun swings high in the heavens,
  And the reapers go shouting home,
She calls to the household, saying,
  " Make haste ! for the binders have come !
And Johnnie will want his dinner—
  He was always a hungry child " ;
And they answer, " Yes, it is waiting " ;
  Then tell you, " Her brain is wild."

Again, in the hush of the evening,
  When the work of the day is done,
And the binders go singing homeward
  In the last red rays of the sun,
She will sit at the threshold waiting,
  And her withered face lights with joy :
" Come, Johnnie," she says, as they pass her,
  " Come into the house, my boy."

POEMS OF REFLECTION

Five summers ago her Johnnie
  Went out in the smile of the morn,
Singing across the meadow,
  Striding down through the corn—
He towered above the binders,
  Walking on either side,
And the mother's heart within her
  Swelled with exultant pride.

For he was the light of the household—
  His brown eyes were wells of truth,
And his face was the face of the morning,
  Lit with its pure, fresh youth,
And his song rang out from the hilltops
  Like the mellow blast of a horn,
And he strode o'er the fresh shorn meadows,
  And down through the rows of corn.

But hushed were the voices of singing,
  Hushed by the presence of death,
As back to the cottage they bore him—
  In the noontide's scorching breath,
For the heat of the sun had slain him,
  Had smitten the heart in his breast,
And he who had towered above them
  Lay lower than all the rest.

The grain grows ripe in the sunshine,
  And the summers ebb and flow,
And the binders stride to their labour
  And sing as they come and go ;

ELLA WHEELER WILCOX

But never again from the hilltops
   Echoes the voice like a horn;
Never up from the meadows,
   Never back from the corn.

Yet the poor, crazed brain of the mother
   Fancies him always near;
She is blest in her strange delusion,
   For she knoweth no pain nor fear,
And always she counts the binders
   As they pass her cottage door;
Are they six, she counts them seven;
   Are they seven, she counts one more.

WHEN I AM DEAD

WHEN I am dead, if some chastened one
      Seeing the "item," or hearing it said
That my play is over and my part done
   And I lie asleep in my narrow bed—
If I could know that some soul would say,
   Speaking aloud or silently,
"In the heat and the burden of the day
   She gave a refreshing draught to me";

Or, "When I was lying nigh unto death
   She nursed me to life and to strength again,
And when I laboured and struggled for breath
   She smoothed and quieted down my pain";

236

Or, " When I was groping in grief and doubt,
   Lost, and turned from the light o' the day,
Her hand reached me and helped me out
   And led me up to the better way " ;

Or, " When I was hated and shunned by all,
   Bowing under my sin and my shame,
She, once in passing me by, let fall
   Words of pity and hope, that came
Into my heart like a blessed calm
   Over the waves of the stormy sea,
Words of comfort like oil and balm,
   She spake, and the desert blossomed for me " ;

Better, by far, than a marble tomb—
   Than a monument towering over my head
(What shall I care, in my quiet room,
   For headboard or footboard when I am dead ?) ;
Better than glory, or honours, or fame
   (Though I am striving for those to-day),
To know that some heart would cherish my name
   And think of me kindly, with blessings, alway.

TWILIGHT THOUGHTS

THE God of the day has vanished,
   The light from the hills has fled,
And the hand of an unseen artist
   Is painting the west all red.

ELLA WHEELER WILCOX

All threaded with gold and crimson,
  And burnished with amber dye,
And tipped with purple shadows,
  The glory flameth high.

Fair, beautiful world of ours !
  Fair, beautiful world, but oh,
How darkened by pain and sorrow,
  How blackened by sin and woe.
The splendour pales in the heavens
  And dies in a golden gleam,
And alone in the hush of twilight,
  I sit, in a chequered dream.

I think of the souls that are straying,
  In shadows as black as night,
Of hands that are groping blindly
  In search of a shining light ;
Of hearts that are mutely crying,
  And praying for just one ray,
To lead them out of the shadows
  Into the better way.

And I think of the Father's children
  Who are trying to walk alone,
Who have dropped the hand of the Parent,
  And wander in ways unknown.
Oh, the paths are rough and thorny,
  And I know they cannot stand.
They will faint and fall by the wayside,
  Unguarded by God's right hand.

And I think of the souls that are yearning
  To follow the good and true ;
They are striving to live unsullied,
  Yet I know not what to do.
And I wonder when God, the Master,
  Shall end this weary strife,
And lead us out of the shadows
  Into the deathless life.

SONG OF THE SPIRIT

TOO sweet and too subtle for pen or for tongue
  In phrases unwritten and measures unsung,
As deep and as strange as the sounds of the sea,
Is the song that my spirit is singing to me.

In the midnight and tempest when forest trees shiver,
In the roar of the surf, and the rush of the river,
In the rustle of leaves and the fall of the rain,
And on the low breezes I catch the refrain.

From the vapours that frame and envelop the earth,
And beyond, from the realms where my spirit had birth,
From the mists of the land and the fogs of the sea,
For ever and ever the song comes to me.

I know not its wording—its import I know—
For the rhythm is broken, the measure runs low,
When vexed or allured by the things of this life
My soul is merged into its pleasures or strife.

ELLA WHEELER WILCOX

When up to the hilltops of beauty and light
My soul like a lark in the ether takes flight,
And the white gates of heaven shine brighter and
    nearer,
The song of the spirit grows sweeter and clearer.

Up, up to the realms where no mortal has trod—
Into space and infinity near to my God—
With whiteness, and silence, and beautiful things,
I am borne when the voice of eternity sings.

When once in the winds or the drop of the rain
Thy spirit shall listen and hear the refrain,
Thy soul shall soar up like a bird on the breeze,
And the things that have pleased thee will never more
    please.

FADING

SHE sits beside the window. All who pass
    Turn once again to gaze on her sweet face.
She is so fair ; but soon, too soon, alas,
    To lie down in her last resting-place.

No gems are brighter than her sparkling eyes,
    Her brow like polished marble, white and fair—
Her cheeks are glowing as the sunset skies—
    You would not dream that Death was lurking there.

But, oh ! he lingers closely at her side,
　And when the forest dons her Autumn dress,
We know that he will claim her as his bride,
　And earth will number one fair spirit less.

She sees the meadow robed in richest green—
　The laughing stream—the willows bending o'er.
With tear-dimmed eyes she views each sylvan scene,
　And thinks earth never was so fair before.

We do not sigh for heaven, till we have known
　Something of sorrow, something of grief and woe,
And as a summer day her life has flown.
　Oh, can we wonder she is loth to go ?

She has no friends in heaven : all are here.
　No lost one waits her in that unknown land,
And life grows doubly, trebly sweet and dear
　As day by day she nears the mystic strand.

We love her and we grieve to see her go.
　But it is Christ who calls her to His breast,
And He shall greet her, and she soon shall know
　The joys of souls that dwell among the blest.

UNTIL THE NIGHT

OVER the ocean of life's commotion
　　We sail till the night comes on,
Sail and sail in a tiny boat,
　Drifting wherever the billows go.

ELLA WHEELER WILCOX

Out on the treacherous sea afloat,
  Beat by the cruel winds that blow,
Hither and thither our boat is drawn,
Till the day dies out and the night comes on.

Over a meadow of light and shadow
  We wander with weary feet,
Seeking a bauble men call " Fame,"
  Grasping the dead-sea fruit named " wealth,"
Finding each but an empty name,
  And the night—the night steals on by stealth
And we count the season of slumber sweet,
When hope lies dead in the arms of defeat.

Over the river a great Forever
  Stretches beyond our sight.
But I know by the glistening pearly gates
  Afar from the region of strife and sin,
A beautiful angel always waits
  To welcome the sheep of the shepherd in.
And out of the shadows of gloom and night,
They enter the mansion of peace and light.

BEYOND

IT seemeth such a little way to me
  Across to that strange country—the Beyond ;
And yet, not strange, for it has grown to be
  The home of those of whom I am so fond ;
They make it seem familiar and most dear,
As journeying friends bring distant regions near.

POEMS OF REFLECTION

So close it lies, that when my sight is clear
    I think I almost see the gleaming strand. .
I know I feel those who have gone from here
    Come near enough sometimes, to touch my hand.
I often think, but for our veilèd eyes,
We should find heaven right round about us lies.

I cannot make it seem a day to dread,
    When from this dear earth I shall journey out
To that still dearer country of the dead,
    And join the lost ones, so long dreamed about.
I love this world, yet shall I love to go
And meet the friends who wait for me, I know.

I never stand above a bier and see
    The seal of death set on some well-loved face
But that I think, " One more to welcome me,
    When I shall cross the intervening space
Between this land and that one ' over there ' ;
One more to make the strange Beyond seem fair."

And so for me there is no sting to death,
    And so the grave has lost its victory.
It is but crossing—with a bated breath,
    And white, set face—a little strip of sea,
To find the loved ones waiting on the shore,
More beautiful, more precious than before.

ELLA WHEELER WILCOX

IDLER'S SONG

I SIT in the twilight dim
   At the close of an idle day,
And I list to the soft, sweet hymn
   That rises far away,
And dies on the evening air.
   Oh, all day long,
   They sing their song,
Who toil in the valley there.

But never a song sing I,
   Sitting with folded hands,
The hours pass me by—
   Dropping their golden sands—
And I list, from day to day,
   To the " tick, tick, tock "
   Of the old brown clock,
Ticking my life away.

And I see the twilight fade,
   And I see the night come on,
And then, in the gloom and shade,
   I weep for the day that's gone—
Weep and wail in pain,
   For the misspent day
   That has flown away,
And will not come again.

POEMS OF REFLECTION

Another morning beams,
    And I forget the last,
And I sit in idle dreams
    Till the day is over—past.
Oh, the toiler's heart is glad !
    When the day is gone
    And the night comes on,
But mine is sore and sad.

For I dare not look behind !
    No shining, golden sheaves
Can I ever hope to find :
    Nothing but withered leaves,
Ah, dreams are very sweet !
    But will not please
    If only these
I lay at the Master's feet.

And what will the Master say
    To dreams and nothing more ?
Oh, Idler, all the day !
    Think, ere thy life is o'er !
And when the day grows late,
    Oh, soul of sin !
    Will He let you in,
There at the pearly gate ?

Oh, idle heart, beware !
    On, to the field of strife !

ELLA WHEELER WILCOX

On, to the valley there!
And live a useful life!
Up, do not wait a day!
For the old brown clock,
With its " tick, tick, tock,"
Is ticking your life away.

A LEAF

SOMEBODY said, in the crowd, last eve,
 That you were married, or soon to be.
I have not thought of you, I believe,
 Since last we parted. Let me see :
Five long Summers have passed since then—
 Each has been pleasant in its own way—
And you are but one of a dozen men
 Who have played the suitor a Summer day.

But, nevertheless, when I heard your name,
 Coupled with some one's, not my own,
There burned in my bosom a sudden flame,
 That carried me back to the day that is flown.
I was sitting again by the laughing brook,
 With you at my feet and the sky above,
And my heart was fluttering under your look—
 The unmistakable look of Love.

Again your breath, like a South wind, fanned
 My cheek, where the blushes came and went ;
And the tender clasp of your strong, warm hand
 Sudden thrills through my pulses sent.

247

ELLA WHEELER WILCOX

Again you were mine by Love's own right—
  Mine for ever by Love's decree :
So for a moment it seemed last night,
  When somebody mentioned your name to me.

Just for the moment I thought you mine—
  Loving me, wooing me, as of old.
The tale remembered seemed half divine—
  Though I held it lightly enough when told.
The past seemed fairer than when it was near,
  As " Blessings brighten when taking flight " ;
And just for the moment I held you dear—
  When somebody mentioned your name last night.

A MARCH SNOW

LET the old snow be covered with the new :
    The trampled snow, so soiled, and stained, and
      sodden.
Let it be hidden wholly from our view
  By pure white flakes, all trackless and untrodden.
When Winter dies, low at the sweet Spring's feet
Let him be mantled in a clean, white sheet.

Let the old life be covered by the new :
  The old past life so full of sad mistakes,
Let it be wholly hidden from the view
  By deeds as white and silent as snow-flakes.

MISCELLANEOUS POEMS

Ere this earth life melts in the eternal Spring
Let the white mantle of repentance fling
Soft drapery about it, fold on fold,
Even as the new snow covers up the old.

AN ANSWER

IF one should bring a rose that had been fair,
    And very fragrant, and surpassing sweet
Before it lost its beauty in the heat
Of crowded ball-rooms or the gas-light's glare,
And beg of me to keep it in my hair
Or in my breast through all the coming hours,
Casting aside all fresher, brighter flowers
Which other hands might offer me to wear,
Would it not seem presumptuous ?
                                    Yet you bring
The remnant of a heart that long ago
Burned all its fire to ashes ; and you say,
" Keep this and cast all other hearts away."
I stooped and blew, and could not raise a glow ;
Square in your face I throw your offering.

ALL FOR ME

THE world grows green on a thousand hills—
    By a thousand willows the bees are humming,
And a million birds by a million rills
Sing of the golden season coming.

ELLA WHEELER WILCOX

But, gazing out in the sun-kiss'd lea,
　And hearing a thrush and a blue-bird singing,
I feel that the Summer is all for me,
　And all for me are the joys it is bringing.

All for me the bumble-bee
　Drones his song in the perfect weather ;
And, just on purpose to sing to me,
　Thrush and blue-bird came North together.
Just for me, in red and white,
　Bloom and blossom the fields of clover ;
And all for me and my delight
　The wild Wind follows and plays the lover.

The mighty sun, with a scorching kiss
　(I have read, and heard, and do not doubt it),
Has burned up a thousand worlds like this,
　And never stopped to think about it.
And yet I believe he hurries up
　Just on purpose to kiss my flowers—
To drink the dew from the lily-cup,
　And help it to grow through golden hours.

I know I am only a speck of dust,
　An individual mite of masses,
Clinging upon the outer crust
　Of a little ball of cooling gases.
And yet, and yet, say what you will,
　And laugh, if you please, at my lack of reason,
For me wholly, and for me still,
　Blooms and blossoms the Summer season.

Nobody else has ever heard
  The story the Wind to me discloses ;
And none but I and the humming-bird
  Can read the hearts of the crimson roses.
Ah,, my Summer—my love—my own !
  The world grows glad in your smiling weather ;
Yet all for me, and me alone,
  You and your Court came North together.

COMRADES

I AND my Soul are alone to-day,
  All in the shining weather ;
We were sick of the world, and we put it away,
  So we could rejoice together.

Our host, the Sun, in the blue, blue sky,
  Is mixing a rare, sweet wine,
In the burnished gold of his cup on high,
  For me, and this Soul of mine.

We find it a safe and a royal drink,
  And a cure for every pain ;
It helps us to love, and helps us to think,
  And strengthens body and brain.

And sitting here, with my Soul alone,
  Where the yellow sun-rays fall,
Of all the friends I have ever known
  I find it the *best* of all.

ELLA WHEELER WILCOX

We rarely meet when the World is near,
  For the World hath a pleasing art,
And brings me so much that is bright and dear
  That my Soul it keepeth apart.

But when I grow weary of mirth and glee,
  Of glitter, and glow, and splendour,
Like a tried old friend it comes to me
  With a smile that is sad and tender.

And we walk together as two friends may,
  And laugh, and drink God's wine.
Oh, a royal comrade any day,
  I find this Soul of mine.

IN THE CROWD

HOW happy they are, in all seeming,
  How gay, or how smilingly proud
How brightly their faces are beaming,
  These people who make up the crowd.
How they bow, how they bend, how they flutter,
  How they look at each other and smile,
How they glow, and what *bons mots* they utter !
  But a strange thought has found me the while !

It is odd, but I stand here and fancy
  These people who now play a part,
All forced by some strange necromancy
  To speak, and to act, from the heart.

MISCELLANEOUS POEMS

What a hush would come over the laughter !
  What a silence would fall on the mirth !
And then what a wail would sweep after,
  As the night-wind sweeps over the earth,

If the secrets held under and hidden,
  In the intricate hearts of the crowd,
Were suddenly called to, and bidden
  To rise up and cry out aloud,
How strange one would look to another !
  Old friends of long standing and years—
Own brothers, would not know each other,
  Robed new in their sorrows and fears.

From broadcloth, and velvet, and laces,
  Would echo the groans of despair,
And there would be blanching of faces
  And wringing of hands and of hair.
That man with his record of honour,
  The lady down there with the rose,
That girl with Spring's freshness upon her,
  Who knoweth the secrets of those ?

Smile on, O ye maskers, smile sweetly !
  Step lightly, bow low and laugh loud !
Though the world is deceived and completely,
  I know ye, O sad-hearted crowd !
I watch you with infinite pity :
  But play on, play ever your part,
Be gleeful, be joyful, be witty !
  'Tis better than showing the heart.

ELLA WHEELER WILCOX

INTO SPACE

IF the sad old world should jump a cog
   Some time, in its dizzy spinning,
And go off the track with a sudden jog,
   What an end would come to the sinning.
What a rest from strife and the burdens of life
   For the millions of people in it,
What a way out of care, and worry and wear,
   All in a beautiful minute.

As 'round the sun with a curving sweep
   It hurries and runs and races,
Should it lose its balance, and go with a leap
   Into the vast sea-spaces,
What a blest relief it would bring to the grief,
   And the trouble and toil about us,
To be suddenly hurled from the solar world
   And let it go on without us.

With not a sigh or a sad good-bye
   For loved ones left behind us,
We would go with a lunge and a mighty plunge
   Where never a grave should find us.
What a wild mad thrill our veins would fill
   As the great earth, like a feather,
Should float through the air to God knows where,
   And carry us all together.

MISCELLANEOUS POEMS

No dark, damp tomb and no mourner's gloom
  No tolling bell in the steeple,
But in one swift breath a painless death
  For a million billion people.
What greater bliss could we ask than this,
  To sweep with a bird's free motion
Through leagues of space to a resting-place
  In a vast and vapoury ocean—
To pass away from this life for aye
  With never a dear tie sundered,
And a world on fire for a funeral pyre,
  While the stars looked on and wondered ?

LA MORT D'AMOUR

WHEN was it that love died ? We were so fond,
  So very fond, a little while ago.
With leaping pulses and blood all aglow,
We dreamed about a sweeter life beyond,

When we should dwell together as one heart,
  And scarce could wait that happy time to come.
  Now side by side we sit with lips quite dumb,
And feel ourselves a thousand miles apart.

How was it that love died ? I do not know.
  I only know that all its grace untold
  Has faded into grey ! I miss the gold
From our dull skies ; but did not see it go.

ELLA WHEELER WILCOX

Why should love die ! We prized it, I am sure ;
  We thought of nothing else when it was ours ;
  We cherished it in smiling, sunlit bowers ;
It was our all ; why could it not endure ?

Alas, we know not how, or when, or why
  This dear thing died. We only know it went,
  And left us dull, cold, and indifferent ;
We who found heaven once in each other's sigh.

How pitiful it is, and yet how true,
  That half the lovers in the world, one day,
  Look questioning in each other's eyes this way
And know love's gone for ever, as we do.

Something I cannot help but think, dear heart,
  As I look out o'er all the wide, sad earth
  And see love's flame gone out on many a hearth,
That those who would keep love must dwell apart.

" LOVE IS ENOUGH "

LOVE is enough. Let us not ask for gold.
  Wealth breeds false aims, and pride and selfishness;
In those serene, Arcadian days of old
  Men gave no thought to princely homes and dress.
The gods who dwelt on fair Olympia's height
Lived only for dear love and love's delight.
                        Love is enough.

MISCELLANEOUS POEMS

Love is enough.   Why should we care for fame ?
  Ambition is a most unpleasant guest :
It lures us with the glory of a name
  Far from the happy haunts of peace and rest.
Let us stay here in this secluded place
Made beautiful by love's endearing grace !
                              Love is enough.

Love is enough.   Why should we strive for power ?
  It brings men only envy and distrust.
The poor world's homage pleases but an hour,
  And earthly honours vanish in the dust.
The grandest lives are ofttimes desolate ;
Let me be loved, and let who will be great.
                              Love is enough.

Love is enough. Why should we ask for more ?
  What greater gift have gods vouchsafed to men ?
What better boon of all their precious store
  Than our fond hearts that love and love again ?
Old love may die ; new love is just as sweet ;
And life is fair and all the world complete :
                              Love is enough !

ELLA WHEELER WILCOX

SNOWED UNDER

OF a thousand things that the Year snowed under—
 The busy Old Year who has gone away—
How many will rise in the Spring, I wonder,
 Brought to life by the sun of May ?
Will the rose-tree branches, so wholly hidden
 That never a rose-tree seems to be,
At the sweet Spring's call come forth unbidden,
 And bud in beauty, and bloom for me ?

Will the fair, green Earth, whose throbbing bosom
 Is hid like a maid's in her gown at night,
Wake out of her sleep, and with blade and blossom
 Gem her garments to please my sight ?
Over the knoll in the valley yonder
 The loveliest buttercups bloomed and grew ;
When the snow has gone that drifted them under,
 Will they shoot up sunward, and bloom anew ?

When wild winds blew, and a sleet-storm pelted,
 I lost a jewel of priceless worth ;
If I walk that way when snows have melted,
 Will the gem gleam up from the bare, brown Earth ?
I laid a love that was dead or dying,
 For the year to bury and hide from sight ;
But out of a trance will it waken, crying,
 And push to my heart, like a leaf to the light ?

MISCELLANEOUS POEMS

Under the snow lie things so cherished—
  Hopes, ambitions, and dreams of men—
Faces that vanished, and trusts that perished,
  Never to sparkle and glow again.
The Old Year greedily grasped his plunder,
  And covered it over and hurried away :
Of the thousand things that he hid, I wonder
  How many will rise at the call of May ?
O wise Young Year, with your hands held under
  Your mantle of ermine, tell me, pray !

NOBLESSE OBLIGE

I HOLD it a duty of one who is gifted
  And specially dowered in all men's sight,
To know no rest till his life is lifted
  Fully up to his great gifts' height.

He must mould the man into rare completeness,
  For gems are set only in gold refined.
He must fashion his thoughts into perfect sweetness,
  And cast out folly and pride from his mind.

For he who drinks from a god's gold fountain
  Of art or music or rhythmic song
Must sift from his soul the chaff of malice,
  And weed from his heart the roots of wrong.

ELLA WHEELER WILCOX

Great gifts should be worn, like a crown befitting !
    And not like gems in a beggar's hands.
And the toil must be constant and unremitting
    Which lifts up the king to the crown's demands.

THE YEAR

WHAT can be said in New-Year rhymes,
    That's not been said a thousand times ?

The new years come, the old years go,
We know we dream, we dream we know.

We rise up laughing with the light,
We lie down weeping with the night.

We hug the world until it stings,
We curse it then and sigh for wings.

We live, we love, we woo, we wed,
We wreathe our brides, we sheet our dead.

We laugh, we weep, we hope, we fear,
And that's the burden of the year.

THE LAND OF CONTENT

I SET out for the Land of Content,
  By the gay crowded pleasure-highway,
With laughter, and jesting, I went
  With the mirth-loving throng for a day;
  Then I knew I had wandered astray,
For I met returned pilgrims, belated,
Who said, " We are weary and sated,
But we found not the Land of Content."

I turned to the steep path of fame.
  I said, " It is over yon height—
This land with the beautiful name—
  Ambition will lend me its light."
  But I passed in my journey ere night,
For the way grew so lonely and troubled;
I said—my anxiety doubled—
" This is not the road to Content."

Then I joined the great rabble and throng
  That frequents the moneyed world's mart;
But the greed, and the grasping and wrong,
  Left me only one wish—to depart.
  And sickened, and saddened at heart,
I hurried away from the gateway,
For my soul and my spirit said straightway,
" This is not the road to Content."

ELLA WHEELER WILCOX

Then weary in body and brain,
  An overgrown path I detected,
And I said, " I will hide with my pain
  In this by-way, unused and neglected."
  Lo ! it led to the realm God selected
To crown with His best gifts of beauty,
And through the great pathway of duty
I came to the Land of Content.

THROUGH DIM EYES

IS it the world, or my eyes, that are sadder ?
  I see not the grace that I used to see
In the meadow-brook whose song was so glad, or
In the boughs of the willow tree.
The brook runs slower—its song seems lower,
And not the song that it sang of old ;
And the tree I admired looks weary and tired
Of the changeless story of heat and cold.

When the sun goes up, and the stars go under,
In that supreme hour of the breaking day,
Is it my eyes, or the dawn, I wonder,
That finds less of the gold, and more of the grey ?
I see not the splendour, the tints so tender,
The rose-hued glory I used to see ;
And I often borrow a vague half-sorrow
That another morning has dawned for me.

MISCELLANEOUS POEMS

When the royal smile of that welcome comer
Beams on the meadow and burns in the sky,
Is it my eyes, or does the Summer
Bring less of bloom than in days gone by ?
The beauty that thrilled me, the rapture that filled me,
To an overflowing of happy tears,
I pass unseeing, my sad eyes being
Dimmed by the shadow of vanished years.

When the heart grows weary, all things seem dreary ;
When the burden grows heavy, the way seems long.
Thank God for sending kind death as an ending,
Like a grand Amen to a minor song.

TRUE CULTURE

THE highest culture is to speak no ill ;
    The best reformer is the man whose eyes
Are quick to see all beauty and all worth ;
And by his own discreet, well-ordered life,
Alone reproves the erring.
                        When thy gaze
Turns it on thy own soul, be most severe.
But when it falls upon a fellow-man,
Let kindliness control it ; and refrain
From that belittling censure that springs forth
From common lips like weeds from marshy soil.

263

ELLA WHEELER WILCOX

· LEAN DOWN

LEAN down and lift me higher, Josephine!
From the Eternal Hills hast thou not seen
How I do strive for heights ? but lacking wings,
I cannot grasp at once those better things
To which I in my inmost soul aspire—
Lean down and lift me higher.

I grope along—not desolate or sad,
For youth and hope and health all keep me glad ;
But too bright sunlight, sometimes, makes us blind,
And I do grope for heights I cannot find.
Oh, thou must know my one supreme desire—
Lean down and lift me higher.

Not long ago we trod the self-same way.
Thou knowest how, from day to fleeting day
Our souls were vexed with trifles, and our feet
Were lured aside to by-paths which seemed sweet,
But only served to hinder and to tire ;
Lean down and lift me higher.

Thou hast gone onward to the heights serene,
And left me here, my loved one, Josephine ;
I am content to stay until the end,
For life is full of promise ; but, my friend,
Canst thou not help me in my best desire
And lean, and lift me higher ?

MISCELLANEOUS POEMS

Frail as thou wert, thou hast grown strong and
    wise,
And quick to understand and sympathise
With all a full soul's needs. It must be so,
Thy year with God hath made thee great, I know.
Thou must see how I struggle and aspire—
Oh, warm me with a breath of heavenly fire,
And lean, and lift me higher.

GOD'S MEASURE

GOD measures souls by their capacity
    For entertaining his best Angel, Love.
Who loveth most is nearest kin to God,
Who is all Love, or Nothing.
                    He who sits
And looks out on the palpitating world,
And feels his heart swell in him large enough
To hold all men within it, he is near
His great Creator's standard, though he dwells
Outside the pale of churches, and knows not
A feast-day from a fast-day, or a line
Of Scripture even. What God wants of us
Is that outreaching bigness that ignores
All littleness of aims, or loves, or creeds,
And clasps all Earth and Heaven in its embrace.

265

ELLA WHEELER WILCOX

WHAT GAIN?

NOW, while thy rounded cheek is fresh and fair,
  While beauty lingers, laughing, in thine eyes,
Ere thy young heart shall meet the stranger, " Care,"
  Or thy blithe soul become the home of sighs,
Were it not kindness should I give thee rest
By plunging this sharp dagger in thy breast ?
Dying so young, with all thy wealth of youth,
What part of life wouldst thou not claim, in sooth ?
    Only the woe,
  Sweetheart, that sad souls know.

Now, in this sacred hour of supreme trust,
  Of pure delight and palpitating joy,
Ere change can come, as come it surely must,
  With jarring doubts and discords, to destroy
Our far too perfect peace, I pray thee, Sweet,
Were it not best for both of us, and meet,
If I should bring swift death to seal our bliss ?
Dying so full of joy, what could we miss ?
    Nothing but tears,
  Sweetheart, and weary years.

How slight the action ! Just one well-aimed blow
  Here where I feel thy warm heart's pulsing beat,
And then another through my own, and so
  Our perfect union would be made complete :
So, past all parting, I should claim thee mine.
Dead with our youth, and faith, and love divine,

266

MISCELLANEOUS POEMS

Should we not keep the best of life that way ?
What shall we gain by living day on day ?
What shall we gain,
Sweetheart, but bitter pain ?

TO THE WEST

[In an interview with Lawrence Barrett, he said : "The literature of the New World must look to the West for its poetry."]

NOT to the crowded East,
    Where, in a well-worn groove,
Like the harnessed wheel of a great machine,
    The trammelled mind must move—
Where Thought must follow the fashion of Thought,
Or be counted vulgar and set at naught.

Not to the languid South,
    Where the mariners of the brain
Are lured by the Sirens of the Sense,
    And wrecked upon its main—
Where Thought is rocked on the sweet wind's breath,
To a torpid sleep that ends in death.

But to the mighty West,
    That chosen realm of God,
Where Nature reaches her hands to men,
    And freedom walks abroad—
Where mind is King, and fashion is naught :
There shall the New World look for Thought.

ELLA WHEELER WILCOX

To the West, the beautiful West,
  She shall look, and not in vain—
For out of its broad and boundless store
  Come muscle, and nerve, and brain,
Let the bards of the East and the South be dumb—
For out of the West shall the Poets come.

They shall come with souls as great
  As the cradle where they were rocked ;
They shall come with brows that are touched with fire,
  Like the Gods with whom they have walked ;
They shall come from the West in royal state,
The Singers and Thinkers for whom we wait.

THE CHRISTIAN'S NEW-YEAR PRAYER

THOU Christ of mine, Thy gracious ear low bending
  Through these glad New-Year days,
To catch the countless prayers to Heaven ascending,—
  For e'en hard hearts do raise
Some secret wish for fame, or gold, or power,
  Or freedom from all care—
Dear, patient Christ, who listened hour on hour,
  Hear now a Christian's prayer.

Let this young year that, silent, walks beside me,
  Be as a means of grace
To lead me up, no matter what betide me,
  Nearer the Master's face.

MISCELLANEOUS POEMS

If it need be that ere I reach the fountain
  Where Living waters play,
My feet should bleed from sharp stones on the mountain,
  Then cast them in my way.

If my vain soul needs blows and bitter losses
  To shape it for Thy crown,
Then bruise it, burn it, burden it with crosses,
  With sorrows bear it down.
Do what Thou wilt to mould me to Thy pleasure,
  And if I should complain,
Heap full of anguish yet another measure
  Until I smile at pain.
Send dangers—deaths! but tell me how to bear them;
  Enfold me in Thy care.
Send trials, tears! but give me strength to bear them—
  This is a Christian's prayer.

AFTER THE BATTLES ARE OVER

[Read at Reunion of the G. A. T., Madison, Wis., July 4, 1872.]

AFTER the battles are over,
    And the war drums cease to beat,
And no more is heard on the hillside
  The sound of hurrying feet;
Full many a noble action,
  That was done in the days of strife,
By the soldier is half forgotten,
  In the peaceful walks of life.

ELLA WHEELER WILCOX

Just as the tangled grasses,
  In Summer's warmth and light,
Grow over the graves of the fallen
  And hide them away from sight,
So many an act of valour,
  And many a deed sublime,
Fade from the mind of the soldier,
  O'ergrown by the grass of time.

Not so should they be rewarded,
  Those noble deeds of old ;
They should live for ever and ever,
  When the heroes' hearts are cold.
Then rally, ye brave old comrades,
  Old veterans, reunite !
Uproot Time's tangled grasses—
  Live over the march, and the fight.

Let Grant come up from the White House,
  And clasp each brother's hand,
First chieftain of the army,
  Last chieftain of the land.
Let him rest from a nation's burdens,
  And go, in thought, with his men,
Through the fire and smoke of Shiloh,
  And save the day again.

This silent hero of battles
  Knew no such word as defeat.
It was left for the rebel's learning,
  Along with the word—retreat.

MISCELLANEOUS POEMS

He was not given to talking,
  But he found that guns would preach
In a way that was more convincing
  Than fine and flowery speech.   .

Three cheers for the grave commander
  Of the grand old Tennessee !
Who won the first great battle—
  Gained the first great victory.
His motto was always " Conquer,"
  " Success " was his counter-sign,
And " though it took all Summer,"
  He kept fighting upon " that line."

Let Sherman, the stern old General,
  Come rallying with his men ;
Let them march once more through Georgia
  And down to the sea again.
Oh ! that grand old tramp to Savannah,
  Three hundred miles to the coast,
It will live in the heart of the nation,
  Forever its pride and boast.

As Sheridan went to the battle,
  When a score of miles away,
He has come to the feast and banquet,
  By the iron horse, to-day.
Its pace is not much swifter
  Than the pace of that famous steed
Which bore him down to the contest
  And saved the day by his speed.

ELLA WHEELER WILCOX

Then go over the ground to-day, boys,
 Tread each remembered spot.
It will be a gleesome journey,
 On the swift-shod feet of thought ;
You can fight a bloodless battle,
 You can skirmish along the route,
But it's not worth while to forage,
 There are rations enough without.

Don't start if you hear the cannon,
 It is not the sound of doom,
It does not call to the contest—
 To the battle's smoke and gloom.
" Let us have peace," was spoken,
 And lo ! peace ruled again ;
And now the nation is shouting,
 Through the cannon's voice, " Amen."

O boys who besieged old Vicksburg,
 Can time e'er wash away
The triumph of her surrender,
 Nine years ago to-day ?
Can you ever forget the moment,
 When you saw the flag of white,
That told how the grim old city
 Had fallen in her might ?

Ah, 'twas a bold brave army,
 When the boys, with a right good will,
Went gaily marching and singing
 To the fight at Champion Hill.

They met with a warm reception,
  But the soul of " Old John Brown "
Was abroad on that field of battle,
  And our flag did NOT go down.

Come, heroes of Look Out Mountain,
  Of Corinth and Donelson,
Of Kenesaw and Atlanta,
  And tell how the day was won !
Hush ! bow the head for a moment—
  There are those who cannot come ;
No bugle-call can arouse them—
  Nor sound of fife or drum.

O boys who died for the country,
  O dear and sainted dead !
What can we say about you
  That has not once been said ?
Whether you fell in the contest,
  Struck down by shot and shell,
Or pined 'neath the hand of sickness
  Or starved in the prison cell,

We know that you died for Freedom,
  To save our land from shame,
To rescue a perilled Nation,
  And we give you deathless fame,
'Twas the cause of Truth and Justice
  That you fought and perished for,
And we say it, oh, so gently,
  " Our boys who died in the war."

ELLA WHEELER WILCOX

Saviours of our Republic,
   Heroes who wore the blue,
We owe the peace that surrounds us—
   And our Nation's strength to you.
We owe it to you that our banner,
   The fairest flag in the world,
Is to-day unstained, unsullied,
   On the Summer air unfurled.

We look on its stripes and spangles,
   And our hearts are filled the while
With love for the brave commanders,
   And the boys of the rank and file.
The grandest deeds of valour
   Were never written out,
The noblest acts of virtue
   The world knows nothing about.

And many a private soldier,
   Who walks in his humble way,
With no sounding name or title,
   Unknow to the world to-day,
In the eyes of God is a hero
   As worthy of the bays,
As any mighty General
   To whom the world gives praise.

Brave men of a mighty army,
   We extend you friendship's hand!
I speak for the " Loyal Women,"
   Those pillars of our land. -

MISCELLANEOUS POEMS

We wish you a hearty welcome,
   We are proud that you gather here
To talk of old times together
   On this brightest day in the year.

And if Peace, whose snow-white pinions,
   Brood over our land to-day,
Should ever again go from us
   (God grant she may ever stay!)
Should our Nation call in her peril
   For " Six hundred thousand more,"
The loyal women would hear her,
   And send you out as before.

We would bring out the treasured knapsack,
   We would take the sword from the wall.
And hushing our own heart's pleadings,
   Hear only the country's call.
For, next to our God, is our Nation;
   And we cherish the honoured name,
Of the bravest of all brave armies
   Who fought for that Nation's fame.

AND THEY ARE DUMB

I HAVE been across the bridges of the years.
      Wet with tears
Were the ties on which I trod, going back
      Down the track
To the valley where I left, 'neath skies of Truth,
      My lost youth.

ELLA WHEELER WILCOX

As I went, I dropped my burdens, one and all—
     Let·them fall ;
All my sorrows, all my wrinkles, all my care,
     My white hair,
I laid down, like some lone pilgrim's heavy pack,
     By the track.

As I neared the happy valley with light feet,
     My heart beat
To the rhythm of a song I used to know
     Long ago,
And my spirits gushed and bubbled like a fountain
     Down a mountain.

On the border of that valley I found you,
     Tried and true ;
And we wandered through the golden Summer-Land
     Hand in hand.
And my pulses beat with rapture in the blisses
     Of your kisses.

And we met there, in those green and verdant places,
     Smiling faces,
And sweet laughter echoed upward from the dells
     Like gold bells.
And the world was spilling over with the glory
     Of Youth's story

MISCELLANEOUS POEMS

It was but a dreamer's journey of the brain ;
    And again
I have left the happy valley far behind,
    And I find
Time stands waiting with his burdens in a pack
    For my back.

As he speeds me, like a rough, well-meaning friend.
    To the end,
Will I find again the lost ones loved so well ?
    Who can tell !
But the dead know what the life will be to come—
    And they are dumb !

NIGHT

AS some dusk mother shields from all alarms
    The tired child she gathers to her breast,
The brunette Night doth fold me in her arms,
    And hushes me to perfect peace and rest.
Her eyes of stars shine on me, and I hear
Her voice of winds low crooning on my ear.
Oh, Night, oh, Night, how beautiful thou art !
Come, fold me closer to thy pulsing heart.

The day is full of gladness, and the light
    So beautifies the common outer things,
I only see with my external sight,
    And only hear the great world's voice which rings.

ELLA WHEELER WILCOX

But silently from daylight and from din
The sweet Night draws me—whispers, " Look within ! "
And looking, as one wakened from a dream,
I see what *is*—no longer what doth seem.

The Night says, " Listen ! " and upon my ear
　Revealed, as are the visions to my sight,
The voices known as " Beautiful " come near
　And whisper of the vasty Infinite.
Great, blue-eyed Truth, her sister Purity,
Their brother Honour, all converse with me,
And kiss my brow, and say, " Be brave of heart ! "
O holy three ! how beautiful thou art !

The Night says, " Child, sleep, that thou may'st arise
　Strong for to-morrow's struggle." And I feel
Her shadowy fingers pressing on my eyes :
　Like thistledown I float to the Ideal—
The Slumberland, made beautiful and bright
As death, by dreams of loved ones gone from sight,
O food for souls, sweet dreams of pure delight,
How beautiful the holy hours of Night !

WARNING

HIGH in the heavens I saw the moon this morning,
　Albeit the sun shone bright ;
Unto my soul it spoke, in voice of warning,
　" Remember Night ! "

MISCELLANEOUS POEMS

PHILOSOPHY

AT morn the wise man walked abroad,
 Proud with the learning of great fools.
He laughed and said, " There is no God—
'Tis force creates, 'tis reason rules."

Meek with the wisdom of great faith,
 At night he knelt while angels smiled,
And wept and cried with anguished breath,
 " Jehovah, *God*, save Thou my child ! "

" CARLOS "

LAST night I knelt low at my lady's feet.
 One soft, caressing hand played with my hair,
And one I kissed and fondled.   Kneeling there,
I deemed my meed of happiness complete.

She was so fair, so full of witching wiles—
Of fascinating tricks of mouth and eye ;
So womanly withal, but not too shy—
And all my heaven was compassed by her smiles.

Her soft touch on my cheek and forehead sent,
Like little arrows, thrills of tenderness
Through all my frame.   I trembled with excess
Of love, and sighed the sigh of great content.

ELLA WHEELER WILCOX

When any mortal dares to so rejoice,
I think a jealous Heaven, bending low,
Reaches a stern hand forth and deals a blow.
Sweet through the dusk I heard my lady's voice.

" My love ! " she sighed, " My Carlos ! " even now
I feel the perfumed zephyr of her breath
Bearing to me those words of living death,
And starting out the cold drops on my brow.

For I am *Paul*—not Carlos !   Who is he
That, in the supreme hour of love's delight,
Veiled by the shadows of the falling night,
She should breathe low his name, forgetting me ?

I will not ask her ! 'twere a fruitless task,
For, womanlike, she would make me believe
Some well-told tale ; and sigh, and seem to grieve,
And call me cruel.   Nay, I will not ask.

But this man Carlos, whosoe'er he be,
Has turned my cup of nectar into gall,
Since I know he has claimed some one or all
Of these delights my lady grants to me.

He must have knelt and kissed her, in some sad
And tender twilight, when the day grew dim.
How else could I remind her so of him ?
Why, reveries like these have made men mad !

He must have felt her soft hand on his brow.
If Heaven was shocked at such presumptuous wrongs,
And plunged him in the grave, where he belongs,
Still she remembers, though she loves me now.

And if he lives, and meets me to his cost,
Why, what avails it ? I must hear and see
That curst name " Carlos " always haunting me—
So has another Paradise been lost.

THROUGH TEARS

AN artist toiled over his pictures ;
    He laboured by night and by day.
He struggled for glory and honour,
    But the world had nothing to say.

Her walls were ablaze with the splendours
    We see in the beautiful skies ;
But the world beheld only the colours—
    They were made out of chemical dyes.

Time sped. And he lived, loved, and suffered :
    He passed through the valley of grief.
Again he toiled over his canvas,
    Since in labour alone was relief.

It showed not the splendour of colours
    Of those of his earlier years,
But the world ? the world bowed down before it,
    Because it was painted with tears.

ELLA WHEELER WILCOX

A poet was gifted with genius,
  And he sang, and he sang all the days.
He wrote for the praise of the people,
  But the people accorded no praise.
Oh, his songs were as blithe as the morning,
  As sweet as the music of birds ;
But the world had no homage to offer,
  Because they were nothing but words.

Time sped. And the poet through sorrow
  Became like his suffering kind.
Again he toiled over his poems
  To lighten the grief of his mind.
They were not so flowing and rhythmic
  As those of his earlier years,
But the world ? lo ! it offered its homage
  Because they were written in tears.

So ever the price must be given
  By those seeking glory in art ;
So ever the world is repaying
  The grief-stricken, suffering heart.
The happy must ever be humble ;
  Ambition must wait for the years,
Ere hoping to win the approval
  Of a world that looks on through its tears.

IN THE NIGHT

SOMETIMES at night, when I sit and write,
    I hear the strangest things,—
As my brain grows hot with burning thought,
  That struggles for form and wings,
I can hear the beat of my swift blood's feet,
  As it speeds with a rush and a whir
From heart to brain and back again,
  Like a race-horse under the spur.

With my soul's fine ear I listen and hear
  The tender Silence speak,
As it leans on the breast of Night to rest,
  And presses his dusky cheek.
And the darkness turns in its sleep, and yearns
  For something that is kin ;
And I hear the hiss of a scorching kiss,
  As it folds and fondles Sin.

In its hurrying race through leagues of space,
  I can hear the Earth catch breath,
As it heaves and moans, and shudders and groans,
  And longs for the rest of Death.
And high and far, from a distant star,
  Whose name is unknown to me,
I hear a voice that says, " Rejoice,
  For I keep ward o'er thee ! "

ELLA WHEELER WILCOX

Oh, sweet and strange are the sounds that range
  Through the chambers of the night ;
And the watcher who waits by the dim, dark gates,
  May hear if he lists aright.

THE PUNISHED

NOT they who know the awful gibbet's anguish,
    Not they who, while sad years go by them, in
The sunless cells of lonely prisons languish,
  Do suffer fullest penalty for sin.

'Tis they who walk the highways unsuspected
  Yet with grim fear for ever at their side,
Who hug the corpse of some sin undetected.
  A corpse no grave or coffin-lid can hide—

'Tis they who are in their own chambers haunted
  By thoughts that like unbidden guests intrude,
And sit down, uninvited and unwanted,
  And make a nightmare of the solitude.

HALF FLEDGED

I FEEL the stirrings in me of great things,
  New half-fledged thoughts rise up and beat their
      wings,
And tremble on the margin of their nest,
Then flutter back, and hide within my breast.

Beholding space, they doubt their untried strength.
Beholding men, they fear them. But at length
Grown all too great and active for the heart
That broods them with such tender mother art,
Forgetting fear, and men, and all, that hour,
Save the impelling consciousness of power
That stirs within them—they shall soar away
Up to the very portals of the Day.

Oh, what exultant rapture thrills me through
When I contemplate all those thoughts may do ;
Like snow-white eagles penetrating space,
They may explore full many an unknown place,
And build their nests on mountain heights unseen
Whereon doth lie that dreamed-of rest serene.
Stay thou a little longer in my breast,
Till my fond heart shall push thee from the nest.
Anxious to see thee soar to heights divine—
Oh, beautiful but half-fledged thoughts of mine.

LOVE'S SLEEP

(VERS DE SOCIÉTÉ)

WE'LL cover Love with roses,
      And sweet sleep he shall take.
None but a fool supposes
      Love always keeps awake.

ELLA WHEELER WILCOX

I've known loves without number,
   True loves were they, and tried ;
And just for want of slumber
   They pined away and died.

Our Love was bright and cheerful
   A little while agone ;
Now he is pale and tearful,
   And—yes, I've seen him yawn.
So tired is he of kisses
   That he can only weep ;
The one dear thing he misses
   And longs for now is sleep.

We could not let him leave us
   One time, he was so dear,
But now it would not grieve us
   If he slept half a year.
For he has had his season,
   Like the lily and the rose,
And it but stands to reason
   That he should want repose.

We prized the smiling Cupid
   Who made our days so bright ;
But he has grown so stupid
   We gladly say good-night.
And if he wakens tender
   And fond, and fair as when
He filled our lives with splendour,
   We'll take him back again.

And should he never waken,
  As that perchance may be,
We will not weep forsaken,
  But sing, " Love, tra-la-lee ! "

THE VOLUPTUARY

OH, I am sick of love reciprocated,
  Of hopes fulfilled, ambitions gratified.
Life holds no thing to be anticipated,
  And I am sad from being satisfied.

The eager joy felt climbing up the mountain
  Has left me now the highest point is gained.
The crystal spray that fell from Fame's fair fountain
  Was sweeter than the waters were when drained.

The gilded apple which the world calls pleasure,
  And which I purchased with my youth and strength,
Pleased me a moment.   But the empty treasure
  Lost all its lustre, and grew dim at length.

And love, all glowing with a golden glory,
  Delighted me a season with its tale.
It pleased the longest, but at last the story
  So oft repeated, to my heart grew stale.

ELLA WHEELER WILCOX

I lived for self, and all I asked was given,
  I have had all, and now am sick of bliss,
No other punishment designed by Heaven
  Could strike me half so forcibly as this.

I feel no sense of aught but enervation
  In all the joys my selfish aims have brought.
And know no wish but for annihilation,
  Since that would give me freedom from the thought.

Oh, blest is he who has some aim defeated ;
  Some mighty loss to balance all his gain.
For him there is a hope not yet completed ;
  For him hath life yet draughts of joy and pain.

But cursed is he who has no balked ambition,
  No hopeless hope, no loss beyond repair,
But sick and sated with complete fruition,
  Keeps not the pleasure even of despair.

GUERDON

UPON the white cheek of the Cherub year
    I saw a tear.
Alas ! I murmured, that the Year should borrow
    So soon a sorrow.
Just then the sunlight fell with sudden flame :
    The tear became
A wond'rous diamond sparkling in the light—
    A beauteous sight.

Upon my soul there fell such woeful loss,
   I said, " The cross
Is grievous for a life as young as mine."
   Just then, like wine,
God's sunlight shone from His high Heavens down ;
   And lo ! a crown
Gleamed in the place of what I thought a burden—
   My sorrow's guerdon.

THE UNATTAINED

A VISION beauteous as the morn,
   With heavenly eyes and tresses streaming,
Slow glided o'er a field late shorn
   Where walked a poet idly dreaming.
He saw her, and joy lit his face.
   " Oh, vanish not at human speaking,"
He cried, " thou form of magic grace,
   Thou art the poem I am seeking.

" I've sought thee long ! I claim thee now—
   My thought embodied, living, real."
She shook the tresses from her brow.
   " Nay, nay ! " she said, " I am ideal.
I am the phantom of desire—
   The spirit of all great endeavour,
I am the voice that says, ' Come higher.'
   That calls men up and up for ever.

ELLA WHEELER WILCOX

" 'Tis not alone the thought supreme
 That here upon thy path has risen ;
I am the artist's highest dream,
 The ray of light he cannot prison.
I am the sweet ecstatic note
 Than all glad music gladder, clearer,
That trembles in the singer's throat,
 And dies without a human hearer.

" I am the greater, better yield,
 That leads and cheers thy farmer neighbour,
For me he bravely tills the field
 And whistles gaily at his labour.
Not thou alone, O poet soul,
 Dost seek me through an endless morrow,
But to the toiling, hoping whole
 I am at once the hope and sorrow.
The spirit of the unattained,
 I am to those who seek to name me,
A good desired but never gained.
 All shall pursue, but none shall claim me."

THE COQUETTE

ALONE she sat with her accusing heart,
 That, like a restless comrade, frightened sleep,
And every thought that found her, left a dart
That hurt her so, she could not even weep.

Her heart that once had been a cup well filled
    With love's red wine, save for some drops of gall
She knew was empty; though it had not spilled
    Its sweets for one, but wasted them on all.

She stood upon the grave of her dead truth,
    And saw her soul's bright armour red with rust,
And knew that all the riches of her youth
    Were Dead Sea apples, crumbling into dust.

Love that had turned to bitter, biting scorn,
    Hearthstones despoiled, and homes made desolate,
Made her cry out that she was ever born,
    To loathe her beauty and to curse her fate.

LIPPO

NOW we must part, my Lippo, even so,
    I grieve to see thy sudden pained surprise;
Gaze not on me with such accusing eyes—
'Twas thine own hand which dealt dear Love's death-
    blow.

I loved thee fondly yesterday. Till then
Thy heart was like a covered golden cup
Always above my eager lip held up.
I fancied thou wert not as other men.

ELLA WHEELER WILCOX

I knew that heart was filled with Love's sweet wine,
Pressed wholly for my drinking.   And my lip
Grew parched with thirsting for one nectared sip
Of what, denied me, seemed a draught divine.

Last evening, in the gloaming that cup spilled
Its precious contents.   Even to the lees
Were offered to me, saying, " Drink of these ! "
And when I saw it empty, Love was killed.

No word was left unsaid, no act undone,
To prove to me thou wert my abject slave.
Ah ! Love, hadst thou been wise enough to save
One little drop of that sweet wine—but one—

I still had lov'd thee, longing for it then.
But even the cup is mine.   I look within,
And find it holds not one last drop to win,
And cast it down.—Thou art as other men.

LOVE'S BURIAL

LET us clear a little space,
     And make Love a burial place.

He is dead, dear, as you see,
     And he wearies you and me,

MISCELLANEOUS POEMS

Growing heavier, day by day,
Let us bury him, I say.

Wings of dead white butterflies,
These shall shroud him, as he lies

In his casket rich and rare,
Made of finest maidenhair.

With the pollen of the rose
Let us his white eyelids close.

Put the rose thorn in his hand,
Shorn of leaves—you understand.

Let some holy water fall
On his dead face, tears of gall—

As we kneel by him and say,
" Dreams to dreams," and turn away.

Those gravediggers, Doubt, Distrust,
They will lower him to the dust.

Let us part here with a kiss—
You go that way, I go this.

Since we buried Love to-day
We will walk a separate way.

ELLA WHEELER WILCOX

HER LOVE (FROM "MAURINE")

THE sands upon the ocean side
    That change about with every tide,
And never true to one abide,
    A woman's love I liken to.

The summer zephyrs, light and vain,
That sing the same alluring strain
To every grass blade on the plain—
    A woman's love is nothing more.

The sunshine of an April day
That comes to warm you with its ray,
But while you smile has flown away—
    A woman's love is like to this.

God made poor woman with no heart,
But gave her skill, and tact, and art,
And so she lives, and plays her part.
    We must not blame, but pity her.

She leans to man—but just to hear
The praise he whispers in her ear ;
Herself, not him, she holdeth dear—
    O fool ! to be deceived by her.

To sate her selfish thirst she quaffs
The love of strong hearts in sweet draughts,
Then throws them lightly by, and laughs,
    Too weak to understand their pain.

As changeful as the winds that blow
From every region to and fro,
Devoid of heart, she cannot know
    The suffering of a human heart.

SONG (FROM "MAURINE")

O PRAISE me not with thy lips, dear one!
    Though thy tender words I prize.
But dearer by far is the soulful gaze
Of your eyes, your beautiful eyes,
    Your tender, loving eyes.

O chide me not with your lips, dear one!
    Though I cause your bosom sighs.
You can make repentance deeper far
    By your sad, reproving eyes,
        Your sorrowful, troubled eyes.

ELLA WHEELER WILCOX

Words, at the best, are but hollow sounds;
  Above, in the beaming skies,
The constant stars say never a word,
  But only smile with their eyes—
    Smile on with their lustrous eyes.

Then breathe no vow with your lips, dear one;
  On the wingèd wind speech flies.
But I read the truth of your noble heart
  In your soulful, speaking eyes—
    In your deep and beautiful eyes.

SONG (FROM " MAURINE ")

O THOU, mine other, stronger part!
  Whom yet I cannot hear, or see,
Come thou, and take this loving heart,
  That longs to yield its all to thee,
  I call mine own—Oh, come to me!
  Love, answer back, I come to thee,
    I come to thee.

This hungry heart, so warm, so large,
  Is far too great a care for me.
I have grown weary of the charge
  I keep so sacredly for thee.
  Come thou, and take my heart from me.
  Love, answer back, I come to thee,
    I come to thee.

I am aweary, waiting here
  For one who tarries long for me.
O ! art thou far, or art thou near ?
  And must I still be sad for thee ?
  Or wilt thou straightway come to me ?
  Love, answer, I am near to thee,
            I come to thee.

IF

DEAR love, if you and I could sail away
  With snowy pennons to the winds unfurled,
Across the waters of some unknown bay,
  And find some island far from all the world ;

If we could dwell there, evermore alone,
  While unrecorded years slip by apace,
Forgetting and forgotten and unknown
  By aught save native song-birds of the place ;

If Winter never visited that land,
  And Summer's lap spilled o'er with fruits and flowers,
And tropic trees cast shade on every hand,
  And twined boughs formed sleep-inviting bowers ;

If from the fashions of the world set free,
  And hid away from all its jealous strife,
I lived alone for you, and you for me—
  Ah ! then, dear love, how sweet were wedded life.

ELLA WHEELER WILCOX

But since we dwell here in the crowded way,
   Where hurrying throngs rush by to seek for gold,
And all is common-place and work-a-day,
   As soon as love's young honeymoon grows old ;

Since fashion rules and nature yields to art,
   And life is hurt by daily jar and fret,
'Tis best to shut such dreams down in the heart
   And go our ways alone, love, and forget.

MAURINE

PART I

I SAT and sewed, and sang some tender tune,
Oh, beauteous was that morn in early June !
Mellow with sunlight, and with blossoms fair :
The climbing rose-tree grew about me there,
And checked with shade the sunny portico
Where, morns like this, I came to read, or sew.

I heard the gate click, and a firm, quick tread
Upon the walk.   No need to turn my head ;
I would mistake, and doubt my own voice sounding,
Before his step upon the gravel bounding.
In an unstudied attitude of grace,
He stretched his comely form ; and from his face
He tossed the dark, damp curls ; and at my knees,
With his broad hat he fanned the lazy breeze,
And turned his head, and lifted his large eyes,
Of that strange hue we see in ocean dyes,
And call it blue sometimes and sometimes green,
And, save in poet eyes, not elsewhere seen.
" Lest I should meet with my fair lady's scorning
For calling quite so early in the morning,

ELLA WHEELER WILCOX

I've brought a passport that can never fail,"
He said, and laughing, laid the morning mail
Upon my lap. " I'm welcome ? so I thought !
I'll figure by the letters that I brought
How glad you are to see me. Only one ?
And that one from a lady ? I'm undone !
That, lightly skimmed, you'll think me *such* a bore,
And wonder why I did not bring you four.
It's ever thus : a woman cannot get
So many letters that she will not fret
O'er one that did not come."

                        " I'll prove you wrong,"
I answered gaily, " here upon the spot !
This little letter, precious if not long,
Is just the one, of all you might have brought,
To please me. You have heard me speak, I'm sure,
Of Helen Trevor : she writes here to say
She's coming out to see me, and will stay
Till autumn, maybe. She is, like her note,
Petite and dainty, tender, loving, pure,
You'd know her by a letter that she wrote,
For a sweet tinted thing. 'Tis always so—
Letters all blots, though finely written, show
A slovenly person. Letters stiff and white
Bespeak a nature honest, plain, upright ;
And tissuey, tinted, perfumed notes, like this,
Tell of a creature formed to pet and kiss."

My listener heard me with a slow, odd smile ;
Stretched in abandon at my feet, the while,

MAURINE

He fanned me idly with his broad-brimmed hat.
" Then all young ladies must be formed for that ! "
He laughed, and said.
             " Their letters read, and look,
As like as twenty copies of one book.
They're written in a dainty, spider scrawl,
To ' darling, precious Kate,' or ' Fan,' or ' Moll.'
The ' dearest, sweetest ' friend they ever had.
They say they ' want to see you, oh, so bad ! '
Vow they'll ' forget you never, *never*, oh ! '
And then they tell about a splendid beau—
A lovely hat—a charming dress, and send
A little scrap of this to every friend.
And then to-close, for lack of something better,
They beg you'll ' read and burn this horrid letter.' "

He watched me, smiling. He was prone to vex
And hector me with flings upon my sex.
He liked, he said, to have me flash and frown,
So he could tease me, and then laugh me down.
My storms of wrath amused him very much :
He liked to see me go off at a touch ;
Anger became me—made my colour rise,
And gave an added lustre to my eyes.
So he would talk—and so he watched me now,
To see the hot flush mantle cheek and brow.

Instead, I answered coolly, with a smile,
Felling a seam with utmost care meanwhile,

ELLA WHEELER WILCOX

" The caustic tongue of Vivian Dangerfield
Is barbed as ever, for my sex, this morn.
Still unconvinced, no smallest point I yield.
Woman I love and trust, despite your scorn.
There is some truth in what you say ?   Well, yes !
Your statements usually hold, more or less.
Some women write weak letters (some men do) ;
Some make professions, knowing them untrue.
And woman's friendship, in the time of need,
I own, too often proves a broken reed.
But I believe, and ever will contend,
Woman can be a sister woman's friend,
Giving from out her large heart's bounteous store
A living love—claiming to do no more
Than, through and by that love, she knows she can ;
And living by her professions, *like a man.*
And such a tie, true friendship's silken tether,
Binds Helen Trevor's heart and mine together.
I love her for her beauty, meekness, grace ;
For her white lily soul and angel face.
She loves me, for my greater strength maybe ;
Loves—and would give her heart's best blood for me.
And I, to save her from a pain or cross,
Would suffer any sacrifice or loss :
Such can be woman's friendship for another.
Could man give more, or ask more from a brother ? "

I paused : and Vivian leaned his massive head
Against the pillar of the portico,
Smiled his slow, sceptic smile, then laughed, and said—

MAURINE

" Nay, surely not—if what you say be so.
You've made a statement, but no proof's at hand.
Wait—do not flash your eyes so !   Understand
I think you quite sincere in what you say :
You love your friend, and she loves you, to-day ;
But friendship is not friendship at the best
Till circumstances put it to the test.
Man's, less demonstrative, stands strain and tear
While woman's, half profession, fails to wear.
Two women love each other passing well—
Say, Helen Trevor and Maurine La Pelle,
                              Just for example.

                              Let them daily meet
At ball and concert, in the church and street,
They kiss and coo, they visit, chat, caress ;
Their love increases, rather than grows less ;
And all goes well, till ' Helen dear ' discovers
That ' Maurine darling ' wins too many lovers.
And then her ' precious friend,' her ' pet,' her ' sweet,'
Becomes a ' minx,' a ' creature of deceit.'
Let Helen smile too oft on Maurine's beaux,
Or wear more stylish or becoming clothes,
Or sport a hat that has a longer feather—
And lo ! the strain has broken ' friendship's tether.'
Maurine's sweet smile becomes a frown or pout ;
' She's just begun to find that Helen out.'
The breach grows wider—anger fills each heart.
They drift asunder, whom ' but death could part.'
You shake your head ?   Oh, well, we'll never know !

303

ELLA WHEELER WILCOX

It is not likely Fate will test you so.
You'll live, and love ; and, meeting twice a year,
While life shall last, you'll hold each other dear.
I pray it may be so ; it were not best
To shake your faith in women by the test.
Keep your belief, and nurse it while you can.
I've faith in woman's friendship too—for man !
They're true as steel, as mothers, friends, and wives :
And that's enough to bless us all our lives.
That man's a selfish fellow, and a bore,
Who is unsatisfied, and asks for more."

" But there is need of more ! " I here broke in.
" I hold that woman guilty of a sin,
Who would not cling to and defend another,
As nobly as she would stand by a brother.
Who would not suffer for a sister's sake,
And, were there need to prove her friendship, make
'Most any sacrifice, nor count the cost.
Who would not do this for a friend is lost
To every nobler principle."

                                    " Shame, shame ! "
Cried Vivian, laughing, " for you now defame
The whole sweet sex ; since there's not one would do
The thing you name, nor would I want her to.
I love the sex. My mother was a woman—
I hope my wife will be, and wholly human,
And if she wants to make some sacrifice
I'll think her far nore sensible and wise

MAURINE

To let her husband reap the benefit,
Instead of some old maid or senseless chit.
Selfish ?   Of course !   I hold all love is so :
And I shall love my wife right well, I know.
Now there's a point regarding selfish love,
You thirst to argue with me, and disprove.
But since these cosy hours will soon be gone,
And all our meetings broken in upon,
No more of these rare moments must be spent
In vain discussions, or in argument.
I wish Miss Trevor was in—Jericho !
(You see the selfishness begins to show.)
She wants to see you ?—So do I : but she
Will gain her wish, by taking you from me.
' Come all the same ? ' that means I'll be allowed
To realise that ' three can make a crowd.'
I do not like to feel myself *de trop*.
With two girl cronies would I not be so ?
My ring would interrupt some private chat.
You'd ask me in and take my cane and hat.
And speak about the lovely summer day.
And think—' The lout !   I wish he'd kept away.'
Miss Trevor'd smile, but just to hide a pout
And count the moments till I was shown out.
And, while I whirled my thumbs, I should sit wishing
That I had gone off hunting birds, or fishing.
No, thanks, Maurine !   The iron hand of Fate
(Or, otherwise, Miss Trevor's dainty fingers,)
Will bar my entrance into Eden's gate ;
And I shall be like some poor soul that lingers

ELLA WHEELER WILCOX

At heaven's portal, paying the price of sin,
Yet hoping to be pardoned and let in."

He looked so melancholy sitting there,
I laughed outright.   " How well you act a part ;
You look the very picture of despair !
You've missed your calling, sir ! suppose you start
Upon a starring tour, and carve your name
With Booth's and Barrett's on the heights of Fame.
But now, tabooing nonsense, I shall send
For you to help me entertain my friend,
Unless you come without it.   ' Cronies ? '   True,
Wanting our ' private chats ' as cronies do.
And we'll take those, while you are reading Greek,
Or writing ' Lines to Dora's brow ' or ' cheek.'
But when you have an hour or two of leisure,
Call as you now do, and afford like pleasure.
For never yet did heaven's sun shine on,
Or stars discover, that phenomenon,
In any country, or in any clime ;
Two maids so bound by ties of mind and heart,
They did not feel the heavy weight of time
In weeks of scenes wherein no man took part.
God made the sexes to associate :
Nor law of man, nor stern decree of Fate,
Can ever undo what His hand has done,
And, quite alone make happy either one.
My Helen is an only child :—a pet
Of loving parents : and she never yet
Has been denied one boon for which she pleaded.

MAURINE

A fragile thing, her lightest wish was heeded.
Would she pluck roses ? they must first be shorn,
By careful hands, of every hateful thorn.
And loving eyes must scan the pathway where
Her feet may tread, to see no stones are there.
She'll grow dull here, in this secluded nook,
Unless you aid me in the pleasant task
Of entertaining. Drop in with your book—
Read, talk, sing for her sometimes. What I ask,
Do once, to please me : then there'll be no need
For me to state the case again, or plead.
There's nothing like a woman's grace and beauty
To waken mankind to a sense of duty."

"I bow before the mandate of my queen :
Your slightest wish is law, Ma Belle Maurine,"
He answered, smiling, " I'm at your command ;
Point but one lily finger, or your wand,
And you will find a willing slave obeying.
There goes my dinner bell ! I hear it saying
I've spent two hours here, lying at your feet,
Not profitable, maybe—surely sweet.
All time is money : now were I to measure
The time I spend here by its solid pleasure,
And that were coined in dollars, then I've laid
Each day a fortune at your feet, fair maid.
There goes that bell again ! I'll say good-bye,
Or clouds will shadow my domestic sky.
I'll come again, as you would have me do,
And see your friend, while she is seeing you.

ELLA WHEELER WILCOX

That's like by proxy being at a feast ;
Unsatisfactory, to say the least."

He drew his fine shape up, and trod the land
With kingly grace.   Passing the gate, his hand
He lightly placed the garden wall upon,
Leaped over like a leopard, and was gone.

And, going, took the brightness from the place,
Yet left the June day with a sweeter grace,
And my young soul so steeped in happy dreams,
Heaven itself seemed shown to me in gleams.

There is a time with lovers, when the heart
First slowly rouses from its dreamless sleep,
To all the tumult of a passion life,
Ere yet have wakened jealousy and strife.
Just as a young, untutored child will start
Out of a long hour's slumber, sound and deep,
And lie and smile with rosy lips, and cheeks,
In a sweet, restful trance, before it speaks.
A time when yet no word the spell has broken,
Save what the heart unto the soul has spoken,
In quickened throbs, and sighs but half-suppressed.
A time when that sweet truth, all unconfessed,
Gives added fragrance to the summer flowers,
A golden glory to the passing hours,
A hopeful beauty to the plainest face,
And lends to life a new and tender grace.

MAURINE

When the full heart has climbed the heights of bliss
And, smiling, looks back o'er the golden past,
I think it finds no sweeter hour than this
In all love-life.   For, later, when the last
Translucent drop o'erflows the cup of joy,
And love, more mighty than the heart's control,
Surges in words of passion from the soul,
And vows are asked and given, shadows rise
Like mists before the sun in noonday skies,
Vague fears, that prove the brimming cup's alloy ;
A dread of change—the crowning moment's curse,
Since what is perfect, change but renders worse ;
A vain desire to cripple Time, who goes
Bearing our joys away, and bringing woes.
And later, doubts and jealousies awaken,
And plighted hearts are tempest-tossed, and shaken,
Doubt sends a test, that goes a step too far,
A wound is made, that, healing, leaves a scar,
Or one heart, full with love's sweet satisfaction,
Thinks truth once spoken always understood,
While one is pining for the tender action
And whispered word by which, of old, 'twas wooed.
But this blest hour, in love's glad, golden day,
Is like the dawning, ere the radiant ray
Of glowing Sol has burst upon the eye,
But yet is heralded in earth and sky,
Warm with its fervour, mellow with its light,
While Care still slumbers in the arms of Night.
But Hope, awake, hears happy birdlings sing,
And thinks of all a summer day may bring.

In this sweet calm, my young heart lay at rest,
Filled with a blissful sense of peace ; nor guessed
That sullen clouds were gathering in the skies
To hide the glorious sun, ere it should rise.

PART II

TO little birds that never tire of humming
    About the garden, in the summer weather,
Aunt Ruth compared us, after Helen's coming,
As we two roamed, or sat and talked together.
Twelve months apart, we had so much to say
Of schooldays gone—and time since passed away ;
Of that old friend, and this ; of what we'd done ;
Of how our separate paths in life had run ;
Of what we would do, in the coming years ;
Of plans and castles, hopes and dreams and fears,
All these, and more, as soon as we found speech,
We touched upon, and skimmed from this to that.
But at the first, each only gazed on each,
And, dumb with joy, that did not need a voice,
Like lesser joys, to say, " Lo ! I rejoice,"
With smiling eyes and clasping hands we sat
Wrapped in that peace, felt but with those dear,
Contented just to know each other near.
But when this silent eloquence gave place
To words, 'twas like the riding of a flood
Above a dam.   We sat there, face to face,
And let our talk glide on where'er it would,

MAURINE

Speech never halting in its speed or zest,
Save when our rippling laughter let it rest ;
Just as a stream will sometimes pause and play
About a bubbling spring, then dash away.
No wonder, then, the third day's sun was nigh
Up to the zenith when my friend and I
Opened our eyes from slumber long and deep ;
Nature demanding recompense for hours
Spent in the portico among the flowers,
Halves of two nights we should have spent in sleep.

So this third day, we breakfasted at one ;
Then walked about the garden in the sun,
Hearing the thrushes and the robins sing,
And looking to see what buds were opening.

The clock chimed three, and we yet strayed at will
About the yard in morning dishabille,
When Aunt Ruth came, with apron o'er her head,
Holding a letter in her hand, and said,
" Here is a note from Vivian, I opine ;
At least his servant brought it.   And now, girls,
You may think this is no concern of mine,
But in my days young ladies did not go
Till almost bed-time roaming to and fro
In morning wrappers, and with tangled curls,
The very pictures of forlorn distress.
'Tis three o'clock, and time for you to dress.
Come ! read your note and hurry in, Maurine,
And make yourself fit object to be seen."

ELLA WHEELER WILCOX

Helen was bending o'er an almond bush,
And ere she looked up I had read the note,
And calmed my heart, that, bounding, sent a flush
To brow and cheek, at sight of aught *he* wrote.
" Ma Belle Maurine : " (so Vivian's billet ran),
" Is it not time I saw your cherished guest ?
' Pity the sorrows of a poor young man,'
Banished from all that makes existence blest.
I'm dying to see—your friend ; and I will come
And pay respects, hoping you'll be at home
To-night at eight.   Expectantly, V. D."

Inside my belt I slipped the billet, saying,
" Helen, go make yourself most fair to see :
Quick ! hurry now ! no time for more delaying !
In just five hours a caller will be here,
And you must look your prettiest, my dear !
Begin your toilet right away.   I know
How long it takes you to arrange each bow—
To twist each curl, and loop your skirts aright.
And you must prove you are *au fait* to-night,
And make a perfect toilet ; for our caller
Is man, and critic, poet, artist, scholar,
And views with eyes of all."
                                        " Oh, oh ! Maurine,"
Cried Helen, with a well-feigned look of fear,
" You've frightened me so I shall not appear ;
I'll hide away, refusing to be seen
By such an ogre.   Woe is me ! bereft
Or all my friends ; my peaceful home I've left,

MAURINE

And strayed away into the dreadful wood
To meet the fate of poor Red Riding Hood.
No, Maurine, no ! you've given me such a fright,
I'll not go near your ugly wolf to-night."

Meantime we'd left the garden, and I stood
In Helen's room, where she had thrown herself
Upon a couch, and lay, a winsome elf,
Pouting and smiling, cheek upon her arm,
Not in the least a portrait of alarm.
" Now, sweet ! " I coaxed, and knelt by her, " be good !
Go curl your hair, and please your own Maurine
By putting on that lovely grenadine.
Not wolf nor ogre, neither Caliban
Nor Mephistopheles you'll meet to-night,
But what the ladies call ' a nice young man ! '
Yet one worth knowing—strong with health and might
Of perfect manhood ; gifted, noble, wise ;
Moving among his kind with loving eyes,
And helpful hand ; progressive, brave, refined,
After the image of his Maker's mind."

" Now, now, Maurine ! " cried Helen, " I believe
It is your lover coming here this eve.
Why have you never written of him, pray ?
Is the day set ?—and when ?   Say, Maurine, say ! "

Had I betrayed by some too fervent word
The secret love that all my being stirred ?
My lover ?   Ay !   My heart proclaimed him so ;

But first *his* lips must win the sweet confession,
Ere even Helen be allowed to know.
I must straightway erase the slight impression
Made by the words just uttered.

                       " Foolish child ! "
I gaily cried, " your fancy's straying wild.
Just let a girl of eighteen hear the name
Of maid and youth uttered about one time,
And off her fancy goes at break-neck pace,
Defying circumstances, reason, space—
And straightway builds romances so sublime
They put all Shakespeare's dramas to the shame.
This Vivian Dangerfield is neighbour, friend,
And kind companion, bringing books and flowers.
And, by his thoughtful actions without end,
Helping me pass some otherwise long hours ;
But he has never breathed a word of love.
If you still doubt me, listen while I prove
My statement by the letter that he wrote.
' Dying to meet—my friend ! ' " (She could not see
The dash between that meant so much to me.)
" ' Will come this eve at eight, and hopes we may
Be in to greet him.' Now, I think you'll say
'Tis not much like a lover's tender note."

We laugh, we jest, not meaning what we say ;
We hide our thoughts by light words lightly spoken,
And pass on heedless, till we find one day
They've bruised our hearts, or left some other broken.

MAURINE

I sought my room, and trilling some blithe air,
Opened my wardrobe, wondering what to wear.
Momentous question ! femininely human !
More than all others vexing mind of woman,
Since that sad day, when in her discontent,
To search for leaves, our fair first mother went.
All undecided what I should put on,
At length I made selection of a lawn—
White, with a tiny pink vine overrun—
My simplest robe, but Vivian's favourite one.
And placing a single floweret in my hair,
I crossed the hall to Helen's chamber, where
I found her with her fair locks all let down,
Brushing the kinks out, with a pretty frown.
'Twas like a picture, or a pleasing play,
To watch her make her toilet.   She would stand,
And turn her head first this, and then that way,
Trying effect of ribbon, bow, or band.
Then she would pick up something else, and curve
Her lovely neck, with cunning, bird-like grace,
And watch the mirror while she put it on,
With such a sweetly grave and thoughtful face ;
And then to view it all would sway, and swerve
Her lithe young body, like a graceful swan.

Helen was over medium height, and slender
Even to frailty.   Her great, wistful eyes
Were like the deep blue of autumnal skies ;
And through them looked her soul, large, loving, tender.
Her long, light hair was lustreless, except

ELLA WHEELER WILCOX

ELLA WHEELER WILCOX

Upon the ends, where burnished sunbeams slept,
And on the earlocks ;_ and she looped the curls
Back with a shell-comb, studded thick with pearls,
Costly yet simple.   Her pale loveliness,
That night, was heightened by her rich, black dress,
That trailed behind her, leaving half in sight
Her taper arms, and shoulders marble white.

I was not tall as Helen, and my face
Was shaped and coloured like my grandsire's race ;
For through his veins my own received the warm,
Red blood of southern France, which curved my form,
And glowed upon my cheek in crimson dyes,
And bronzed my hair, and darkled in my eyes,
And as the morning trails the skirts of night,
And dusky night puts on the garb of morn,
And walk together when the day is born,
So we two glided down the hall and stair,
Arm clasping arm, into the parlour, where
Sat Vivian, bathed in sunset's gorgeous light.
He rose to greet us.   Oh ! his form was grand ;
And he possessed that power, strange, occult,
Called magnetism, lacking better word,
Which moves the world, achieving great result
Where genius fails completely.   Touch his hand,
It thrilled through all your being—meet his eye,
And you were moved, yet knew not how, or why ;
Let him but rise, you felt the air was stirred
By an electric current.

MAURINE

                        This strange force
Is mightier than genius.   Rightly used,
It leads to grand achievements ; all things yield
Before its mystic presence, and its field
Is broad as earth and heaven.   But abused,
It sweeps like a poison simoon on its course,
Bearing miasma in its scorching breath,
And leaving all its touches struck with death.

Far-reaching science shall yet·tear away
The mystic garb that hides it from the day,
And drag it forth and bind it with its laws,
And make it serve the purposes of men,
Guided by common sense and reason.   Then
We'll hear no more of seance, table-rapping,
And all that trash, o'er which the world is gaping,
Lost in effect, while science seeks the cause.

Vivian was not conscious of his power ;
Or, if he was, knew not its full extent.
He knew his glance would make a wild beast cower,
And yet he knew not that his large eyes sent
Into the heart of woman the same thrill
That made the lion servant of his will.
And even strong men felt it.

                        He arose,
Reached forth his hand, and in it clasped my own,
While I held Helen's ; and he spoke some word
Of pleasant greeting in his low, round tone,

ELLA WHEELER WILCOX

Unlike all other voices I have heard.
Just as the white cloud, at the sunrise, glows
With roseate colours, so the pallid hue
Of Helen's cheek, like tinted sea-shells grew.
Through mine, his hand caused hers to tremble : such
Was the all-mast'ring magic of his touch.

Then we sat down, and talked about the weather,
The neighbourhood—some author's last new book.
But, when I could, I left the two together
To make acquaintance, saying I must look
After the chickens—my especial care ;
And ran away, and left them, laughing, there.

Knee-deep, through clover, to the poplar grove,
I waded, where my pets were wont to rove :
And there I found the foolish mother hen
Brooding her chickens underneath a tree,
An easy prey for foxes. " Chick-a-dee,"
Quoth I, while reaching for the downy things
That, chirping, peeped from out the mother-wings,
" How very human is your folly ! When
There waits a haven, pleasant, bright, and warm,
And one to lead you thither from the storm
And lurking dangers, yet you turn away,
And, thinking to be your own protector, stray
Into the open jaws of death ; for, see !
An owl is sitting—in this very tree
You thought safe shelter. Go now to your pen."

MAURINE

And followed by the clucking, clamorous hen,
So like the human mother here again,
Moaning because a strong, protecting arm
Would shield her little ones from cold and harm,
I carried back my garden hat brimful
Of chirping chickens, like white balls of wool,
And snugly housed them.

                                And just then I heard
A sound like gentle winds among the trees,
Or pleasant waters in the summer, stirred
And set in motion by a passing breeze.
'Twas Helen singing : and, as I drew near,
Another voice, a tenor full and clear,
Mingled with hers, as murmuring streams unite,
And flow on stronger in their wedded might.

It was a way of Helen's not to sing
The songs that other people sang. She took
Sometimes an extract from an ancient book ;
Again some floating, fragmentary thing
And such she fitted to old melodies,
Or else composed the music. One of these
She sang that night ; and Vivian caught the strain,
And joined her in the chorus, or refrain.

SONG
O thou, mine other, stronger part !
  Whom yet I cannot hear, or see,
Come thou, and take this loving heart,
  That longs to yield its all to thee,

ELLA WHEELER WILCOX

I call mine own—Oh, come to me !
Love, answer back, I come to thee,
      I come to thee.

This hungry heart, so warm, so large,
  Is far too great a care for me.
I have grown weary of the charge
  I keep so sacredly for thee.
    Come thou, and take my heart from me.
Love, answer back, I come to thee,
      I come to thee.

I am aweary, waiting here
  For one who tarries long from me.
O ! art thou far, or art thou near ?
  And must I still be sad for thee ?
  Or wilt thou straightway come to me ?
Love, answer, I am near to thee,
      I come to thee.

The melody, so full of plaintive chords,
Sobbed into silence—echoing down the strings
Like voice of one who walks from us, and sings.
Vivian had leaned upon the instrument
The while they sang. But, as he spoke those words,
" Love, I am near to thee, I come to thee,"
He turned his grand head slowly round, and bent
His lustrous, soulful, speaking gaze on me.
And my young heart, eager to own its king,
Sent to my eyes a great, glad, trustful light
Of love and faith, and hung upon my cheek
Hope's rose-hued flag. There was no need to speak
I crossed the room, and knelt by Helen. " Sing
That song you sang a fragment of one night,
Out on the porch, beginning ' Praise me not,' "

MAURINE

I whispered : and her sweet and plaintive tone
Rose, low and tender, as if she had caught
From some sad passing breeze, and made her own
The echo of the wind-harp's sighing strain,
Or the soft music of the falling rain.

SONG

O praise me not with your lips, dear one !
   Though your tender words I prize.
But dearer by far is the soulful gaze
   Of your eyes, your beautiful eyes,
      Your tender, loving eyes.

O chide me not with your lips, dear one !
   Though I cause your bosom sighs.
You can make repentance deeper far
   By your sad, reproving eyes,
      Your sorrowful, troubled eyes.

Words, at the best, are but hollow sounds ;
   Above, in the beaming skies,
The constant stars say never a word,
   But only smile with their eyes—
      Smile on with their lustrous eyes.

Then breathe no vow with your lips, dear one ;
   On the wingèd wind speech flies.
But I read the truth of your noble heart
   In your soulful, speaking eyes—
      In your deep and beautiful eyes.

The twilight darkened 'round us, in the room,
While Helen sang ; and, in the gathering gloom,
Vivian reached out, and took my hand in his,
And held it so ; while Helen made the air
Languid with music.   Then a step drew near,

ELLA WHEELER WILCOX

And voice of Aunt Ruth broke the spell :

                                   " Dear ! dear !
Why, Maurie, Helen, children ! how is this ?
I hear you, but you have no light in there.
Your room is dark as Egypt.   What a way
For folk to visit !—Maurie, go, I pray,
And order lamps."

                       And so there came a light,
And all the sweet dreams hovering around
The twilight shadows flitted in affright :
And e'en the music had a harsher sound.

In pleasant converse passed an hour away :
And Vivian planned a picnic for next day—
A drive the next, and rambles without end,
That he might help me entertain my friend.
And then he rose, bowed low, and passed from sight,
Like some great star that drops out from the night ;
And Helen watched him through the shadows go,
And turned and said, her voice subdued and low,
" How tall he is ! in all my life, Maurine,
A grander man I never yet have seen."

PART III

ONE golden twelfth-part of a chequered year ;
    One summer month of sunlight, moonlight, mirth,
With not a hint of shadows lurking near,
Or storm-clouds brewing.

322

MAURINE

'Twas a royal day ;
Voluptuous July held her lover, Earth,
With her warm arms, upon her glowing breast,
And twined herself about him as he lay
Smiling and panting in his dream-stirred rest.
She bound him with her limbs of perfect grace,
And hid him with her trailing robe of green,
And wound him in her long hair's shimmering sheen,
And rained her ardent kisses on his face.

Through the glad glory of the summer land
Helen and I went wandering, hand in hand,
In winding paths, hard by the ripe wheat field,
White with the promise of a bounteous yield,
Across the late shorn meadow—down the hill,
Red with the tiger-lily blossoms, till
We stood upon the borders of the lake,
That, like a pretty placid infant, slept
Low at its base ; and little ripples crept
Along its surface, just as dimples chase
Each other o'er an infant's sleeping face.
Helen in idle hours had learned to make
A thousand pretty, feminine knick-knacks
For brackets, ottomans, and toilet stands—
Labour just suited to her dainty hands.
That morning she had been at work in wax,
Moulding a wreath of flowers for my room—
Taking her patterns from the living blows,
In all their dewy beauty and sweet bloom,
Fresh from my garden.   Fuchsia, tulip, rose,

ELLA WHEELER WILCOX

And trailing ivy, grew beneath her touch,
Resembling the living plants as much
As life is copied in the form of death ;
These lacking but the perfume, and that, breath.

And now the wreath was all completed, save
The mermaid blossom of all flowerdom,
The water-lily, dripping from the wave.
And 'twas in search of it that we have come
Down to the lake, and wandered on the beach,
To see if any lilies grew in reach.
Some broken stalks, where flowers late had been ;
Some buds, with all their beauties folded in,
We found, but not the treasure that we sought.
And then we turned our footsteps to the spot
Where, all impatient of its chain, my boat,
The Swan, rocked, asking to be set afloat.
It was a dainty row-boat—strong, yet light ;
Each side a swan was painted snowy white—
A present from my uncle, just before
He sailed, with Death, to that mysterious strand,
Where freighted ships go sailing evermore,
But none return to tell us of the land.
I freed *The Swan*, and slowly rowed about,
Wherever sea-weeds, grass, or green leaves lifted
Their tips above the water. So we drifted,
While Helen, opposite, leaned idly out
And watched for lilies in the waves below,
And softly crooned some sweet and dreamy air,
That soothed me like a mother's lullabies.

MAURINE

I dropped the oars, and closed my sun-kissed eyes,
And let the boat go drifting here and there.
Oh, happy day! the last of that brief time
Of thoughtless youth, when all the world seems bright,
Ere that disguisèd angel men call Woe
Leads the sad heart through valleys dark as night,
Up to the heights exalted and sublime.
On each blest, happy moment, I am fain
To linger long, ere I pass on to pain
And sorrow that succeeded.

                    From day-dreams,
As golden as the summer noontide's beams,
I was awakened by a voice that cried—
" Strange ship, ahoy! Fair frigate, whither bound ? "
And, starting up, I cast my gaze around,
And saw a sail-boat o'er the water glide
Close to *The Swan*, like some live thing of grace ;
And from it looked the glowing, handsome face
Of Vivian.

              " Beauteous sirens of the sea,
Come sail across the raging main with me."
He laughed ; and leaning, drew our drifting boat
Beside his own. " There now ! step in," he said,
" I'll land you anywhere you want to go—
My boat is safer far than yours, I know ;
And much more pleasant with its sails all spread.
The Swan ? We'll take the oars, and let it float
Ashore at leisure. You, Maurine, sit there ;
Miss Helen here. Ye gods and little fishes !

ELLA WHEELER WILCOX

I've reached the height of pleasure, and my wishes.
Adieu despondency ! farewell to care ! "

'Twas done so quickly ; that was Vivian's way.
He did not wait for either yea or nay.
He gave commands, and left you with no choice
But just to do the bidding of his voice.
His rare, kind smile, low tones, and manly face
Lent to his quick imperiousness a grace
And winning charm, completely stripping it
Of what might otherwise have seemed unfit,
Leaving no trace of tyranny, but just
That nameless force that seemed to say, " You must."
Suiting its pretty title of *The Dawn*
(So named, he said, that it might rhyme with *Swan*),
Vivian's sail-boat was carpeted with blue,
While all its sails were of a pale rose hue.
The daintiest craft that flirted with the breeze ;
A poet's fancy in an hour of ease.
Whatever Vivian had was of the best.
His room was like some Sultan's in the East.
His board was always spread as for a feast,
Whereat, each meal, he was both host and guest.
He would go hungry sooner than he'd dine
At his own table if 'twere illy set.
He so loved things artistic in design—
Order and beauty all about him.   Yet
So kind he was, if it befell his lot
To dine within the humble peasant's cot,
He made it seem his native soil to be,

MAURINE

And thus displayed the true gentility.
Under the rosy banners of *The Dawn*,
Around the lake we drifted on, and on.
It was a time for dreams, and not for speech.
And so we floated on in silence, each
Weaving the fancies suiting such a day.
Helen leaned idly o'er the sail-boat's side,
And dipped her rosy fingers in the tide ;
And I among the cushions half reclined,
Half sat, and watched the fleecy clouds at play,
While Vivian with his blank-book, opposite,
In which he seemed to either sketch or write,
Was lost in inspiration of some kind.

No time, no change, no scene, can e'er efface
My mind's impression of that hour and place :
It stands out like a picture.   O'er the years,
Black with their robes of sorrow—veiled with tears,
Lying with all their lengthened shapes between,
Untouched, undimmed, I still behold that scene.
Just as the last of Indian-summer days,
Replete with sunlight, crowned with amber haze,
Followed with dark and desolate December,
Through all the months of winter we remember.

The sun slipped westward.   That peculiar change
Which creeps into the air, and speaks of night
While yet the day is full of golden light,
We felt steal o'er us.
                              Vivian broke the spell

327

ELLA WHEELER WILCOX

Of dream-fraught silence, throwing down his book :
" Young ladies, please allow me to arrange
These wraps about your shoulders.   I know well
The fickle nature of our atmosphere—
Her smile swift followed by a frown or tear—
And go prepared for changes.' Now, you look,
Like—like—oh, where's a pretty simile ?
Had you a pocket mirror here you'd see
How well my native talent is displayed
In shawling you.   Red on the brunette maid :
Blue on the blonde—and quite without design
(Oh, where *is* that comparison of mine ?)
Well—like a June rose and a violet blue
In one bouquet !   I fancy that will do.
And now, I crave your patience and a boon,
Which is to listen, while I read my rhyme,
A floating fancy of the summer time.
'Tis neither witty, wonderful, nor wise,
So listen kindly, but don't criticise
My maiden effort of the afternoon—

> If all the ships I have at sea
> Should come a-sailing home to me,
> Ah, well ! the harbour could not hold
> So many sails as there would be
> If all my ships came in from sea.

> If half my ships came home from sea,
> And brought their precious freight to me,
> Ah, well ! I should have wealth as great
> As any King who sits in state—
> So rich the treasures that would be
> In half my ships now out at sea.

MAURINE

If just one ship I have at sea
Should come a-sailing home to me,
Ah, well! the storm-clouds then might frown,
For if the others all went down,
Still rich and proud and glad I'd be
If that one ship came back to me.

If that one ship went down at sea,
And all the others came to me,
Weighed down with gems and wealth untold,
With glory, honours, riches, gold,
The poorest soul on earth I'd be
If that one ship came not to me.

O skies be calm! O winds blow free—
Blow all my ships safe home to me.
But if thou sendest some a-wrack,
To never more come sailing back,
Send any—all that skim the sea,
But bring my love-ship home to me.

Helen was leaning by me, and her head
Rested against my shoulder. As he read
I stroked her hair, and watched the fleecy skies,
And when he finished did not turn my eyes.
I felt too happy and too shy to meet
His gaze just then. I said, " 'Tis very sweet,
And suits the day; does it not, Helen, dear?"
But Helen, voiceless, did not seem to hear.
" 'Tis strange," I added, " how you poets sing
So feelingly about the very thing
You care not for! And dress up an ideal
So well, it looks a living, breathing real!
Now, to a listener, your love song seemed
A heart's outpouring; yet I've heard you say
Almost the opposite; or that you deemed

329

ELLA WHEELER WILCOX

Position, honour, glory, power, fame,
Gained without loss of conscience or good name,
The things to live for."

                        " Have you ? Well, you may,"
Laughed Vivian, " but 'twas years—or months ago !
And Solomon says wise men change, you know !
I now speak truth ! if she I hold most dear
Slipped from my life, and no least hope were left,
My heart would find the years more lonely here
Than if I were of wealth, fame, friends bereft,
And sent an exile to a foreign land."

His voice was low and measured ; as he spoke
New, unknown chords of melody awoke
Within my soul. I felt my heart expand
With that sweet fulness born of love. I turned
To hide the blushes on my cheek that burned,
And leaning over Helen, breathed her name.
She lay so motionless I thought she slept :
But, as I spoke, I saw her eyes unclose,
And o'er her face a sudden glory swept,
And a slight tremor thrilled all through her frame.
" Sweet friend," I said, " your face is full of light :
What were the dreams that made your eyes so
    bright ? "

She only smiled for answer, and arose
From her reclining posture at my side,
Threw back the clust'ring ringlets from her face
With a quick gesture, full of easy grace,

MAURINE

And, turning, spoke to Vivian. "Will you guide
The boat up near that little clump of green
Off to the right? There's where the lilies grow.
We quite forgot our errand here, Maurine,
And our few moments have grown into hours.
What will Aunt Ruth think of our ling'ring so?
There—that will do—now I can reach the flowers."

"Hark! just hear that!" and Vivian broke forth
    singing,
"Row, brothers, row." "The six o'clock bell's ring-
    ing!
Who ever knew three hours to go so fast
In all the annals of the world, before?
I could have sworn not over one had passed.
Young ladies, I am forced to go ashore!
I thank you for the pleasure you have given;
This afternoon has been a glimpse of heaven.
Good-night—sweet dreams! and, by your gracious
    leave,
I'll pay my compliments to-morrow eve."
A smile, a bow, and he had gone his way:
And, in the waning glory of the day,
Down cool, green lanes, and through the length'ning
    shadows,
Silent, we wandered back across the meadows.
The wreath was finished, and adorned my room;
Long afterward, the lilies' copied bloom
Was like a horrid spectre in my sight,
Staring upon me morning, noon, and night.

ELLA WHEELER WILCOX

The sun went down.   The sad new moon rose up,
And passed before me, like an empty cup,
The Great Unseen brims full of pain or bliss,
And gives His children, saying, " Drink of this."

A light wind, from the open casement, fanned
My brow and Helen's, as we, hand in hand,
Sat looking out upon the twilight scene,
In dreamy silence.   Helen's dark blue eyes,
Like two lost stars that wandered from the skies
Some night adown the meteor's shining track,
And always had been grieving to go back,
Now gazed up, wistfully, at heaven's dome,
And seemed to recognise and long for home.
Her sweet voice broke the silence : " Wish, Maurine,
Before you speak ! you know the moon is new,
And anything you wish for will come true
Before it wanes.   I do believe the sign !
Now tell me your wish, and I'll tell you mine."

I turned and looked up at the slim young moon ;
And, with an almost superstitious heart,
I sighed, " Oh, new moon ! help me, by thine art,
To grow all grace and goodness, and to be
Worthy the love a true heart proffers me."
Then smiling down, I said, " Dear one ! my boon,
I fear, is quite too silly or too sweet
For my repeating ; so we'll let it stay
Between the moon and me.   But if I may
I'll listen now to your wish.   Tell me, please ! "

MAURINE

All suddenly she nestled at my feet,
And hid her blushing face upon my knees,
Then drew my hand against her glowing cheek,
And, leaning on my breast, began to speak,
Half sighing out the words my tortured ear
Reached down to catch, while striving not to hear.

" Can you not guess who 'twas about, Maurine ?
Oh, my sweet friend ! you must ere this have seen
The love I tried to cover from all eyes
And from myself.   Ah, foolish little heart !
As well it might go seeking for some art
Whereby to hide the sun in noonday skies.
When first the strange sound of his voice I heard,
Looked on his noble face, and touched his hand, .
My slumb'ring heart thrilled through and through, and
    stirred
As if to say, ' I hear, and understand.'
And day by day mine eyes were blest beholding
The inner beauty of his life, unfolding
In countless words and actions, that portrayed
The noble stuff of which his soul was made.
And more and more I felt my heart upreaching
Toward the truth, drawn gently by his teaching,
As flowers are drawn by sunlight.   And there grew
A strange, shy something in its depths, I knew
At length was love, because it was so sad,
And yet so sweet, and made my heart so glad,
Yet seemed to pain me.   Then, for very shame,
Lest all should read my secret and its name,

333

ELLA WHEELER WILCOX

I strove to hide it in my breast away,
Where God could see it only. But each day
It seemed to grow within me, and would rise,
Like my own soul, and look forth from my eyes,
Defying bonds of silence ; and would speak,
In its red-lettered language, on my cheek,
If but his name was uttered. You were kind,
My own Maurine ! as you alone could be,
So long the sharer of my heart and mind,
While yet you saw, in seeming not to see.
In all the years we have been friends, my own,
And loved as women very rarely do,
My heart no sorrow and no joy has known
It has not shared at once, in full, with you.
And I so longed to speak to you of this,
When first I felt its mingled pain and bliss ;
Yet dared not, lest you, knowing him, should say,
In pity for my folly—' Lack-a-day !
You are undone : because no mortal art
Can win the love of such a lofty heart.'
And so I waited, silent and in pain,
Till I could know I did not love in vain.
And now I know, beyond a doubt or fear.
Did he not say, ' If she I hold most dear
Slipped from my life, and no least hope were left,
My heart would find the years more lonely here
Than if I were of wealth, fame, friends, bereft,
And sent, an exile, to a foreign land ? '
Oh, darling, you must *love*, to understand
The joy that thrilled all through me at those words.

MAURINE

It was as if a thousand singing birds
Within my heart broke forth in notes of praise.
I did not look up, but I knew his gaze
Was on my face, and that his eyes must see
The joy I felt almost transfigured me.
He loves me—loves me ! so the birds kept singing,
And all my soul with that sweet strain is ringing.
If there were added but one drop of bliss,
No more my cup would hold : and so, this eve,
I made a wish that I might feel his kiss
Upon my lips, ere yon pale moon should leave
The stars all lonely, having waned away,
Too old and weak and bowed with care to stay."
Her voice sighed into silence.   While she spoke
My heart writhed in me, praying she would cease—
Each word she uttered falling like a stroke
On my bare soul.   And now a hush like death,
Save that 'twas broken by a quick-drawn breath,
Fell 'round me, but brought not the hoped-for peace ;
For when the lash no longer leaves its blows,
The flesh still quivers, and the blood still flows.

She nestled on my bosom like a child,
And 'neath her head my tortured heart throbbed wild
With pain and pity.   She had told her tale—
Her self-deceiving story to the end.
How could I look down on her as she lay
So fair, and sweet, and lily-like, and frail—
A tender blossom on my breast, and say,
" Nay, you are wrong—you do mistake, dear friend !

335

'Tis I am loved, not you " ?   Yet that were truth,
And she must know it later.

                     Should I speak,
And spread a ghastly pallor o'er the cheek
Flushed now with joy ?   And while I, doubting,
    pondered,
She spoke again.   " Maurine ! I oft have wondered
Why you and Vivian were not lovers.   He
Is all a heart could ask its king to be ;
And you have beauty, intellect, and youth.
I think it strange you have not loved each other—
Strange how he could pass by you for another
Not half so fair or worthy.   Yet I know
A loving Father pre-arranged it so.
I think my heart has known him all these years,
And waited for him.   And if when he came
It had been as a lover of my friend,
I should have recognised him, all the same,
As my soul mate, and loved him to the end,
Hiding my grief, and forcing back my tears
Till on my heart, slow dropping, day by day,
Unseen they fell, and wore it all away.
And so a tender Father kept him free,
With all the largeness of his love, for me—
For me, unworthy such a precious gift !
Yet I will bend each effort of my life
To grow in grace and goodness, and to lift
My soul and spirit to his lofty height,
So to deserve that holy name, his wife.
Sweet friend, it fills my whole heart with delight

MAURINE

To breathe its long-hid secret in your ear.
Speak, my Maurine, and say you love to hear ! "

The while she spoke, my active brain gave rise
To one great thought of mighty sacrifice
And self-denial. Oh ! it blanched my cheek,
And wrung my soul ; and from my heart it drove
All life and feeling. Coward-like, I strove
To send it from me : but I felt it cling
And hold fast on my mind like some live thing ;
And all the Self within me felt its touch
And cried, " No, no ! I cannot do so much—
I am not strong enough—there is no call."
And then the voice of Helen bade me speak,
And with a calmness borne of nerve, I said,
Scarce knowing what I uttered—" Sweetheart, all
Your joys and sorrows are with mine own wed.
I thank you for your confidence, and pray
I may deserve it always. But, dear one,
Something—perhaps our boat-ride in the sun,
Has set my head to aching. I must go
To bed directly ; and you will, I know,
Grant me your pardon, and another day
We'll talk of this together. Now, good-night,
And angels guard you with their wings of light."

I kissed her lips, and held her on my heart,
And viewed her as I ne'er had done before.
I gazed upon her features o'er and o'er ;
Marked her white, tender face—her fragile form,

ELLA WHEELER WILCOX

Like some frail plant that withers in the storm;
Saw she was fairer in her new-found joy
Than e'er before; and thought, " Can I destroy
God's handiwork, or leave it at the best
A broken harp, while I close clasp my bliss ? "
I bent my head, and gave her one last kiss,
And sought my room, and found there such relief
As sad hearts feel when first alone with grief.

The moon went down, slow sailing from my sight,
And left the stars to watch away the night.
O stars, sweet stars, so changeless and serene !
What depths of woe your pitying eyes have seen !
The proud sun sets, and leaves us with our sorrow,
To grope alone in darkness till the morrow.
The languid moon, e'en if she deigns to rise,
Soon seeks her couch, grown weary of our sighs;
But from the early gloaming till the day
Sends golden-liveried heralds forth to say
He comes in might; the patient stars shine on,
Steadfast and faithful, from twilight to dawn.
And, as they shone upon Gethsemane,
And watched the struggle of a God-like soul,
Now from the same far height they shone on me,
And saw the waves of anguish o'er me roll.

The storm had come upon me all unseen :
No sound of thunder fell upon my ear;
No cloud arose to tell me it was near;
But under skies all sunlit and serene,

MAURINE

I floated with the current of the stream,
And thought life all one golden-haloed dream.
When lo! a hurricane, with awful force,
Swept swift upon its devastating course,
Wrecked my frail barque, and cast me on the wave
Where all my hopes had found a sudden grave.
Love makes us blind and selfish : otherwise
I had seen Helen's secret in her eyes ;
So used I was to reading every look
In her sweet face, as I would read a book.
But now, made sightless by love's blinding rays,
I had gone on, unseeing, to the end
Where Pain dispelled the mist of golden haze
That walled me in, and lo! I found my friend
Who journeyed with me—at my very side,
Had been sore wounded to the heart, while I
Both deaf and blind, saw not, nor heard her cry.
And then I sobbed, " O God! I would have died
To save her this."   And as I cried in pain
There leaped forth from the still, white realm of Thought
Where Conscience dwells, that unimpassioned spot
As widely different from the heart's domain
As north from south—the impulse felt before,
And put away ; but now it rose once more,
In greater strength, and said, "Heart, wouldst thou prove
What lips have uttered ?   Then go lay thy love
On Friendship's altar, as thy offering."
" Nay! " cried my heart, " ask any other thing—
Ask life itself—'twere easier sacrifice.
But ask not love, for that I cannot give."

ELLA WHEELER WILCOX

" But," spoke the voice, " the meanest insect dies
And is no hero ! Heroes dare to live
When all that makes life sweet is snatched away."
So with my heart, in converse, till the day
In gold and crimson billows, rose and broke,
The voice of Conscience, all unwearied, spoke.
Love warred with Friendship : heart with Conscience
. fought,
Hours rolled away, and yet the end was not.
And wily Self, tricked out like tenderness,
Sighed, " Think how one, whose life thou wert to bless,
Will be cast down, and grope in doubt and fear !
Wouldst thou wound him, to give thy friend relief ?
Can wrong make right ? "
        " Nay ! " Conscience said, " but Pride
And Time can heal the saddest hurts of Love.
While Friendship's wounds gape wide and yet more wide,
And bitter fountains of the spirit prove."

At length, exhausted with the wearing strife,
I cast the new-found burden of my life
On God's broad breast, and sought that deep repose
That only he who watched with sorrow knows.

PART IV

" MAURINE, Maurine ! 'tis ten o'clock ! arise,
My pretty sluggard ! open those dark eyes,
And see where yonder sun is ! Do you know
I made my toilet just four hours ago ? "

340

MAURINE

'Twas Helen's voice : and Helen's gentle kiss
Fell on my cheek. As from a deep abyss,
I drew my weary self from that strange sleep
That rests not, nor refreshes. Scarce awake
Or conscious, yet there seemed a heavy weight
Bound on my breast, as by a cruel Fate.
I knew not why, and yet I longed to weep.
Some dark cloud seemed to hang upon the day ;
And, for a moment, in that trance I lay ;
When suddenly the truth did o'er me break,
Like some great wave upon a helpless child.
The dull pain in my breast grew like a knife—
The heavy throbbing of my heart grew wild,
And God gave back the burden of the life
He kept what time I slumbered.   " You are ill,"
Cried Helen, " with that blinding headache still !
You look so pale and weary. Now let me
Play nurse, Maurine, and care for you to-day !
And first I'll suit some dainty to your taste,
And bring it to you, with a cup of tea,"
And off she ran, not waiting my reply.
But, wanting most the sunshine and the light,
I left my couch, and clothed myself in haste,
And, kneeling, sent to God an earnest cry
For help and guidance.
                          " Show Thou me the way
Where duty leads, for I am blind ! my sight
Obscured by self. Oh, lead my steps aright !
Help me see the path, and, if it may,

ELLA WHEELER WILCOX

Let this cup pass—and yet, Thou heavenly One,
Thy will in all things, not mine own, be done."
Rising, I went upon my way, receiving
The strength prayer gives alway to hearts believing
I felt that unseen hands were leading me,
And knew the end was peace.

                      " What ! are you up ? "
Cried Helen, coming with a tray and cup
Of tender toast, and fragrant, smoking tea.
" You naughty girl, you should have stayed in bed
Until you ate your breakfast, and were better !
I've something hidden from you here—a letter.
But drink your tea before you read it, dear !
'Tis from some distant cousin, auntie said,
And so you need not hurry. Now, be good,
And mind your Helen."

                    So, in passive mood,
I laid the still unopened letter near,
And loitered at my breakfast, more to please
My nurse than any hunger to appease.
Then listlessly I broke the seal and read
The few lines written in a bold, free hand—
" New London, Canada.   Dear Coz. Maurine !
(In spite of generations stretched between
Our natural right to that most handy claim
Of cousinship, we'll use it all the same)
I'm coming to see you ! honestly, in truth !
I've threatened often—now I mean to act.
You'll find my coming is a stubborn fact.
Keep quiet, though, and do not tell Aunt Ruth.

MAURINE

I wonder if she'll know her petted boy
In spite of changes.   Look for me until
You see me coming.   As of old, I'm still
Your faithful friend, and loving cousin, Roy."

So Roy was coming !   He and I had played
As boy and girl, and later, youth and maid,
Full half our lives together.   He had been,
Like me, an orphan ; and the roof of kin
Gave both kind shelter.   Swift years sped away
Ere change was felt ; and then one summer day
A long-lost uncle sailed from India's shore—
Made Roy his heir, and he was ours no more.

" He'd write us daily, and we'd see his face
Once every year."   Such was his promise given
The morn he left.   But now the years were seven
Since last he looked upon the olden place.
He'd been through college, travelled in all lands,
Sailed over seas, and trod the desert sands.
Would write and plan a visit, then, ere long,
Would write again from Egypt or Hong-Kong—
Some fancy called him thither unforeseen.
So years had passed, till seven lay between
His going and the coming of this note,
Which I hid in my bosom, and replied
To Aunt Ruth's queries, " What the truant wrote ? "
By saying he was still upon the wing,
And merely dropped a line, while journeying,
To say he lived : and she was satisfied.

ELLA WHEELER WILCOX

Sometimes it happens, in this world so strange,
A human heart will pass through mortal strife,
And writhe in torture : while the old sweet life,
So full of hope and beauty, bloom and grace,
Is slowly strangled by remorseless Pain :
And one stern, cold, relentless, takes its place—
A ghastly, pallid spectre of the slain.
Yet those in daily converse see no change
Nor dream the heart has suffered.

So that day
I passed along toward the troubled way
Stern duty pointed, and no mortal guessed
A mighty conflict had disturbed my breast.

I had resolved to yield up to my friend
The man I loved.   Since she, too, loved, him so
I saw no other way in honour left.
She was so weak and fragile, once bereft
Of this great hope, that held her with such power,
She would wilt down, like some frost-bitten flower,
And swift, untimely death would be the end.
But I was strong : and hardy plants, which grow
In out-door soil, can bear bleak winds that blow
From Arctic lands, whereof a single breath
Would lay the hot-house blossom low in death.

The hours went by, too slow, and yet too fast.
All day I argued with my foolish heart
That bade me play the shrinking coward's part
And hide from pain.   And when the day had passed
And time for Vivian's call drew near and nearer,

344

MAURINE

It pleaded, " Wait, until the way seems clearer :
Say you are ill,—or busy : keep away
Until you gather strength enough to play
The part you have resolved on."

        " Nay, not so,"
Made answer clear-eyed Reason, " Do you go
And put your resolution to the test.
Resolve, however nobly formed, at best
Is but a still-born babe of Thought, until
It proves existence of its life and will
By sound or action."

      So when Helen came
And knelt by me, her fair face all aflame
With sudden blushes, whispering, " My sweet !
My heart can hear the music of his feet—
Go down with me to meet him," I arose,
And went with her all calmly, as one goes
To look upon the dear face of the dead.
That eve, I know not what I did or said.
I was not cold—my manner was not strange :
Perchance I talked more freely than my wont,
But in my speech was naught could give affront ;
Yet I conveyed, as only woman can,
That nameless *something*, which bespeaks a change.

'Tis in the power of woman, if she be
Whole-souled and noble, free from coquetry—
Her motives all unselfish, worthy, good,
To make herself and feelings understood
By nameless acts—thus sparing what to man,

345

ELLA WHEELER WILCOX

However gently answered, causes pain,
The offering of his hand and heart in vain.

She can be friendly, unrestrained, and kind,
Assume no airs of pride or arrogance ;
But in her voice, her manner, and her glance,
Convey that mystic something, undefined,
Which men fail not to understand and read,
And, when not blind with egoism, heed.
My task was harder.   'Twas the slow undoing
Of long sweet months of unimpeded wooing.
It was to hide and cover and conceal
The truth—assuming what I did not feel.
It was to dam love's happy singing tide
That blessed me with its hopeful, tuneful tone,
By feigned indiff'rence, till it turned aside,
And changed its channel, leaving me alone
To walk parched plains, and thirst for that sweet
    draught
My lips had tasted, but another quaffed.
It could be done.   For no words yet were spoken—
None to recall—no pledges to be broken.
" He will be grieved, then angry, cold, then cross,"
I reasoned, thinking what would be his part
In this strange drama.   " Then, because his heart
Feels something lacking, to make good his loss
He'll turn to Helen : and her gentle grace
And loving acts will win her soon the place
I hold to-day : and like a troubled dream
At length, our past, when he looks back, will seem."

MAURINE

That evening passed with music, chat, and song :
But hours that once had flown on airy wings
Now limped on weary, aching limbs along,
Each moment like some dreaded step that brings
A twinge of pain.
        As Vivian rose to go,
Slow bending to me, from his greater height,
He took my hand, and, looking in my eyes,
With tender questioning and pained surprise,
Said, " Maurine, you are not yourself to-night !
What is it ? Are you ailing ? "
                    " Ailing ? no ? "
I answered, laughing lightly, " I am not :
Just see my cheek, sir ! is it thin, or pale ?
Now tell me, am I looking very frail ? "
" Nay, nay ! " he answered, " it cannot be *seen,*
The change I speak of—'twas more in your mien :
Preoccupation, or—I know not what !
Miss Helen, am I wrong, or does Maurine
Seem to have something on her mind this eve ? "
" She does," laughed Helen, " and I do believe
I know what 'tis ! A letter came to-day
Which she read shyly, and then hid away
Close to her heart, not knowing I was near ;
And since she's been as you have seen her here.
See how she blushes ! So my random shot,
We must believe, has struck a tender spot."

Her rippling laughter floated through the room,
And redder yet I felt the hot blood rise,

347

ELLA WHEELER WILCOX

Then surge away to leave me pale as death,
Under the dark and swiftly gathering gloom
Of Vivian's questioning, accusing eyes
That searched my soul.   I almost shrieked beneath
That stern, fixed gaze, and stood spell-bound until
He turned with sudden movement, gave his hand
To each in turn, and said, " You must not stand
Longer, young ladies, in this open door.
The air is heavy with a cold, damp chill.
We shall have rain to-morrow, or before.
Good-night."

             He vanished in the darkling shade ;
And so the dreaded evening found an end,
That saw me grasp the conscience-whetted blade,
And strike a blow for honour and for friend.

" How swiftly passed the evening ! " Helen sighed.
" How long the hours ! " my tortured heart replied.
Joy, like a child, with lightsome steps doth glide
By Father Time, and, looking in his face,
Cries, snatching blossoms from the fair roadside,
" I could pluck more but for my hurried pace."
The while her elder brother Pain, man grown,
Whose feet are hurt by many a thorn and stone,
Looks to some distant hill-top, high and calm,
Where he shall find not only rest, but balm
For all his wounds, and cries in tones of woe,
" O Father Time ! why is thy pace so slow ? "

Two days, all sad with lonely wind and rain,
Went sobbing by, repeating o'er and o'er

348

MAURINE

The miserere, desolate and drear,
Which every human heart must sometime bear.
Pain is but little varied.   Its refrain,
Whate'er the words are, is for aye the same.
The third day brought a change, for with it came
Not only sunny smiles to Nature's face,
But Roy, our Roy, came back to us.   Once more
We looked into his laughing, handsome eyes,
Which, while they gave Aunt Ruth a glad surprise,
In no way puzzled her ; for one glance told
What each succeeding one confirmed—that he
Who bent above her with the lissome grace
Of his fine form, though grown so tall, could be
No other than the Roy Montaine of old.
It was a sweet reunion ; and he brought
So much of sunshine with him, that I caught,
Just from his smile alone, enough of gladness
To make my heart forget a time its sadness.
We talked together of the dear old days.
Leaving the present, with its depths and heights
Of life's maturer sorrows and delights,
I turned back to my childhood's level land,
And Roy and I, dear playmates, hand in hand,
Wandered in mem'ry, through the olden ways.

It was the second evening of his coming.
Helen was playing dreamily, and humming
Some wordless melody of white-souled thought
While Roy and I sat by the open door,
Re-living childish incidents of yore.

349

ELLA WHEELER WILCOX

My eyes were glowing, and my cheeks were hot
With warm young blood, excitement, joy, or pain
Alike would send swift coursing through each
   vein.
Roy, always eloquent, was waxing fine,
And bringing vividly before my gaze
· Some old adventure of those halcyon days,
When suddenly, in pauses of the talk,
I heard a well-known step upon the walk,
And looked up quickly to meet full in mine
The eyes of Vivian Dangerfield.   A flash
Shot from their depths—a sudden blaze of light
Like that swift followed by the thunder's crash,
Which said, " Suspicion is confirmed by sight,"
As they fell on the pleasant doorway scene.
Then o'er his clear-cut face a cold white look
Crept, like the pallid moonlight o'er a brook,
And, with a slight proud bending of the head,
He stepped toward us haughtily, and said,
" Please pardon my intrusion, Miss Maurine :
I called to ask Miss Trevor for a book
She spoke of lending me : nay, sit you still !
And I, by grant of your permission, will
Pass by to where I hear her playing."
                                    " Stay ! "
I said, " one moment, Vivian, if you please " ;
And suddenly bereft of all my ease,
And scarcely knowing what to do, or say,
Confused as any school-girl, I arose,
And some way made each to the other known.

MAURINE

They bowed, shook hands : then Vivian turned away
And sought out Helen, leaving us alone.

" One of Miss Trevor's, or of Maurine's beaux ?
Which may he be, who cometh like a prince
With haughty bearing, and an eagle eye ? "
Roy queried, laughing : and I answered, " Since
You saw him pass me for Miss Trevor's side,
I leave your own good judgment to reply."
And straightway caused the tide of talk to glide
In other channels, striving to dispel
The sudden gloom that o'er my spirit fell.

We mortals are such hypocrites at best !
When Conscience tries our courage with a test,
And points to some steep pathway, we set out
Boldly, denying any fear or doubt ;
But pause before the first rock in the way,
And, looking back, with tears, at Conscience, say,
" We are so sad, dear Conscience ! for we would
Most gladly do what to thee seemeth good ;
But lo ! this rock ! we cannot climb it, so
Thou must point out some other way to go."
Yet secretly we are rejoicing : and,
When right before our faces, as we stand
In seeming grief, the rock is cleft in twain,
Leaving the pathway clear, we shrink in pain !
And loth to go, by every act reveal
What we so tried from Conscience to conceal.

ELLA WHEELER WILCOX

I saw that hour, the way made plain, to do
With scarce an effort, what had seemed a strife
That would require the strength of my whole life.

Women have quick perceptions : and I knew
That Vivian's heart was full of jealous pain,
Suspecting—nay, *believing*—Roy Montaine
To be my lover.   First my altered mien—
And next the letter—then the doorway scene—
My flushed face gazing in the one above
That bent so near me, and my strange confusion—
When Vivian came, all led to one conclusion—
That I had but been playing with his love,
As women sometimes cruelly do play
With hearts, when their true lovers are away.

There could be nothing easier, than just
To let him linger on in this belief
Till hourly-fed Suspicion and Distrust
Should turn to scorn and anger all his grief.
Compared with me, so doubly sweet and pure
Would Helen seem, my purpose would be sure,
And certain of completion in the end.
But now, the way was made so straight and clear,
My coward heart shrank back in guilty fear,
Till Conscience whispered with her " still small
      voice,"
" The precious time is passing—make thy choice—
Resign thy love, or slay thy trusting friend."

MAURINE

The growing moon, watched by the myriad eyes
Of countless stars, went sailing through the skies,
Like some young prince, rising to rule a nation,
To whom all eyes are turned in expectation.
A woman who possesses tact and art
And strength of will can take the hand of doom,
And walk on, smiling sweetly as she goes,
With rosy lips, and rounded cheeks of bloom,
Cheating a loud-tongued world that never knows
The pain and sorrow of her hidden heart.
And so I joined in Roy's bright changing chat ; ·
Answered his sallies—talked of this and that,
My brow unruffled as the calm, still wave
That tells not of the wrecked ship, and the grave
Beneath its surface.
                              Then we heard, ere long,
The sound of Helen's gentle voice in song,
And, rising, entered where the subtle power
Of Vivian's eyes, forgiving while accusing,
Finding me weak, had won me, in that hour ;
But Roy, alway polite and *debonair*
Where ladies were, now hung about my chair
With nameless delicate attentions, using
That air devotional, and those small arts
Acquaintance with society imparts
To men gallant by nature.
                              'Twas my sex
And not myself he bowed to. Had my place
Been filled that evening by a dowager,
Twice his own age, he would have given her

The same attentions. But they served to vex
Whatever hope in Vivian's heart remained.
The cold, white look crept back upon his face,
Which told how deeply he was hurt and pained.

Little by little all things had conspired
To bring events I dreaded, yet desired.
We were in constant intercourse : walks, rides,
Picnics, and sails, filled weeks of golden weather,
And almost hourly we were thrown together.
No words were spoken of rebuke or scorn :
Good friends we seemed. But as a gulf divides
This land and that, though lying side by side,
So rolled a gulf between us—deep and wide—
The gulf of doubt, which widened slowly, morn
And noon and night.
                          Free and informal were
These picnics and excursions. Yet, although
Helen and I would sometimes choose to go
Without our escorts, leaving them quite free,
It happened alway Roy would seek out me
Ere passed the day, while Vivian walked with her.
I had no thought of flirting. Roy was just
Like some dear brother, and I quite forgot
The kinship was so distant it was not
Safe to rely upon in perfect trust,
Without reserve or caution. Many a time
When there was some steep mountain side to climb,
And I grew weary, he would say, " Maurine,
Come rest you here." And I would go and lean

MAURINE

My head upon his shoulder, or would stand
And let him hold in his my willing hand,
The while he stroked it gently with his own.
Or I would let him clasp me with his arm,
Nor entertained a thought of any harm,
Nor once supposed but Vivian was alone
In his suspicions. But ere long the truth
I learned in consternation !—both Aunt Ruth
And Helen, honestly, in faith believed
That Roy and I were lovers.

                         Undeceived,
Some careless words might open Vivian's eyes
And spoil my plans. So, reasoning in this wise,
To all their sallies I in jest replied,
To naught assented, and yet naught denied,
With Roy unchanged remaining, confident
Each understood just what the other meant.

If I grew weary of this double part,
And self-imposed deception caused my heart
Sometimes to shrink, I needed but to gaze
On Helen's face : that wore a look ethereal,
As if she dwelt above the things material
And held communion with the angels. So
I fed my strength and courage through the days.
What time the harvest moon rose full and clear,
And cast its ling'ring radiance on the earth,
We made a feast ; and called from far and near
Our friends, who came to share the scene of mirth.

355

ELLA WHEELER WILCOX

Fair forms and faces flitted too and fro,
But none more sweet than Helen's.   Robed in white,
She floated like a vision through the dance.
So frailly fragile and so phantom fair,
She seemed like some stray spirit of the air,
And was pursued by many an anxious glance
That looked to see her fading from the sight
Like figures that a dreamer sees at night.

And noble men and gallants graced the scene :
Yet none more noble or more grand of mien
Than Vivian—broad of chest and shoulder, tall,
And finely formed as any Grecian god
Whose high-arched foot on Mount Olympus trod.
His clear-cut face was beardless ; and, like those
Same Grecian statues, when in calm repose,
Was it in hue and feature.   Framed in hair
Dark and abundant ; lighted by large eyes
That could be cold as steel in winter air,
Or warm and sunny as Italian skies.

Weary of mirth and music, and the sound
Of tripping feet, I sought a moment's rest
Within the lib'ry, where a group I found
Of guests, discussing with apparent zest
Some theme of interest—Vivian, near the while,
Leaning and listening with his slow, odd smile.

" Now, Miss La Pelle, we will appeal to you,"
Cried young Guy Semple as I entered.   " We

MAURINE

Have been discussing right before his face,
All unrebuked by him, as you may see,
A poem lately published by our friend;
And we are quite divided. I contend
The poem is a libel, and untrue.
I hold the fickle women are but few,
Compared with those who are like yon fair moon
That, ever faithful, rises in her place
Whether she's greeted by the flowers of June,
Or cold and dreary stretches of white space."

" Oh ! " cried another, " Mr. Dangerfield,
Look to your laurels ! or you needs must yield
The crown to Semple, who, 'tis very plain,
Has mounted Pegasus and grasped his mane."

All laughed ; and then, as Guy appealed to me,
I answered lightly, " My young friend, I fear
You chose a most unlucky simile
To prove the truth of woman. To her place
The moon does rise—but with a different face
Each time she comes. But now I needs must hear
The poem read before I can consent
To pass my judgment on the sentiment."

All clamoured that the author was the man
To read the poem ; and, with tones that said
More than the cutting, scornful words he read,
Taking the book Guy gave him, he began—

ELLA WHEELER WILCOX

HER LOVE

The sands upon the ocean side
That change about with every tide,
And never true to one abide,
  A woman's love I liken to.

The summer zephyrs, light and vain,
That sing the same alluring strain
To every grass blade on the plain—
  A woman's love is nothing more.

The sunshine of an April day
That comes to warm you with its ray,
But while you smile has flown away—
  A woman's love is like to this.

God made poor woman with no heart,
But gave her skill, and tact, and art,
And so she lives, and plays her part.
  We must not blame, but pity her.

She leans to man—but just to hear
The praise he whispers in her ear;
Herself, not him, she holdeth dear—
  O fool! to be deceived by her.

To sate her selfish thirst she quaffs
The love of strong hearts in sweet draughts,
Then throws them lightly by and laughs,
  Too weak to understand their pain.

As changeful as the winds that blow
From every region to and fro,
Devoid of heart, she cannot know
  The suffering of a human heart.

I knew the cold, fixed gaze of Vivian's eyes
Saw the slow colour to my forehead rise ;
But lightly answered, toying with my fan,
" That sentiment is very like a man !

MAURINE

Men call us fickle, but they do us wrong ;
We're only frail and helpless—men are strong ;
And when love dies they take the poor dead thing
And make a shroud out of their suffering,
And drag the corpse about with them for years.
But we ?—we mourn it for a day with tears !
And then we robe it for its last long rest,
And being women, feeble things at best,
We cannot dig the grave ourselves.   And so
We call strong-limbed New Love to lay it low.
Immortal sexton he ! whom Venus sends
To do this service for her earthly friends.
The trusty fellow digs the grave so deep,
Nothing disturbs the dead laid there to sleep."

The laugh that followed had not died away
Ere Roy Montaine came seeking me, to say
The band was tuning for our waltz, and so
Back to the ballroom bore me.   In the glow
And heat and whirl my strength ere long was spent,
And I grew faint and dizzy, and we went
Out on the cool, moonlighted portico,
And, sitting there, Roy drew my languid head
Upon the shelter of his breast, and bent
His smiling eyes upon me as he said,
" I'll try the mesmerism of my touch
To work a cure : be very quiet now,
And let me make some passes o'er your brow.
Why, how it throbs ! you've exercised too much !
I shall not let you dance again to-night."

ELLA WHEELER WILCOX

Just then before us, in the broad moonlight,
Two forms were mirrored : and I turned my face
To catch the teasing and mischievous glance
Of Helen's eyes, as, heated by the dance,
Leaning on Vivian's arm, she sought this place.
" I beg your pardon," came in that round tone
Of his low voice.   " I think we do intrude."
Bowing, they turned, and left us quite alone
Ere I could speak, or change my attitude.

PART V

A VISIT to a cave some miles away
Was next in order.   So, one sunny day,
Four prancing steeds conveyed a laughing load
Of merry pleasure-seekers o'er the road.
A basket picnic, music and croquet
Were in the programme.   Skies were blue and clear,
And cool winds whispered of the autumn near.
The merry-makers filled the time with pleasure
Some floated to the music's rhythmic measure,
Some played, some promenaded on the green.

Ticked off by happy hearts, the moments passed.
The afternoon, all glow and glimmer, came.
Helen and Roy were leaders of some game,
And Vivian was not visible.
                                    " Maurine,

MAURINE

I challenge you to climb yon cliff with me !
And who shall tire, or reach the summit last
Must pay a forfeit," cried a romping maid.
" Come ! start at once, or own you are afraid."
So challenged I made ready for the race,
Deciding first the forfeit was to be
A handsome pair of bootees to replace
The victor's loss who made the rough ascent.
The cliff was steep and stony. On we went
As eagerly as if the path was Fame,
And what we climbed for, glory and a name.
My hands were bruised ; my garments sadly rent,
But on I clambered. Soon I heard a cry,
" Maurine ! Maurine ! my strength is wholly spent !
You've won the boots ! I'm going back—good-bye ! "
And back she turned, in spite of laugh and jeer.

I reached the summit : and its solitude,
Wherein no living creature did intrude,
Save some sad birds that wheeled and circled near,
I found far sweeter than the scene below.
Alone with One who knew my hidden woe,
I did not feel so much alone as when
I mixed with th'unthinking throngs of men.

Some flowers that decked the barren, sterile place
I plucked, and read the lesson they conveyed,
That in our lives, albeit dark with shade
And rough and hard with labour, yet may grow
The flowers of Patience, Sympathy, and Grace.

ELLA WHEELER WILCOX

As I walked on in meditative thought,
A serpent writhed across my pathway ; not
A large or deadly serpent ; yet the sight
Filled me with ghastly terror and affright.
I shrieked aloud : a darkness veiled my eyes—
And I fell fainting 'neath the watchful skies.

I was no coward.   Country-bred and born,
I had no feelings but the keenest scorn
For those fine lady " ah's " and " oh's " of fear
So much assumed (when any man is near).
But God implanted in each human heart
A natural horror, and a sickly dread
Of that accursed, slimy, creeping thing
That squirms a limbless carcase o'er the ground.
And where that inborn loathing is not found
You'll find the serpent qualities instead.
Who fears it not, himself is next of kin,
And in his bosom holds some treacherous art
Whereby to counteract its venomed sting.
And all are sired by Satan—Chief of Sin.

Who loathes not that foul creature of the dust,
However fair in seeming, I distrust.

I woke from my unconsciousness, to know
I leaned upon a broad and manly breast,
And Vivian's voice was speaking, soft and low,
Sweet whispered words of passion, o'er and o'er.
I dared not breathe.   Had I found Eden's shore ?

MAURINE

Was this a foretaste of eternal bliss ?
" My love," he sighed, his voice like winds that moan
Before a rain in summer time, " my own,
For one sweet stolen moment, lie and rest
Upon this heart that loves and hates you both !
O fair false face ! Why were you made so fair !
O mouth of Southern sweetness ! that ripe kiss
That hangs upon you, I do take an oath,
His lips shall never gather.   There—and there !
I steal it from him.   Are you his—all his ?
Nay, you are mine, this moment, as I dreamed—
Blind fool—believing you were what you seemed—
You would be mine in all the years to come
Fair fiend !   I love and hate you in a breath.
O God ! if this white pallor were but *death*,
And I were stretched beside you, cold and dumb,
My arms about you, so—in fond embrace !
My lips pressed so—upon your dying face !

" Woman, how dare you bring me to such shame !
How dare you drive me to an act like this,
To steal from your unconscious lips the kiss
You lured me on to think my rightful claim !
O frail and puny woman ! could you know
The devil that you waken in the hearts
You snare and bind in your enticing arts,
The thin, pale stuff that in your veins doth flow
Would freeze in terror.
                        Strange you have such power
To please, **or pain** us, poor, weak, soulless things—

ELLA WHEELER WILCOX

Devoid of passion as a senseless flower !
Like butterflies, your only boast, your wings.
There, now, I scorn you—scorn you from this hour,
And hate myself for having talked of love ! "

He pushed me from him.   And I felt as those
Doomed angels must, when pearly gates above
Are closed against them.

                With a feigned surprise
I started up and opened wide my eyes,
And looked about.   Then in confusion rose
And stood before him.

                  " Pardon me, I pray ! "
He said quite coldly.   " Half an hour ago
I left you with the company below,
And sought this cliff.   A moment since you cried,
It seemed, in sudden terror and alarm.
I came in time to see you swoon away.
You'll need assistance down the rugged side
Of this steep cliff.   I pray you take my arm."

So, formal and constrained, we passed along,
Rejoined our friends, and mingled with the throng
To have no further speech again that day.
Next morn there came a bulky document,
The legal firm of Blank & Blank had sent,
Containing news unlooked for.   An estate
Which proved a cosy fortune—nowise great
Or princely—had in France been left to me,

MAURINE

My grandsire's last descendant.   And it brought
A sense of joy and freedom in the thought
Of foreign travel, which I hoped would be
A panacea for my troubled mind,
That longed to leave the olden scenes behind
With all their recollections, and to flee
To some strange country.

I was in such haste
To put between me and my native land
The briny ocean's desolating waste,
I gave Aunt Ruth no peace, until she planned
To sail that week two months, though she was fain
To wait until the springtime.   Roy Montaine
Would be our guide and escort.

No one dreamed
The cause of my strange hurry, but all seemed
To think good fortune had quite turned my brain.
One bright October morning, when the woods
Had donned their purple mantles and red hoods
In honour of the Frost King, Vivian came,
Bringing some green leaves, tipped with crimson flame—
First trophies of the autumn time.

And Roy
Made a proposal that we all should go
And ramble in the forest for a while.
But Helen said she was not well—and so
Must stay at home.   Then Vivian, with a smile,
Responded, " I will stay and talk to you,
And they may go " ; at which her two cheeks grew

365

ELLA WHEELER WILCOX

Like twin blush roses ; dyed with love's red wave,
Her fair face shone transfigured with great joy.

And Vivian saw—and suddenly was grave.

Roy took my arm in that protecting way
Peculiar to some men, which seems to say,
" I shield my own," a manner pleasing, e'en
When we are conscious that it does not mean
More than a simple courtesy.   A woman,
Whose heart is wholly feminine and human,
And not unsexed by hobbies, likes to be
The object of that tender chivalry—
That guardianship which man bestows on her,
Yet mixed with deference ; as if she were
Half child, half angel.
                        Though she may be strong,
Noble and self-reliant, not afraid
To raise her hand and voice against all wrong
And all oppression, yet if she be made,
With all the independence of her thought,
A woman womanly, as God designed,
Albeit she may have as great a mind
As man, her brother, yet his strength of arm,
His muscle and his boldness she has not,
And cannot have without she loses what
Is far more precious, modesty and grace.
So walking on in her appointed place,
She does not strive to ape him, nor pretend

MAURINE

But that she needs him for a guide and friend,
To shield her with his greater strength from harm.

We reached the forest ; wandered to and fro
Through many a winding path and dim retreat,
Till I grew weary ; when I chose a seat
Upon an oak tree, which had been laid low
By some wind storm, or by some lightning stroke.
. And Roy stood just below me, where the ledge
On which I sat sloped steeply to the edge
Of sunny meadows lying at my feet.
One hand held mine ; the other grasped a limb
That cast its chequered shadows over him ;
And, with his head thrown back, his dark eyes raised
And fixed upon me, silently he gazed
Until I, smiling, turned to him and spoke—
" Give words, my cousin, to those thoughts that rise,
And, like dumb spirits, look forth from your eyes."
The smooth and even darkness of his cheek
Was stained one moment by a flush of red.
He swayed his lithe form nearer as he stood
Still clinging to the branch above his head.
His brilliant eyes grew darker, and he said,
With sudden passion, " Do you bid me speak ?
I cannot, then, keep silence if I would.
That hateful fortune, coming as it did,
Forbade my speaking sooner, for I knew
A harsh-tongued world would quickly misconstrue
My motive for a meaner one.   But, sweet,
So big my heart has grown with love for you

367

ELLA WHEELER WILCOX

I cannot shelter it, or keep it hid.
And so I cast it throbbing at your feet,
For you to guard and cherish, or to break.
Maurine, I love you better than my life.
My friend—my cousin—be still more, my wife !
Maurine, Maurine, what answer do you make ? "

I scarce could breathe for wonderment ; and, numb
With truth that fell too suddenly, sat dumb
With sheer amaze, and stared at Roy with eyes
That looked no feeling but complete surprise.
He swayed so near his breath was on my cheek.
" Maurine, Maurine," he whispered, " will you speak ? "

Then suddenly, as o'er some magic glass
One picture in a score of shapes will pass,
I seemed to see Roy glide before my gaze.
First, as the playmate of my earlier days ;
Next, as my kin ; and then my valued friend ;
And last, my lover.   As when colours blend
In some unlooked-for group before our eyes,
We hold the glass, and look them o'er and o'er,
So now I gazed on Roy in his new guise,
In which he ne'er appeared to me before.

His form was like a panther's in its grace,
So lithe and supple, and of medium height,
And garbed in all the elegance of fashion.
His large black eyes were full of fire and passion,
And in expression fearless, firm, and bright,

MAURINE

His hair was like the very deeps of night,
And hung in raven clusters 'round a face
Of dark and flashing beauty.
                                        He was more
Like some romantic maiden's grand ideal
Than like a common being.   As I gazed
Upon the handsome face to mine upraised,
I saw before me—living, breathing, real—
The hero of my early day-dreams ; though
So full my heart was with that clear-cut face,
Which, all unlike, yet claimed the hero's place,
I had not recognised him so before,
Or thought of him, save as a valued friend.
So now I called him, adding,
                                        " Foolish boy !
Each word of love you utter aims a blow
At that sweet trust I had reposed in you.
I was so certain I had found a true,
Steadfast man friend, on whom I could depend,
And go on wholly trusting, to the end.
Why did you shatter my delusion, Roy,
By turning to a lover ? "
                                        " Why, indeed !
Because I loved you more than any brother,
Or any friend could love."   Then he began
To argue like a lawyer, and to plead
With all his eloquence.   And, listening,
I strove to think it was a goodly thing
To be so fondly loved by such a man,
And it were best to give his wooing heed,

ELLA WHEELER WILCOX

And not deny him.   Then before my eyes
In all its clear-cut majesty, that other
Haughty and poet-handsome face would rise
And rob my purpose of all life and strength,
Roy urged and argued, as Roy only could,
With that impetuous, boyish eloquence.
He held my hands, and vowed I must, and should
Give some least hope ; till, in my own defence,
I turned upon him, and replied at length :
" I thank you for the noble heart you offer :
But it deserves a true one in exchange.
I could love you if I loved not another
Who keeps my heart ; so I have none to proffer."

Then, seeing how his dark eyes flashed, I said,
" Dear Roy ! I know my words seem very strange ;
But I love one I cannot hope to wed.
A river rolls between us, dark and deep.
To cross it were to stain with blood my hand.
You force my speech on what I fain would keep
In my own bosom, but you understand ?
My heart is given to love that's sanctified,
And now can feel no other.
                    Be you kind,
Dear Roy, my brother ! speak of this no more,
Lest pleading and denying should divide
The hearts so long united.   Let me find
In you my cousin and my friend of yore.
And now come home.   The morning, all too
    soon

370

MAURINE

And unperceived, has melted into noon.
Helen will miss us, and we must return."

He took my hand, and helped me to arise,
Smiling upon me with his sad, dark eyes,
Where passion's fires had, sudden, ceased to burn.

" And so," he said, " too soon and unforeseen
My friendship melted into love, Maurine.
But, sweet ! I am not wholly in the blame,
For what you term my folly.   You forgot,
So long we'd known each other, I had not
In truth a brother's or a cousin's claim.
But I remembered, when through every nerve
Your lightest touch went thrilling ; and began
To love you with that human love of man
For comely woman.   By your coaxing arts,
You won your way into my heart of hearts,
And all Platonic feelings put to rout.
A maid should never lay aside reserve
With one who's not her kinsman out and out.
But as we now, with measured steps, retrace
The path we came, e'en so my heart I'll send,
At your command, back to the olden place,
And strive to love you only as a friend."
I felt the justice of his mild reproof,
But answered, laughing, " 'Tis the same old cry :
' The woman tempted me, and I did eat.'
Since Adam's time we've heard it.   But I'll try
And be more prudent, sir, and hold aloof

ELLA WHEELER WILCOX

The fruit I never once had thought so sweet
'Twould tempt you any.   Now go dress for dinner,
Thou sinned against ! as also will the sinner.
And guard each act, that no least look betray
What's passed between us."
                                    Then I turned away
And sought my room, low humming some old air
That ceased upon the threshold ; for mine eyes
Fell on a face so glorified and fair
All other senses, merged in that of sight,
Were lost in contemplation of the bright
And wond'rous picture, which had otherwise
Made dim my vision.
                                    Waiting in my room,
Her whole face lit as by an inward flame
That shed its halo 'round her, Helen stood ;
Her fair hands folded like a lily's leaves
Weighed down by happy dews of summer eves.
Upon her cheek the colour went and came
As sunlight flickers o'er a bed of bloom ;
And, like some slim young sapling of the wood,
Her slender form leaned slightly ; and her hair
Fell 'round her loosely, in long curling strands
All unconfined, and as by loving hands
Tossed into bright confusion.
                                    Standing there,
Her starry eyes uplifted, she did seem
Like some unearthly creature of a dream ;
Until she started forward, gliding slowly,
And broke the breathless silence, speaking lowly,

MAURINE

As one grown meek and humble in an hour,
Bowing before some new and mighty power.
" Maurine, Maurine ! " she murmured, and again,
" Maurine, my own sweet friend, Maurine ! "

                                        And then,

Laying her love-light hands upon my head,
She leaned, and looked into my eyes, and said,
With voice that bore her joy in ev'ry tone,
As winds that blow across a garden bed
Are weighed with fragrance, " He is mine alone,
And I am his—all his—his very own.
So pledged this hour, by that most sacred tie
Save one beneath God's over-arching sky.
I could not wait to tell you of my bliss :
I want your blessing, sweetheart ! and your kiss."
So hiding my heart's trouble with a smile,
I leaned and kissed her dainty mouth ; the while
I felt a guilt-joy, as of some sweet sin,
When my lips fell where his so late had been.
And all day long I bore about with me
A sense of shame—yet mixed with satisfaction,
As some starved child might steal a loaf, and be
Sad with the guilt resulting from her action,
While yet the morsel in her mouth was sweet.
That ev'ning when the house had settled down
To sleep and quiet, to my room there crept
A lithe young form, robed in a long white gown :
With steps like fall of thistledown she came,
Her mouth smile-wreathed ; and, breathing low my
    name,

ELLA WHEELER WILCOX

Nestled in graceful beauty at my feet.

" Sweetheart," she murmured softly, " ere I sleep,
I needs must tell you all my tale of joy,
Beginning where you left us—you and Roy.
You saw the colour flame upon my cheek
When Vivian spoke of staying.   So did he—
And, when we were alone, he gazed at me
With such a strange look in his wond'rous eyes.
The silence deepened ; and I tried to speak
Upon some common topic, but could not,
My heart was in such tumult.
                                                In this wise
Five happy moments glided by us, fraught
With hours of feeling.   Vivian rose up then,
And came and stood by me, and stroked my hair.
And, in his low voice, o'er and o'er again,
Said, ' Helen, little Helen, frail and fair.'
Then took my face, and turned it to the light,
And looking in my eyes, and seeing what
Was shining from them, murmured, sweet and low,
' Dear eyes, you cannot veil the truth from sight.
You love me, Helen ! answer, is it so ? '
And I made answer straightway, ' With my life
And soul and strength I love you, O my love ! '
He leaned and took me gently to his breast,
And said, ' Here then this dainty head shall rest
Henceforth for ever : O my little dove !
My lily-bud—my fragile blossom-wife ! '

MAURINE

" And then I told him all my thoughts ; and he
Listened, with kisses for his comments, till
My tale was finished.   Then he said, ' I will
Be frank with you, my darling, from the start,
And hide no secret from you in my heart.
I love you, Helen, but you are not first
To rouse that love to being.   Ere we met
I loved a woman madly—never dreaming
She was not all in truth she was in seeming.
Enough ! she proved to be that thing accursed
Of God and man—a wily, vain coquette.
I hate myself for having loved her.   Yet
So much my heart spent on her, it must give
A love less ardent, and less prodigal,
Albeit just as tender and as true—
A milder, yet a faithful love to you.
Just as some evil fortune might befall
A man's great riches, causing him to live
In some low cot, all unpretending, still
As much his home—as much his loved retreat,
As was the princely palace on the hill,
E'en so I gave you all that's left, my sweet !
Of my heart-fortune.'
                              " ' That were more to me,'
I made swift smiling answer, ' than to be
The worshipped consort of a king.'   And so
Our faith was pledged.   But Vivian would not go
Until I vowed to wed him New Year Day.
And I am sad because you go away
Before that time.   I shall not feel half wed

MAURINE

Striving to keep away that unloved guest
Who comes unbiden, making hearts to mourn.

Through all the nxious weeks I watched beside
The suff'rer's coch—Roy was my help and stay ;
Others were kin, but he alone each day
Brought strengt and comfort, by his cheerful face
And hopeful wods, that fell in that sad place
Like rays of ligt upon a darkened way.
November passd ; and winter, crisp and chill,
In robes of ermie walked on plain and hill.
Returning lightnd life dispelled the gloom
That cheated Dath had brought us from the tomb.
Aunt Ruth wasaved, and slowly getting better—
Was dressed eah day, and walked about the room.
Then came onenorning in the Eastern mail,
A little white-wnged birdling of a letter.
I broke the seaand read,

                    " Maurine, my own !
I hear Aunt Rth is better, and am glad.
I felt so sorry or you ; and so sad
To think I leftyou when I did—alone
To bear your pin and worry, and those nights
Of weary, anxous watching.

                    Vivian writes
Your plans archanged now, and you will not sail
Before the spngtime. So you'll come and be
My bridesmai darling ! Do not say me nay.
But three wees more of girlhood left to me.
Come, if you un, just two weeks from to-day,

ELLA WHEELER WILCOX

Without you here.   Postpone your trip and stay,
And be my bridesmaid."
                         " Nay, I cannot, dear !
'Twould disarrange our plans for half a year.
I'll be in Europe New Year Day," I said,
" And send congratulations by the cable."
And from my soul thanked Providence for sparing
The pain, to me, of sharing in, and wearing
The festal garments of a wedding scene,
While all my heart was hung with sorrow's sable.
Forgetting for a season, that between
The cup and lip lies many a chance of loss,
I lived in my near future, confident
All would be as I planned it ; and, across
The briny waste of waters, I should find
Some balm and comfort for my troubled mind.
The sad Fall days, like maidens auburn-tressed
And amber-eyed, in purple garments dressed,
Passed by, and dropped their tears upon the tomb
Of fair Queen Summer, buried in her bloom.
Roy left us for a time, and Helen went
To make the nuptial preparations.   Then,
Aunt Ruth complained one day of feeling ill :
Her veins ran red with fever ; and the skill
Of two physicians could not stem the tide.
The house, that rang so late with laugh and jest,
Grew ghostly with low-whispered sounds ; and when
The autumn day that I had thought to be
Bounding upon the billows of the sea,
Came sobbing in, it found me pale and worn,

MAURINE

Striving to keep away that unloved guest
Who comes unbidden, making hearts to mourn.

Through all the anxious weeks I watched beside
The suff'rer's couch—Roy was my help and stay ;
Others were kind, but he alone each day
Brought strength and comfort, by his cheerful face
And hopeful words, that fell in that sad place
Like rays of light upon a darkened way.
November passed ; and winter, crisp and chill,
In robes of ermine walked on plain and hill.
Returning light and life dispelled the gloom
That cheated Death had brought us from the tomb.
Aunt Ruth was saved, and slowly getting better—
Was dressed each day, and walked about the room.
Then came one morning in the Eastern mail,
A little white-winged birdling of a letter.
I broke the seal and read,

                          " Maurine, my own !
I hear Aunt Ruth is better, and am glad.
I felt so sorry for you ; and so sad
To think I left you when I did—alone
To bear your pain and worry, and those nights
Of weary, anxious watching.

                         Vivian writes
Your plans are changed now, and you will not sail
Before the springtime. So you'll come and be
My bridesmaid, darling ! Do not say me nay.
But three weeks more of girlhood left to me.
Come, if you can, just two weeks from to-day,

And make your preparations here.   My sweet !
Indeed, I am not glad Aunt Ruth was ill—
I'm sorry she has suffered so ; and still
I'm thankful something happened, so you stayed.
I'm sure my wedding would be incomplete
Without your presence.   Selfish, I'm afraid
You'll think your Helen.   But I love you so,
How can I be quite willing you should go ?
Come Christmas Eve, or earlier.   Let me know
And I will meet you, dearie ! at the train.
Your happy, loving Helen."
                              Then the pain
That, hidden under later pain and care,
Had made no moan, but silent, seemed to sleep,
Woke from its trance-like lethargy, to steep
My tortured heart in anguish and despair.

I had relied too fully on my skill
In bending circumstances to my will :
And now I was rebuked and made to see
That God alone knoweth what is to be.
Then came a message from Vivian, who
Came not himself, as he was wont to do,
But sent his servant each new day to bring
A kindly message, or an offering
Of juicy fruits to cool the lips of fever,
Or dainty hot-house blossoms, with their bloom
To brighten up the convalescent's room.
But now the servant only brought a line
From Vivian Dangerfield to Roy Montaine,

MAURINE

" Dear Sir, and Friend "—in letters bold and plain,
Written on cream-white paper, so it ran :
" It is the will and pleasure of Miss Trevor,
And therefore doubly so a wish of mine,
That you shall honour me next New Year Eve,
My wedding hour, by standing as best man.
Miss Trevor has six bridesmaids I believe.
Being myself a novice in the art—
If I should fail in acting well my part, ·
I'll need protection 'gainst the regiment
Of outraged ladies.   So, I pray, consent
To stand by me in time of need, and shield
Your friend sincerely, Vivian Dangerfield,"

The last least hope had vanished ; I must drain,
E'en to the dregs, this bitter cup of pain.

PART VI

THERE was a week of bustle and of hurry ;
    A stately home echoed to voices sweet,
Calling, replying ; and to tripping feet
Of busy bridesmaids, running to and fro,
With all that girlish fluttering and flurry
Preceding such occasions.
                Helen's room
Was like a lily-garden, all in bloom,
Decked with the dainty robes of her trousseau.
My robe was fashioned by swift, skilful hands—

ELLA WHEELER WILCOX

A thing of beauty, elegant and rich,
A mystery of loopings, puffs, and bands ;
And as I watched it growing, stitch by stitch,
I felt as one might feel who should behold
With vision trance-like, where his body lay
In deathly slumber, simulating clay,
His grave-cloth sewed together, fold on fold.

I lived with ev'ry nerve upon the strain,
As men go into battle ; and the pain,
That, more and more to my sad heart revealed,
Grew ghastly with its horrors, was concealed
From mortal eyes by superhuman power,
That God bestowed upon me, hour by hour.
What night the Old Year gave unto the New
The key of human happiness and woe,
The pointed stars, upon their field of blue,
Shone, white and perfect, o'er a world below,
Of snow-clad beauty ; all the trees were dressed
In gleaming garments, decked with diadems,
Each seeming like a bridal-bidden guest,
Coming o'erladen with a gift of gems.

The bustle of the dressing-room ; the sound
Of eager voices in discourse ; the clang
Of " sweet bells jangled " ; thud of steel-clad feet
That beat swift music on the frozen ground—
All blent together in my brain and rang
A medley of strange noises, incomplete,
And full of discords.

MAURINE

      Then out on the night
Streamed from the open vestibule, a light
That lit the velvet blossoms which we trod,
With all the hues of those that deck the sod.
The grand cathedral windows were ablaze
With gorgeous colours ; through a sea of bloom
Up the long aisle, to join the waiting groom,
The bridal cortège passed.

        As some lost soul
Might surge on with the curious crowd, to gaze
Upon its coffined body, so I went
With that glad festal throng. The organ sent
Great waves of melody along the air,
That broke and fell, in liquid drops, like spray,
On happy hearts that listened. But to me
It sounded faintly, as if miles away,
A troubled spirit, sitting in despair,
Beside the sad and ever-moaning sea,
Gave utterance to sighing sounds of dole.
We paused before the altar. Framed in flowers,
The white-robed man of God stood forth.

           I heard
The solemn service open ; through long hours
I seemed to stand and listen, while each word
Fell on my ear as falls the sound of clay
Upon the coffin of the worshipped dead.
The stately father gave the bride away :
The bridegroom circled with a golden band
The taper finger of her dainty hand.
The last imposing, binding words were said—

ELLA WHEELER WILCOX

" What God has joined let no man put asunder "—
And all my strife with self was at an end ;
My lover was the husband of my friend.

How strangely, in some awful hour of pain,
External trifles with our sorrows blend !
I never hear the mighty organ's thunder,
I never catch the scent of heliotrope,
Nor see stained windows all ablaze with light,
Without the dizzy whirling of the brain,
And all the ghastly feeling of that night,
When my sick heart relinquished love and hope.

The pain we feel so keenly may depart,
And e'en its memory cease to haunt the heart ;
But some slight thing, a perfume or a sound,
Will probe the closed recesses of the wound,
And for a moment bring the old-time smart,
Congratulations, kisses, tears, and smiles,
Good-byes and farewells given ; then across
The snowy waste of weary winter miles,
Back to my girlhood's home, where, through each room
For evermore pale phantoms of delight
Should aimless wander, always in my sight,
Pointing, with ghostly fingers, to the tomb
Wet with the tears of living pain and loss.
The sleepless nights of watching and of care,
Followed by that one week of keenest pain,
Taxed my weakened system, and my brain,
Brought on a ling'ring illness.

MAURINE

                                   Day by day,
In that strange, apathetic state I lay,
Of mental and of physical despair.
I had no pain, no fever, and no chill,
But lay without ambition, strength, or will,
Knowing no wish for anything but rest,
Which seemed, of all God's store of gifts, the best.

Physicians came and shook their heads and sighed,
And to their score of questions I replied,
With but one languid answer, o'er and o'er,
" I am so weary—weary—nothing more."

I slept, and dreamed I was some feathered thing,
Flying through space with ever-aching wing,
Seeking a ship called Rest, all snowy white,
That sailed and sailed before me, just in sight,
But always one unchanging distance kept,
And woke more weary than before I slept.

I slept, and dreamed I ran to win a prize
A hand from heaven held down before my eyes.
All eagerness I sought it—it was gone,
But shone in all its beauty farther on.
I ran, and ran, and ran, in eager quest
Of that great prize, whereon was written " rest,"
Which ever just beyond my reach did gleam,
And wakened doubly weary with my dream.
I dreamed I was a crystal drop of rain,
That saw a snow-white lily on the plain,

ELLA WHEELER WILCOX

And left the cloud to nestle in her breast.
I fell and fell, but nevermore found rest—
I fell and fell, but found no stopping place,
Through leagues and leagues of never-ending space,
While space illimitable stretched before.

And all these dreams but wearied me the more.

Familiar voices sounded in my room—
Aunt Ruth's, and Roy's, and Helen's ; but they seemed
A part of some strange fancy I had dreamed,
And now remembered dimly.
                                Wrapped in gloom,
My mind, o'ertaxed, lost hold of time at last,
Ignored its future, and forgot its past,
And groped along the present as a light,
Carried, uncovered, through the fogs of night,
Will flicker faintly.
                                But I felt, at length,
When March winds brought vague rumours of the
        spring,
A certain sense of " restlessness with rest."
My aching frame was weary of repose,
And wanted action.
                                Then slow-creeping strength
Came back with Mem'ry hand in hand, to bring,
And lay upon my sore and bleeding breast,
Grim-visaged Recollection's thorny rose,
I gained, and failed.   One day could ride and walk,

MAURINE

The next would find me prostrate ; while a flock
Of ghostly thoughts, like phantom birds, would flit
About the chambers of my heart, or sit,
Pale spectres of the past, with folded wings,
Perched, silently, upon the voiceless strings,
That once resounded to Hope's happy lays.

So passed the ever-changing April days.
When May came, lightsome footed, o'er the lea,
Accompanied by kind Aunt Ruth and Roy
I bade farewell to home with secret joy,
And turned my wan face eastward to the sea.
Roy planned our route of travel : for all lands
Were one to him.   Or Egypt's burning sands,
Or Alps of Switzerland, or stately Rome—
All were familiar as the fields of home.
There was a year of wand'ring to and fro,
Like restless spirits ; scaling mountain heights ;
Dwelling among the countless, rare delights
Of lands historic ; turning dusty pages,
Stamped with the tragedies of mighty ages ;
Gazing upon the scenes of bloody acts,
Of kings long buried—bare, unvarnished facts,
Surpassing wildest fictions of the brain ;
Rubbing against all people, high and low,
And by this contact feeling Self to grow
Smaller and less important, and the vein
Of human kindness deeper, seeing God,
Unto the humble delver of the sod,
And to the ruling monarch on the throne,

ELLA WHEELER WILCOX

Has given hope, ambition, joy, and pain,
And that all hearts have feelings like our own.

There is no school that disciplines the mind,
And broadens thought, like contact with mankind.
The college-prisoned greybeard, who has burned
The midnight lamp, and book-bound knowledge learned,
Till sciences and classics hold no lore
He has not conned and studied o'er and o'er,
Is but a babe in wisdom, when compared
With some unlettered wand'rer, who has shared
The hospitalities of every land ;
Felt touch of brother in each proffered hand ;
Made man his study, and the world his college,
And gained this grand epitome of knowledge :
Each human being has a heart and soul,
And Self is but an atom of the whole.
I hold he is best learnèd and most wise,
Who best and most can love and sympathise.
Book-wisdom makes us vain and self-contained ;
Our banded minds go round in little grooves ;
But constant friction with the world removes
These iron foes to freedom, and we rise
To grander heights, and, all untrammelled, find
A better atmosphere and clearer skies ;
And through its broadened realm, no longer chained,
Thought travels freely, leaving Self behind.

Where'er we chanced to wander or to roam,
Glad letters came from Helen ; happy things,

MAURINE

Like little birds that followed on swift wings,
Bringing their tender messages from home.
Her days were poems, beautiful, complete,
The rhythm perfect, and the burden sweet.
She was so happy—happy, and so blest.

My heart had found contentment in that year.
With health restored, my life seemed full of cheer.
The heart of youth turns ever to the light ;
Sorrow and gloom may curtain it like night,
But, in its very anguish and unrest,
It beats and tears the pall-like folds away,
And finds again the sunlight of the day.

And yet, despite the changes without measure,
Despite sight-seeing, round on round of pleasure,
Despite new friends, new suitors, still my heart
Was conscious of a something lacking, where
Love once had dwelt, and afterward despair.
Now love was buried ; and despair had flown
Before the healthful zephyrs that had blown
From heights serene and lofty ; and the place
Where both had dwelt was empty, voiceless space.
And so I took my long-loved study, art,
The dreary vacuum in my life to fill,
And worked, and laboured, with a right good will.
Aunt Ruth and I took rooms in Rome ; while Roy
Lingered in Scotland, with his new-found joy.
A dainty little lassie, Grace Kildare,
Had snared him in her flossy, flaxen hair,
And made him captive.

ELLA WHEELER WILCOX

                We were thrown, by chance,
In contact with her people while in France
The previous season : she was wholly sweet
And fair and gentle ; so naïve, and yet
So womanly, she was at once the pet
Of all our party ; and, ere many days,
Won by her fresh face, and her artless ways,
Roy fell a helpless captive at her feet.
Her home was in the Highlands ; and she came
Of good old stock, of fair untarnished fame.
Through all these months Roy had been true as
    steel ;
And by his every action made me feel
He was my friend and brother, and no more—
The same big-souled and trusty friend of yore.
Yet, in my secret heart, I wished I knew
Whether the love he felt one time was dead,
Or only hidden, for my sake, from view.
So when he came to me one day and said,
The velvet blackness of his eyes ashine
With light of love and triumph, " Cousin mine,
Congratulate me ! She whom I adore
Has pledged to me the promise of her hand ;
Her heart I have already," I was glad
With double gladness, for it freed my mind
Of fear that he, in secret, might be sad.

From March till June had left her moons behind,
And merged her rose-red beauty in July,
There was no message from my native land.

MAURINE

Then came a few brief lines, by Vivian penned :
Death had been near to Helen, but passed by ;
The danger was now over.   God was kind ;
The mother and the child were both alive ;
No other child was ever known to thrive
As throve this one, nurse had been heard to say;
The infant was a wonder, every way.
And, at command of Helen, he would send
A lock of baby's golden hair to me.
And did I, on my honour, ever see
Such hair before ?   Helen would write, ere long :
She gained quite slowly, but would soon be strong—
Stronger than ever, so the doctors said.
I took the tiny ringlet, golden—fair,
Mayhap his hand had severed from the head
Of his own child, and pressed it to my cheek
And to my lips, and kissed it o'er and o'er.
All my maternal instincts seemed to rise,
And clamour for their rights, while my wet eyes
Rained tears upon the silken tress of hair.
The woman struggled with her heart before !
It was the mother in me now did speak,
Moaning, like Rachel, that her babes were not,
And crying out against her barren lot.

Once I bemoaned the long and lonely years
That stretched before me, dark with love's eclipse ;
And thought how my unmated heart would miss
The shelter of a broad and manly breast—
The strong, bold arm—the tender, clinging kiss—

389

ELLA WHEELER WILCOX

And all pure love's possessions, manifold ;
But now I wept a flood of bitter tears,
Thinking of little heads of shining gold,
That would not on my bosom sink to rest ;
Of little hands that would not touch my cheek ;
Of little lisping voices, and sweet lips,
That never in my list'ning ear would speak
The blessed name of mother.
                              Oh, in woman
How mighty is the love of offspring !   Ere
Unto her wond'ring, untaught mind unfolds
The myst'ry that is half divine, half human,
Of life and birth, the love of unborn souls
Within her, and the mother-yearning creeps
Through her warm heart, and stirs its hidden
      deeps,
And grows and strengthens with each riper year.
As storms may gather in a placid sky,
And spend their fury, and then pass away,
Leaving again the blue of cloudless day,
E'en so the tempest of my grief passed by.
'Twas weak to mourn for what I had resigned,
With the deliberate purpose of my mind,
To my sweet friend.
                    Relinquishing my love,
I gave my dearest hope of joy to her.
If God, from out His boundless store above,
Had chosen added blessings to confer,
I would rejoice, for her sake—not repine
That th'immortal treasures were not mine.

MAURINE

Better my lonely sorrow, than to know
My selfish joy had been another's woe ;
Better my grief and my strength to control,
Than the despair of her frail-bodied soul ;
Better to go on, loveless, to the end,
Than wear love's rose,.whose thorn had slain my
    friend.

Work is the salve that heals the wounded heart.
With will most resolute I set my aim
To enter on the weary race for Fame,
And if I failed to climb the dizzy height,
To reach some point of excellence in art.

E'en as the Maker held earth incomplete,
Till man was formed, and placed upon the sod,
The perfect, living image of his God,
All landscape scenes were lacking in my sight
Wherein the human figure had no part.
In that, all lines of symmetry did meet—
All hues of beauty mingle. So I brought
Enthusiasm in abundance, thought,
Much study, and some talent day by day
To help me in my efforts to portray
The wond'rous power, majesty, and grace
Stamped on some form, or looking from some face.
This was to be my specialty—To take
Human emotion for my theme, and make
The unassisted form divine express
Anger or Sorrow, Pleasure, Pain, Distress ;

ELLA WHEELER WILCOX

And thus to build Fame's monument above
The grave of my departed hope and love.

This is not Genius. Genius spreads its wings
And soars beyond itself, or selfish things.
Talent has need of stepping-stones ; some cross,
Some cheated purpose, some great pain or loss
Must lay the groundwork, and arouse ambition,
Before it labours onward to fruition.

But, as the lark from beds of bloom will rise
And sail and sing among the very skies,
Still mounting near and nearer to the light,
Impelled alone by love of upward flight,
So Genius soars—it does not need to climb—
Upon God-given wings to heights sublime.
Some sportsman's shot, grazing the singer's throat,
Some venomous assault of birds of prey,
May speed its flight toward the realm of day,
And tinge with triumph every liquid note.
So deathless Genius mounts but higher yet,
When Strife and Envy think to slay or fret.

There is no baulking Genius. Only death
Can silence it, or hinder. While there's breath
Or sense of feeling it will spurn the sod,
And lift itself to glory, and to God.
The acorn sprouted—weeds nor flowers can choke
The certain growth of th'upreaching oak.
Talent was mine, not Genius ; and my mind

MAURINE

Seemed bound by chains, and would not leave behind
Its selfish love and sorrow.
                              Did I strive
To picture some emotion, lo ! *his* eyes,
Of emerald beauty, dark as ocean dyes,
Looked from the canvas ; and my buried pain
Rose from its grave, and stood by me alive.
Whate'er my subject, in some hue or line,
The glorious beauty of his face would shine.

So for a time my labour seemed in vain,
Since it but freshened, and made keener yet,
The grief my heart was striving to forget.

While in his form all strength and magnitude
With grace and supple sinews were entwined,
While in his face all beauties were combined
Of perfect features, intellect, and truth,
With all that fine, rich colouring of youth,
How could my brush portray aught good or fair
Wherein no fatal likeness should intrude
Of him my soul had worshipped ?
                                 But at last,
Setting a watch upon my unwise heart
That thus would mix its sorrow with my art,
I resolutely shut away the past,
And made the toilsome present passing bright
With dreams of what was hidden from my sight
In the far distant future, when the soil
Should yield me golden fruit for all my toil.

ELLA WHEELER WILCOX

PART VII

WITH much hard labour and some pleasure
        fraught
The months rolled by me noiselessly, that taught
My hand to grow more skilful in its art,
Strengthened my daring dream of fame, and brought
Sweet hope and resignation to my heart.

Brief letters came from Helen now and then :
She was quite well—oh, yes ! quite well, indeed !
But still so weak and nervous. By and by,
When baby, being older, should not need
Such constant care, she would grow strong again.
She was as happy as a soul could be ;
No least cloud hovered in her azure sky ;
She had not thought life held such depths of bliss.
Dear baby sent Maurine a loving kiss,
And said she was a naughty, naughty girl,
Not to come home and see ma's little pearl.

No gift of costly jewels, or of gold,
Had been so precious or so dear to me,
As each brief line wherein her joy was told.
It lightened toil, and took the edge from pain,
Knowing my sacrifice was not in vain.
Roy purchased fine estates in Scotland, where

MAURINE

He built a pretty villa-like retreat.
And when the Roman summer's languid heat
Made work a punishment, I turned my face
Toward the Highlands, and with Roy and Grace
Found rest and freedom from all thought and care.

I was a willing worker. Not an hour
Passed idly by me : each, I would employ
To some good purpose, ere it glided on
To swell the tide of hours forever gone.
My first completed picture, known as " Joy,"
Won pleasant words of praise. " Possesses power,"
" Displays much talent," " Very fairly done."
So fell the comments on my grateful ear.

Swift in the wake of Joy, and always near,
Walks her sad sister Sorrow. So my brush
Began depicting Sorrow, heavy-eyed,
With pallid visage, ere the rosy flush
Upon the beaming face of Joy had dried.
The careful study of long months, it won
Golden opinions ; even bringing forth
That certain sign of merit—a critique
Which set both pieces down as daubs, and weak
As empty heads that sang their praises—so
Proving conclusively the pictures' worth.
These critics and reviewers do not use
Their precious ammunition to abuse
A worthless work. That, left alone, they know
Will find its proper level ; and they aim

ELLA WHEELER WILCOX

Their batteries at rising works which claim
Too much of public notice.   But this shot
Resulted only in some noise, which brought
A dozen people, where one came before
To view my pictures ; and I had my hour
Of holding those frail baubles, Fame and Pow'r.
An English Baron who had lived two score
Of his allotted three score years and ten,
Bought both the pieces.   He was very kind,
And so attentive, I, not being blind,
Must understand his meaning.

                    Therefore, when
He said,
       " Sweet friend, whom I would make my wife,
The ' Joy ' and ' Sorrow ' this dear hand portrayed
I have in my possession : now resign
Into my careful keeping, and make mine,
The joy and sorrow of your future life "—
I was prepared to answer, but delayed,
Grown undecided suddenly.

                  My mind
Argued the matter coolly pro and con,
And made resolve to speed his wooing on
And grant him favour.   He was good and kind ;
Not young, no doubt he would be quite content
With my respect, nor miss an ardent love ;
Could give me ties of family and home ;
And then, perhaps, my mind was not above
Setting some value on a titled name—
Ambitious woman's weakness !

MAURINE

                                   Then my art
Would be encouraged and pursued the same,
And I could spend my winters all in Rome.
Love never more could touch my wasteful heart
That all its wealth upon one object spent,
Existence would be very bleak and cold,
After long years, when I was grey and cold,
With neither home nor children.
                                   Once a wife,
I would forget the sorrow of my life,
And pile new sods upon the grave of pain.
My mind so argued ; and my sad heart heard,
But made no comment.
                                   Then the Baron spoke, .
And waited for my answer.   All in vain
I strove for strength to utter that one word
My mind dictated.   Moments rolled away—
Until at last my torpid heart awoke,
And forced my trembling lips to say him nay.
And then my eyes with sudden tears o'erran,
In pity for myself and for this man
Who stood before me, lost in pained surprise.
" Dear friend," I cried, " Dear generous friend, forgive
A troubled woman's weakness !   As I live,
In truth I meant to answer otherwise.
From out its store my heart can give you naught
But honour and respect ; and yet methought
I would give willing answer did you sue.
But now I know 'twere cruel wrong I planned ;
Taking a heart that beat with love more true,

ELLA WHEELER WILCOX

And giving in exchange an empty hand.
Who weds for love alone, may not be wise ;
Who weds without it, angels must despise.
Love and respect together must combine
To render marriage holy and divine ;
And lack of either, sure as Fate, destroys
Continuation of the nuptial joys,
And brings regret, and gloomy discontent,
To put to rout each tender sentiment.
Nay, nay !   I will not burden all your life
By that possession—an unloving wife ;
Nor will I take the sin upon my soul
Of wedding where my heart goes not in whole.
However bleak may be my single lot,
I will not stain my life with such a blot.
Dear friend, farewell ! the earth is very wide ;
It holds some fairer woman for your bride.
I would I had a heart to give to you,
But, lacking it, can only say—adieu ! "

He whom temptation never has assailed,
Knows not that subtle sense of moral strength :
When sorely tried, we waver, but at length,
Rise up and turn away, not having failed.

———

The autumn of the third year came and went ;
The mild Italian winter was half spent,
When this brief message came across the sea—
" My darling !   I am dying.   Come to me.

MAURINE

Love, which so long the growing truth concealed,
Stands pale within the shadow.   O my sweet !
This heart of mine grows fainter with each beat—
Dying with very weight of bliss.   O come !
And take the legacy I leave to you,
Before these lips for evermore are dumb.
In life or death.   Yours, Helen Dangerfield."

This plaintive letter bore a month old date ;
And, wild with fears lest I had come too late,
I bade the old world and new friends adieu,
And with Aunt Ruth, who long had sighed for home,
I turned my back on glory, art, and Rome.
All selfish thoughts were merged in one wild fear
That she for whose dear sake my heart had bled,
Rather than her sweet eyes should know one tear,
Was passing from me ; that she might be dead ;
And, dying, had been sorely grieved with me,
Because I made no answer to her plea.

" O ship, that sailest slowly, slowly on,
Make haste before a wasting life is gone !
Make haste that I may catch a fleeting breath !
And true in life, be true e'en unto death.

" O ship, sail on ! and bear me o'er the tide
To her for whom my woman's heart once died.
Sail, sail, O ship ! for she hath need of me,
And I would know what her last wish may be !
I have been true, so true, through all the past,

399

ELLA WHEELER WILCOX

Sail, sail, O ship ! I would not fail at last."
So prayed my heart still o'er, and ever o'er,
Until the weary lagging ship reached shore.
All sad with fears that I had come too late,
By that strange source whence men communicate,
Though miles on miles of space between them lie,
I spoke with Vivian : " Does she live ?   Reply."
The answer came, " She lives, but hasten, friend !
Her journey draweth swiftly to its end."
Ah me ! ah me ! when each remembered spot,
My own dear home, the lane that led to his—
The fields, the woods, the lake, burst on my sight,
Oh ! then, Self rose up in asserting might ;
Oh ! then, my bursting heart all else forgot
But those sweet early years of lost delight,
Of hope, defeat, of anguish, and of bliss.

I have a theory, vague, undefined,
That each emotion of the human mind,
Love, pain or passion, sorrow or despair,
Is a live spirit, dwelling in the air,
Until it takes possession of some breast ʃ
And, when at length, grown weary of unrest,
We rise up strong and cast it from the heart,
And bid it leave us wholly, and depart ;
It does not die, it cannot die, but goes
And mingles with some restless wind that blows
About the region where it had its birth,
And though we wander over all the earth,
That spirit waits, and lingers, year by year,

MAURINE

Invisible, and clothèd like the air,
Hoping that we may yet again draw near,
And it may haply take us unaware,
And once more find safe shelter in the breast
It stirred of old with pleasure or unrest.
Told by my heart, and wholly positive,
Some old emotion long had ceased to live ;
That, were it called, it could not hear or come,
Because it was so voiceless and so dumb ;
Yet, passing where it first sprang into life,
My very soul has suddenly been rife
With all the old intensity of feeling.
It seemed a living spirit, which came stealing
Into my heart from that departed day ;
Exiled emotion, which I fancied clay.

So now into my troubled heart, above
The present's pain and sorrow, crept the love
And strife and passion of a bygone hour,
Possessed of all their olden might and power,
'Twas but a moment, and the spell was broken
By pleasant words of greeting, gently spoken,
And Vivian stood before us.
                              But I saw
In him the husband of my friend alone.
The old emotions might at times return,
And smould'ring fires leap up an hour and burn ;
But never yet had I transgressed God's law,
By looking on the man I had resigned,
With any hidden feeling in my mind,

ELLA WHEELER WILCOX

Which she, his wife, my friend, might not have known,
He was but little altered. From his face
The nonchalant and almost haughty grace,
The lurking laughter waiting in his eyes,
The years had stolen, leaving in their place
A settled sadness, which was not despair,
Nor was it gloom, nor weariness, nor care,
But something like the vapour o'er the skies
Of Indian summer, beautiful to see,
But spoke of frosts, which had been and would be
There was that in his face which cometh not,
Save when the soul has many a battle fought,
And conquered self by constant sacrifice.

There are two sculptors, who, with chisels fine,
Render the plainest features half divine.
All other artists strive, and strive in vain,
To picture beauty perfect and complete.
Their statues only crumble at their feet,
Without the master touch of Faith and Pain.
And now his face, that perfect seemed before,
Chiselled by these two careful artists, wore
A look exalted, which the spirit gives
When soul has conquered, and the body lives
Subservient to its bidding.
                              In a room
Which curtained out the February gloom,
And, redolent with perfume, bright with flowers,
Rested the eye like one of summer's bowers,
I found my Helen, who was less mine now

Than Death's ; for on the marble of her brow,
His seal was stamped indelibly.

                          Her form
Was like the slender willow, when some storm
Has stripped it bare of foliage. Her face,
Pale always, now was ghastly in its hue ;
And, like two lamps, in some dark, hollow place,
Burned her large eyes, grown more intensely blue.
Her fragile hands displayed each cord and vein,
And on her mouth was that drawn look, of pain
Which is not uttered. Yet an inward light
Shone through and made her wasted features bright
With an unearthly beauty ; and an awe
Crept o'er me, gazing on her, for I saw
She was so near to Heaven that I seemed
To look upon the face of one redeemed.
She turned the brilliant lustre of her eyes
Upon me. She had passed beyond surprise,
Or any strong emotion linked with clay.
But as I glided to her where she lay,
A smile, celestial in its sweetness, wreathed
Her pallid features. " Welcome home ! " she breathed.
" Dear hands ! dear lips ! I touch you and rejoice."
And like the dying echo of a voice
Were her faint tones that thrilled upon my ear.
I fell upon my knees beside her bed ;
All agonies within my heart were wed,
While to the aching numbness of my grief,
Mine eyes refused the solace of a tear—
The tortured soul's most merciful relief.

ELLA WHEELER WILCOX

Her wasted hand caressed my bended head
For one sad, sacred moment. Then she said,
In that low tone so like the wind's refrain,
" Maurine, my own ! give not away to pain ;
The time is precious. Ere another dawn
My soul may hear the summons and pass on.
Arise, sweet sister ! rest a little while,
And when refreshed, come hither. I grow weak
With every hour that passes. I must speak
And make my dying wishes known to-night.
Go now." And in the halo of her smile,
Which seemed to fill the room with golden light,
I turned and left her.

     Later, in the gloom
Of coming night I entered that dim room,
And sat down by her. Vivian held her hand :
And on the pillow at her side there smiled
The beauteous count'nance of a sleeping child.

" Maurine," spoke Helen, " for three blissful years,
My heart has dwelt in an enchanted land ;
And I have drank the sweetened cup of joy,
Without one drop of anguish or alloy.
And so, ere Pain embitters it with gall,
Or sad-eyed Sorrow fills it full of tears,
And bids me quaff, which is the fate of all
Who linger long upon this troubled way,
God takes me to the realm of Endless Day,
To mingle with His angels, who alone
Can understand such bliss as I have known.

MAURINE

I do not murmur. God has heaped my measure,
In three short years, full to the brim with pleasure ;
And, from the fullness of an earthly love,
I pass to th'Immortal arms above,
Before I even brush the skirts of Woe.

" I leave my aged parents here below,
With none to comfort them. Maurine, sweet friend !
Be kind to them, and love them to the end,
Which may not be far distant.

      And I leave
A soul immortal in your charge, Maurine.
From this most holy, sad and sacred eve,
Till God shall claim her, she is yours to keep,
To love and shelter, to protect and guide."
She touched the slumb'ring cherub at her side,
And Vivian gently bore her, still asleep,
And laid the precious burden on my breast.
A solemn silence fell upon the scene.
And when the sleeping infant smiled, and pressed
My yielding bosom with her waxen cheek,
I felt it would be sacrilege to speak,
Such wordless joy possessed me.
      Oh l at last
This infant, who in that tear-blotted past,
Had caused my soul such travail, was my own :
Through all the lonely coming years to be
Mine own to cherish—wholly mine alone.

405

ELLA WHEELER WILCOX

And what I mourned so hopelessly as lost
Was now restored, and given back to me.
The dying voice continued :
                                        " In this child
You yet have me, whose mortal life she cost.
But all that was most pure and undefiled,
And good within me, lives in her again.
Maurine, my husband loves me ; yet I know,
Moving about the wide world, to and fro,
And through, and in the busy haunts of men,
Not always will his heart be dumb with woe,
But sometime waken to a later love.
Nay, Vivian, hush ! my soul has passed above
All selfish feelings ! I would have it so.
While I am with the angels, blest and glad,
I would not have you sorrowing and sad,
In loneliness go mourning to the end.
But, love ! I could not trust to any other
The sacred offer of a foster-mother
To this sweet cherub, save my own heart-friend.

" Teach her to love her father's name, Maurine,.
Where'er he wanders. Keep my memory green
In her young heart, and lead her in her youth,
To drink from th'eternal fount of Truth ;
Vex her not with sectarian discourse,
Nor strive to teach her piety by force ;
Ply not her mind with harsh and narrow creeds
Nor frighten her with an avenging God,
Who rules His subjects with a burning rod ;

MAURINE

But teach her that each mortal simply needs
To grow in hate of hate and love of love,
To gain a kingdom in the courts above.

" Let her be free and natural as the flowers,
That smile and nod throughout the summer hours.
Let her rejoice in all the joys of youth,
But first impress upon her mind this truth,
No lasting happiness is e'er attained
Save when the heart some *other* seeks to please.
The cup of selfish pleasures soon is drained,
And full of gall and bitterness the lees.
Next to her God, teach her to love her land ;
In her young bosom light the patriot's fame
Until the heart within her shall expand
With love and fervour at her country's name.

" No coward-mother bears a valiant son.
And this, my last wish, is an earnest one.

" Maurine, my o'er-taxed strength is waning ; you
Have heard my wishes, and you will be true
In death as you have been in life, my own !
Now leave me for a little while alone
With him—my husband. Dear love ! I shall rest
So sweetly with no care upon my breast.
Good-night, Maurine, come to me in the morning."

But lo l the bridegroom, with no further warning,
Came for her at the dawning of the day.

ELLA WHEELER WILCOX

She heard his voice, and smiled, and passed away
Without a struggle.
     Leaning o'er her bed
To give her greeting, I found but her clay,
And Vivian bowed beside it.
       And I said,
" Dear friend ! my soul shall treasure thy request,
And when the night of fever and unrest
Melts in the morning of Eternity,
Like a freed bird, then I will come to thee.

" I will come to thee in the morning, sweet !
I have been true ; and soul with soul shall meet
Before God's throne, and shall not be afraid :
Thou gav'st me trust, and it was not betrayed.

" I will come to thee in the morning, dear !
The night is dark. I do not know how near
The morn may be of that Eternal Day ;
I can but keep my faithful watch and pray.

" I will come to thee in the morning, love !
Wait for me on the Eternal Heights above.
The way is troubled where my feet must climb,
Ere I shall tread the mountain-top sublime.

" I will come in the morning, O mine own !
But for a time must grope my way alone,
Through tears and sorrow, till the Day shall dawn,
And I shall hear the summons, and pass on.

MAURINE

" I will come in the morning. Rest secure !
My hope is certain and my faith is sure.
After the gloom and darkness of the night
I will come to thee with the morning light."

.   .   .   .   .   .

Three peaceful years slipped silently away.

We dwelt together in my childhood's home,
Aunt Ruth and I, and sunny-hearted May.
She was a fair and most exquisite child ;
Her pensive face was delicate and mild
Like her dead mother's ; but through her dear eyes
Her father smiled upon me, day by day.
Afar in foreign countries did he roam,
Now resting under Italy's blue skies,
And now with Roy in Scotland.
                              And he sent
Brief, friendly letters, telling where he went
And what he saw, addressed to May or me.
And I would write and tell him how she grew—
And how she talked about him o'er the sea
In her sweet baby fashion ; how she knew
His picture in the album ; how each day
She knelt and prayed the blessèd Lord would bring
Her own papa back to his little May.

It was a warm bright morning in the spring.
I sat in that same sunny portico,
Where I was sitting seven years ago

409

ELLA WHEELER WILCOX

When Vivian came. My eyes were full of tears
As I looked back across the chequered years.
How many were the changes they had brought!
Pain, death, and sorrow! but the lesson taught
To my young heart had been of untold worth.
I had learned how to " suffer and grow strong "—
That knowledge which best serves us here on earth,
And brings reward in Heaven.

                    Oh! how long
The years had been since that June morning, when
I heard his step upon the walk, and yet
I seemed to hear its echo still.

                    Just then
Down that same path I turned my eyes, tear-wet,
And lo! the wanderer from a foreign land
Stood there before me—holding out his hand
And smiling with those wondrous eyes of old.

To hide my tears, I ran and brought his child;
But she was shy, and clung to me when told
This was papa, for whom her prayers were said.
She dropped her eyes and shook her little head,
And would not by his coaxing be beguiled,
Or go to him.

            Aunt Ruth was not at home,
And we two sat and talked, as strangers might,
Of distant countries which we both had seen.
But once I thought I saw his large eyes light
With sudden passion, when there came a pause
In our chit-chat, and then he spoke:

MAURINE

"Maurine,
I saw a number of your friends in Rome.
We talked of you.   They seemed surprised, because
You were not 'mong the seekers for a name.
They thought your whole ambition was for fame."

"It might have been," I answered, "when my heart
Had nothing else to fill it.   Now my art
Is but a recreation.   I have *this*
To love and live for, which I had not then."
And, leaning down, I pressed a tender kiss
Upon my child's fair brow.

                              "And yet," he said,
The old light leaping to his eyes again,
"And yet, Maurine, they say you might have wed
A noble Baron ! one of many men
Who laid their hearts and fortunes at your feet.
Why won the bravest of them no return ? "

I bowed my head nor dared, his gaze to meet.
On cheek and brow I felt the red blood burn,
And strong emotion strangled speech.
                                        He rose,
And came and knelt beside me.
                                  " Sweet, my sweet ! "
He murmured softly, " God in Heaven knows
How well I loved you seven years ago.
He only knows my anguish, and my grief,
When your own acts forced on me the belief

411

ELLA WHEELER WILCOX

That I had been your plaything and your toy.
Yet from his lips I since have learned that Roy
Held no place nearer than a friend and brother.
And then a faint suspicion, undefined,
Of what had been—was—might be, stirred my mind,
And that great love, I thought died at a blow,
Rose up within me, strong with hope and life.
Before all heaven and the angel mother
Of this sweet child that slumbers on your heart,
Maurine, Maurine, I claim you for my wife—
Mine own, forever, until death shall part ! "

Through happy mists of upward welling tears
I leaned, and looked into his beauteous eyes.
" Dear heart," I said, " if she who dwells above
Looks down upon us from yon azure skies,
She can but bless us, knowing all these years
My soul had yearned in silence for the love
That crowned her life, and left mine own so bleak.
I turned you from me for her fair, frail sake.
For her sweet child's, and for my own, I take
You back to be all mine, for evermore."

Just then the child upon my breast awoke
From her light sleep, and laid her downy cheek
Against her father as he knelt by me.
And this unconscious action seemed to be
A silent blessing which the mother spoke,
Gazing upon us from the mystic shore.

POEMS OF HOPE

PAIN'S PROOF

I THINK man's great capacity for pain
   Proves his immortal birthright. I am sure
No merely human mind could bear the strain
   Of some tremendous sorrows we endure.

Art's most ingenious breastworks fail at length,
   Beat by the mighty billows of the sea ;
Only the God-formed shores possess the strength
   To stand before their onslaughts, and not flee.

The structure that we build with careful toil,
   The tempest lays in ruins in an hour ;
While some grand tree that springs forth from the soil
   Is bended but not broken by its power.

Unless our souls had root in soil divine
   We could not bear earth's overwhelming strife.
The fiercest pain that racks this heart of mine,
   Convinces me of everlasting life.

ELLA WHEELER WILCOX

THE MASTER HAND

IT is something too strange to understand,
  How all the chords on the instrument,
Whether sorrowful, blithe, or grand,
Under the touch of your master hand
  Were into one melody blent.
Major, minor, everything—all—
Came at your magic fingers' call.

Why ! famed musicians had turned in despair
  Again and again from those self-same keys ;
They mayhap brought forth a simple air,
But a discord always crept in somewhere,
  In their fondest efforts to please ;
Or a jarring, jangling, meaningless strain
Angered the silence to noisy pain.

" Out of tune," they would frown and say !
  Or " a loosened key " or " a broken string " ;
But sure and certain they were alway,
That no man living on earth could play
  Measures more perfect, or bring
Sweeter sounds or a truer air
Out of that curious instrument there.

And then you came. You swept the scale
  With a mighty master's wonderful art.
You made the minor keys sob and wail,

While the low notes rang like a bell in the gale,
  And every chord in my heart,
From the deep bass tones to the shrill ones above,
Joined into that glorious harmony—Love.

And now, though I live for a thousand years,
  On no new chord can a new hand fall.
The chords of sorrow, of pain, of tears,
The chord of raptures and hopes and fears,
  I say you have struck them all ;
I say all the meaning put into each strain
By the Great Composer, you have made plain.

THE LAW

LIFE is a Shylock ; always it demands
  The fullest usurer's interest for each pleasure.
Gifts are not freely scattered by its hands :
  We make returns for every-borrowed treasure.

Each talent, each achievement, and each gain
  Necessitates some penalty to pay.
Delight imposes lassitude and pain,
  As certainly as darkness follows day.

All you bestow on causes or on men,
  Of love or hate, of malice or devotion,
Somehow, sometime, shall be returned again—
  There is no wasted toil, no lost emotion.

ELLA WHEELER WILCOX

The motto of the world is give and take.
  It gives you favours—out of sheer goodwill,
But unless speedy recompense you make,
  You'll find yourself presented with its bill.

When rapture comes to thrill the heart of you,
  Take it with tempered gratitude.   Remember,
Some later time the interest will fall due,
  No year brings June that does not bring December.

RECOMPENSE

STRAIGHT through my heart this fact to-day,
    By Truth's own hand is driven:
God never takes one thing away,
  But something else is given.

I did not know in earlier years,
  This law of love and kindness;
I only mourned through bitter tears
  My loss, in sorrow's blindness.

But, ever following each regret
  O'er some departed treasure,
My sad repining heart was met
  With unexpected pleasure.

I thought it only happened so;
  But Time this truth has taught me—
No least thing from my life can go,
  But something else is brought me.

It is the Law, complete, sublime ;
  And now with Faith unshaken,
In patience I but bide my time.
  When any joy is taken.

No matter if the crushing blow
  May for the moment down me,
Still, behind it waits Love, I know,
  With some new gift to crown me.

AN OLD COMRADE

ALL suddenly between me and the light,
  That brightly shone, and warm,
Robed in the pall-like garments of the night,
  There rose a shadowy form.

" Stand back," I said ; " you quite obscure the sun ;
  What do you want with me ? "
" Dost thou not know, then ? " quoth the mystic one ;
  " Look on my face and see ! "

I looked, and, lo ! it was my old despair,
  Robed in a new disguise ;
In blacker garments than it used to wear,
  But with the same sad eyes.

So ghostly were the memories it awoke,
  I shrank in fear away.
" Nay, be more kind," 'twas thus the dark shape spoke,
  " For I have come to stay.

ELLA WHEELER WILCOX

" So long thy feet have trod on sunny heights,
  Such joys thy heart has known,
Perchance thou hast forgotten those long nights,
  When we two watched alone.

" Though sweet and dear the Pleasures thou hast met,
  And comely to thine eye,
Has one of them, in all that bright throng yet,
  Been half so true as I ?

" And that last rapture which ensnared thee so
  With pleasure twin to pain,
It was the swiftest of them all to go—
  But I—I will remain.

" Again we two will live a thousand years,
  In desperate nights of grief,
That shall refuse the bitter balm of tears,
  For thy bruised heart's relief.

" Again we two will watch the hopeless dawn
  Creep up a lonely sky—
Again we'll urge the drear day to be gone,
  Yet dread to see it die.

" Nay, shrink not from me, for I am thy friend,
  One whom the Master sent ;
And I shall help thee, ere we reach the end,
  To find a great content.

" And I will give thee courage to attain,
  The heights supremely fair,
Wherein thou'lt cry, ' How blessèd was my pain !
  How God sent my despair 1 ' "

THE MOTHER-IN-LAW

SHE was my dream's fulfilment and my joy,
  This lovely woman whom you call your wife,
You sported at your play, an idle boy,
  When I first felt the stirring of her life
Within my startled being. I was thrilled
With such intensity of love, it filled
The very universe ! But words are vain—
No man can comprehend that wild, sweet pain.

You smiled in childhood's slumber while I felt
  The agonies of labour ; and the nights
I, weeping, o'er the little sufferer knelt,
You, wandering on through dreamland's fair delights,
Flung out your lengthening limbs and slept and grew ;
While I, awake, saved this dear wife for you.

She was my heart's loved idol and my pride.
  I taught her all those graces which you praise,
I dreamed of coming years, when at my side
  She would lend lustre to my fading days,
Should cling to me (as she to you clings now),
The young fruit hanging to the withered bough.

But lo ! the blossom was so fair a sight,
You plucked it from me—for your own delight.

Well, you are worthy of her—oh, thank God—
   And yet I think you do not realise
How burning were the sands o'er which I trod,
   To bear and rear this woman you so prize.
It was no easy thing to see her go—
Even into the arms of the one she worshipped so.

How strong, how vast, how awful seems the power
   Of this new love which fills a maiden's heart,
For one who never bore a single hour
   Of pain for her ; which tears her life apart
From all its moorings, and controls her more
Than all the ties the years have held before ;
Which crowns a stranger with a kingly grace—
And gives the one who bore her—second place.

She loves me still ! and yet, were Death to say,
   " Choose now between them ! " you would be her
     choice.
God meant it to be so—it is His way.
   But can you wonder if, while I rejoice
In her content, this thought hurts like a knife—
" No longer necessary to her life ! "

My pleasure in her joy is bitter sweet.
   Your very goodness sometimes hurts my heart,

Because, for her, life's drama seems complete
　Without the mother's oft-repeated part.
Be patient with me ! She was mine so long
Who now is yours. One must indeed be strong,
　To meet the loss without the least regret.
And so, forgive me, if my eyes *are* wet.

THE OLD STAGE QUEEN

BACK in the box by the curtains shaded,
　She sits alone by the house unseen ;
Her eye is dim, her cheek is faded,
　She who was once the people's queen.

The curtain rolls up, and she sees before her
　A vision of beauty and youth and grace.
Ah ! no wonder all hearts adore her,
　Silver-throated and fair of face.

Out of her box she leans and listens ;
　Oh, is it with pleasure or with despair
That her thin cheek pales and her dim eye glistens,
　While that fresh young voice sings the grand old air ?

She is back again in the Past's bright splendour—
　When life seemed worth living, and love a truth,
Ere Time had told her she must surrender
　Her double dower of fame and youth.

ELLA WHEELER WILCOX

It is she herself who stands there singing
  To that sea of faces that shines and stirs ;
And the cheers and cheers that go up ringing
  And rousing the echoes—are hers—all hers.

Just for one moment the sweet delusion
  Quickens her pulses and blurs her sight,
And wakes within her that wild confusion
  Of joy that is anguish and fierce delight.

Then the curtain goes down and the lights are gleaming
  Brightly o'er circle and box and stall.
She starts like a sleeper who wakes from dreaming—
  Her past lies under a funeral pall.

Her day is dead and her star descended,
  Never to rise or shine again ;
Her reign is over—her Queenship ended—
  A new name is sounded and sung by men.

All the glitter and glow and splendour,
  All the glory of that lost day,
With the friends that seemed true, and the love that
    seemed tender,
  Why, what is it all but a dead bouquet ?

She rises to go. Has the night turned colder ?
  The new Queen answers to call and shout ;
And the old Queen looks back over her shoulder,
  Then all unnoticed she passes out.

FAITH

I WILL not doubt, though all my ships at sea
   Come drifting home with broken masts and sails ;
  I shall believe the Hand which never fails,
From seeming evil worketh good for me ;
   And though I weep because those sails are battered,
   Still will I cry, while my best hopes lie shattered,
                   " I trust in thee."

I will not doubt, though all my prayers return
   Unanswered from the still, white Realm above ;
  I shall believe it is an all-wise Love
Which has refused those things for which I yearn ;
   And though at times I cannot keep from grieving,
   Yet the pure ardour of my fixed believing
                   Undimmed shall burn.

I will not doubt, though sorrows fall like rain,
   And troubles swarm like bees about a hive ;
  I shall believe the heights for which I strive
Are only reached by anguish and by pain ;
   And though I groan and tremble with my crosses,
   I yet shall see, through my severest losses,
                  The greater gain,

I will not doubt ; well anchored in the faith,
   Like some staunch ship, my soul braves every gale,
  So strong its courage that it will not fail

ELLA WHEELER WILCOX

To breast the mighty unknown sea of Death.
  Oh, may I cry when body parts with spirit,
  "I do not doubt," so listening worlds may hear it,
                        With my last breath.

THE TRUE KNIGHT

WE sigh above historic pages,
    Brave with the deeds of courtly men,
And wish those peers of middle ages
    In our dull day could live again.
And yet no knight or troubadour began
In chivalry with the American.

He does not frequent joust or tourney
    And flaunt his lady's colours there ;
But in the tedium of a journey,
    He shows that deferential care—
That thoughtful kindness to the sex at large,
Which makes each woman feel herself his charge.

He does not challenge foes to duel,
    To win his lady's cast-off glove,
But proves in ways less rash and cruel,
    The truth and fervour of his love.
Not by bold deeds, but by his reverent mien,
He pays his public tribute to his Queen.

424

He may not shine with courtly graces,
   But yet, his kind, respectful air
To woman, whatsoe'er her place is,
   It might be well if kings could share.
So, for the chivalric true gentleman,
Give me, I say, our own American.

THIMBLE ISLANDS

(OFF LONG ISLAND SOUND)

BETWEEN the shore and the distant sky-lands,
   Where a ship's dim shape seems etched on space,
There lies this cluster of lovely islands,
   Like laughing mermaids grouped in grace.

I look out over the waves and wonder,
   Are they not sirens who dwell in the sea?
When the tide runs high they dip down under
   Like mirthful bathers who sport in glee.

When the tide runs low they lift their shoulders
   Above the billows and gaily spread
Their soft green garments along the boulders
   Of grim grey granite that form their bed.

Close by the group, in sheltered places,
   Many a ship at anchor lies,
And drinks the charm of their smiling faces,
   As lover's drink smiles from maiden's eyes.

But true to the harsh and stern old ocean,
　As maids in a harem are true to one,
They give him all of their heart's devotion,
　Though wooed for ever by moon and sun.

A ship sails on that has bravely waded
　Through foaming billows to sue in vain ;
A whip-poor-will flies that has serenaded
　And sung unanswered his plaintive strain.

In the sea's great arms I see them lying,
　Bright and beaming and fond and fair,
While the jealous July day is dying
　In a crimson fury of mad despair.

The desolate moon drifts slowly over,
　And covers its face with the lace of a cloud,
While the sea, like a glad triumphant lover,
　Clasps close his islands and laughs aloud.

THE SOUTH

A QUEEN of indolence and idle grace,
　　Robed in the vestments of a costly gown,
She turns the languor of her lovely face
　Upon progression with a lazy frown.
　Her throne is built upon a marshy down ;
Malarial mosses wreathe her like old lace ;

POEMS OF HOPE

With slim crossed feet, unshod and bare and brown,
She sits indifferent to the world's swift race.
Across the seas there stalks an ogre grim:
    Too languid she for even fear's alarms,
    While frightened nations rally in defence,
She lifts her smiling Creole eyes to him,
    And reaching out her shapely unwashed arms,
    She clasps her rightful lover—Pestilence.

MY GRAVE

IF, when I die, I must be buried, let
    No cemetery engulf me—no lone grot,
Where the great palpitating world comes not,
Save when, with heart bowed down and eyelids wet,
It pays its last sad melancholy debt
To some out-journeying pilgrim. May my lot
Be rather to lie in some much-used spot,
Where human life, with all its noise and fret,
Throbs on about me. Let the roll of wheels,
With all earth's sounds of pleasure, commerce, love,
And rush of hurrying feet surge o'er my head.
Even in my grave I shall be one who feels
Close kinship with the pulsing world above;
And too deep silence would distress me, dead.

ELLA WHEELER WILCOX

A SAILOR'S WIFE

(HER MEMORY)

SUN in my lattice, and sun on the sea
  (Oh, but the sun is fair),
And a sky of blue and a sea of green,
And a ship with a white, white sail between,
  And a light wind blowing free—
And back from the stern, and forth from the land,
The last farewell of a waving hand.

Mist on the window and mist on the sea
  (Oh, but the mist is gray),
And the weird, tall shape of a spectral mast
Gleams out of the fog like a ghost of my past
  And the old hope stirs in me—
The old, old hope that warred with doubt,
While the years with the tides surged in and out.

Rain on my window and rain on the sea
  (Oh, but the rain is sad),
And only the dreams of a vanished barque
And a vanished youth shine through the dark,
  And torture the night and me.
But somewhere, I think, near some fair strand,
That lost ship lies with its waving hand.

THE DISAPPOINTED

THERE are songs enough for the hero
   Who dwells on the heights of fame ;
I sing for the disappointed—
   For those who missed their aim.

I sing with a tearful cadence
   For one who stands in the dark,
And knows that his last, best arrow
   Has bounded back from the mark.

I sing for the breathless runner,
   The eager, anxious soul,
Who falls with his strength exhausted,
   Almost in sight of the goal ;

For the hearts that break in silence
   With a sorrow all unknown,
For those who need companions,
   Yet walk their ways alone.

There are songs enough for the lovers
   Who share love's tender pain,
I sing for the one whose passion
   Is given all in vain.

ELLA WHEELER WILCOX

For those whose spirit comrades
　　Have missed them on the way
I sing with a heart o'erflowing,
　　This minor strain to-day.

And I know the Solar system
　　Must somewhere keep in space
A prize for that spent runner
　　Who barely lost the race.

For the plan would be imperfect
　　Unless it held some sphere
That paid for the toil and talent
　　And love that are wasted here.

THE BIRTH OF THE OPAL

THE Sunbeam loved the Moonbeam,
　　And followed her low and high,
But the Moonbeam fled and hid her head,
　　She was so shy—so shy.

The Sunbeam wooed with passion ;
　　Ah, he was a lover bold !
And his heart was afire with mad desire
　　For the Moonbeam pale and cold.

She fled like a dream before him,
　　Her hair was a shining sheen,
And oh, that Fate would annihilate
　　The space that lay between !

POEMS OF HOPE

Just as the day lay panting
  In the arms of the twilight dim,
The Sunbeam caught the one he sought
  And drew her close to him.

But out of his warm arms, startled
  And stirred by Love's first shock,
She sprang afraid, like a trembling maid,
  And hid in the niche of a rock.

And the Sunbeam followed and found her,
  And led her to Love's own feast ;
And they were wed on that rocky bed,
  And the dying Day was their priest.

And lo 1 the beautiful Opal—
  That rare and wondrous gem—
Where the moon and sun blend into one,
  Is the child that was born to them.

TWO LOVES

THE woman he loved, while he dreamed of her,
  Danced on till the stars grew dim,
But alone with her heart, from the world apart,
  Sat the woman who loved him.

The woman he worshipped only smiled,
  When he poured out his passionate love.
But the other somewhere, kissed her treasure most rare,
  A book he had touched with his glove.

ELLA WHEELER WILCOX

The woman he loved betrayed his trust,
  And he wore the scars for life ;
And he cared not, nor knew, that the other was true
  But no man called her his wife.

The woman he loved trod festal halls,
  While they sang his funeral hymn,
But the sad bells tolled, ere the year was old,
  For the woman who lovèd him.

ABSENCE

AFTER you went away, our lovely room
  Seemed like a casket whence the soul had fled.
I stood in awful and appalling gloom,
  The world was empty and all joy seemed dead.

I think I felt as one might feel who knew
  That Death had left him on the earth alone.
For " all the world " to my fond heart means you ;
  And there is nothing left when you are gone.

Each way I turned my sad, tear-blinded gaze,
  I found fresh torture to augment my grief ;
Some new reminder of the perfect days
  We passed together, beautiful as brief.

There lay a pleasing book that we had read—
  And there your latest gift ; and everywhere
Some tender act, some loving word you said,
  Seemed to take form and mock at my despair.

All happiness that human heart may know
Find with you ; and when you go away,
Thee hours become a winding-sheet of woe,
Ad make a ghastly phantom of To-day.

FISHING

MA'BE this is fun, sitting in the sun,
  With a book and a parasol, as my Angler wishes,
While h dips his line in the ocean brine,
  Undethe impression that his bait will catch the fishes.

'Tis romntic, yes, but I must confess
  Thoubts of shady rooms at home somehow seem
    more inviting.
But I dre not move—" Quiet, there, my love ! "
  Says ıy Angler, " for I think a monster fish is biting."

Oh, of curse it's bliss, but how hot it is !
  And he rock I'm sitting on grows harder every
    mnute ;
Still myfisher waits, trying various baits,
  But tè basket at his side I see has nothing in it.

Oh, it's ust the way to pass a July day,
  Arcaàn and sentimental, dreamy, idle, charming,
But ho\ fierce the sunlight falls ! and the way that
    isect crawls
  Alongmy neck and down my back is really quite
    aırming.

FISHING

All happiness that human heart may know
I find with you ; and when you go away,
Those hours become a winding-sheet of woe,
And make a ghastly phantom of To-day.

FISHING

MAYBE this is fun, sitting in the sun,
    With a book and a parasol, as my Angler wishes,
While he dips his line in the ocean brine,
    Under the impression that his bait will catch the fishes.

'Tis romantic, yes, but I must confess
    Thoughts of shady rooms at home somehow seem
        more inviting.
But I dare not move—" Quiet, there, my love ! "
Says my Angler, " for I think a monster fish is biting."

Oh, of course it's bliss, but how hot it is !
    And the rock I'm sitting on grows harder every
        minute ;
Still my fisher waits, trying various baits,
    But the basket at his side I see has nothing in it.

Oh, it's just the way to pass a July day,
    Arcadian and sentimental, dreamy, idle, charming,
But how fierce the sunlight falls ! and the way that
        insect crawls
    Along my neck and down my back is really quite
        alarming.

ELLA WHEELER WILCOX

" Any luck ? " I gently ask of the Angler at his task,
  " There's something pulling at my line," he says ;
    " I've almost caught it."
But when with blistered face, we our homeward steps
    retrace,
  We take the little basket just as empty as we brought it.

NEW YEAR

I SAW on the hills of the morning,
  The form of the New Year arise,
He stood like a statue adorning
  The world with a background of skies.
There were courage and grace in his beautiful face,
  And hope in his glorious eyes.

" I come from Time's boundless forever,"
  He said, with a voice like a song,
" I come as a friend to endeavour,
  I come as a foe to all wrong.
To the sad and afraid I bring promise of aid,
  And the weak I will gird and make strong.

" I bring you more blessings than terrors,
  I bring you more sunlight than gloom,
I tear out your page of old errors,
  And hide them away in Time's tomb.
I reach you clean hands, and lead on to the lands
  Where the lilies of peace are in bloom."

THE DIFFERENCE

PASSION is what the sun feels for the earth
  When harvests ripen into golden birth.

Lust is the hot simoon whose burning breath
Sweeps o'er the fields with devastating death.

Passion is what God felt, the Holy One,
Who loved the world so, He begot His Son.

Lust is the impulse Satan peering in
To Eden had, when he taught Eve to sin.

One sprang from light, and one from darkness grew !
How dim the vision that confounds the two !

THE SEA-BREEZE AND THE SCARF

HUNG on the casement that looked o'er the main,
  Fluttered a scarf of blue ;
And a gay, bold breeze paused to flatter and tease
  This trifle of delicate hue.
" You are lovelier far than the proud skies are,"
  He said with a voice that sighed ;
" You are fairer to me than the beautiful sea—
  Oh, why do you stay here and hide ?

ELLA WHEELER WILCOX

" You are wasting your life in that dull, dark room "
   (And he fondled her silken folds),
" O'er the casement lean but a little, my Queen,
   And see what the great world holds.
How the wonderful blue of your matchless hue
   Cheapens both sea and sky—
You are far too bright to be hidden from sight,
   Come, fly with me, darling—fly."

Tender his whisper and sweet his caress,
   Flattered and pleased was she,
The arms of her lover lifted her over
   The casement out to sea.
Close to his breast she was fondly pressed,
   Kissed once by his laughing mouth ;
Then dropped to her grave in the cruel wave,
   While the wind went whistling south.

HER REVERIE

WE were both of us—aye, we were *both* of us there,
   In the self-same house at the play together,
To her it was summer, with bees in the air—
   To me it was winter weather.

We never had met and yet we two
   Had played in desperate woman fashion,
A game of life, with a prize in view,
   And oh ! I played with passion.

Twas a game that meant heaven and sweet home-life,
  For the one who went forth with a crown upon her ;
For the one who lost—it meant lone strife,
  Sorrow, despair, and dishonour.

Well, she won (yet it was not she—
  I am told that she was a praying woman :
No earthly power could outwit me—
  But hers was superhuman).

She has the prize, and I have—well,
  Memories sweeter than joys of heaven ;
Memories fierce as the fires of hell—
  Those unto me were given.

And we sat in the self-same house last night ;
  And *he* was there.   It is no error
When I say (and it gave me keen delight)
  That his eye met mine with terror.

When the love we have won at any cost
  Has grown familiar as some old story,
Naught seems so dear as the love we lost,
  All bright with the Past's weird glory.

And tho' he is fond of that woman, I know—
  I saw in his eyes the brief confession—
That the love seemed sweeter which he let go
  Than that in his possession.

ELLA WHEELER WILCOX

So I am content.   It would be the same
   Were I the wife love-crowned and petted,
And she the woman who lost the game—
   Then *she* were the one regretted.

And loving him so, I would rather be
   The one he let go—and then vaguely desired,
Than, winning him, once in his face to see
   The look of a love grown tired.

QUERIES

WELL, how has it been with you since we met
   That last strange time of a hundred times ?
When we met to swear that we could forget—
   I your caresses, and you my rhymes—
The rhyme of my lays that rang like a bell,
And the rhyme of my heart with yours, as well ?

How has it been since we drank that last kiss,
   That was bitter with lees of the wasted wine ;
When the tattered remains of a threadbare bliss,
   And the worn-out shreds of a joy divine,
With a year's best dreams and hopes, were cast
Into the ragbag of the Past ?

438

POEMS OF HOPE

Since Time, the rag-buyer, hurried away
  With a chuckle of glee at the bargain made,
Did you discover, like me, one day,
  That hid in the folds of those garments frayed
With priceless jewels and diadems—
The soul's best treasures, the heart's best gems ?

Have you, too, found that you could not supply
  The place of those jewels so rare and chaste ?
Do all that you borrow, or beg, or buy,
  Prove to be nothing but skilful paste ?
Have you found pleasure, as I find art,
Not all sufficient to fill your heart ?

Do you sometimes sigh for the tattered shreds
  Of the old delight that we cast away,
And find no worth in the silken threads
  Of newer fabrics we wear to-day ?
Have you thought the bitter of that last kiss
Better than sweets of a later bliss ?

What idle queries !—or yes or no—
  Whatever your answer, I understand
That there is no pathway by which we can go
  Back to the dead past's wonderland ;
And the gems he purchased from me and you,
There is no rebuying, from Time the Jew.

ELLA WHEELER WILCOX

SLEEP AND DEATH

WHEN Sleep drops down beside my love and me,
    Although she wears the countenance of a friend,
  A jealous foe we prove her in the end.
In separate barques far out on dreamland's sea,
She lures our wedded souls. Wild winds blow free,
    And drift us wide apart by tides that tend
Tow'rd unknown worlds. Not once our strange ways
    blend
Through the long night, while Sleep looks on in glee.

O Death 1 be kinder than thy sister seems,
    When at thy call we journey forth some day,
    Through that mysterious and unatlased strait,
To lands more distant than the lands of dreams ;
    Close, close together let our spirits stay,
    Or else, with one swift stroke, annihilate'l

GUILO

YES, yes ! I love thee, Guilo ; thee alone.
    Why dost thou sigh, and wear that face of
    sorrow ?
The sunshine is to-day's, although it shone
    On yesterday, and may shine on to-morrow.

POEMS OF HOPE

I love but thee, my Guilo ! be content,
   The greediest heart can claim but present pleasure.
The future is thy God's. The past is spent.
   To-day is thine ; clasp close the precious treasure.

See how I love thee, Guilo ! Lips and eyes
   Could never under thy fond gaze dissemble.
I could not feign these passion-laden sighs,
   Deceiving thee, my pulses would not tremble.

" So I loved Romney." Hush, thou foolish one—
   I should forget him wholly, wouldst thou let me ;
Or but remember that his day was done
   From that most supreme hour when first I met thee.

" And Paul ? " Well, what of Paul ? Paul had blue
     eyes,
   And Romney grey, and thine are darkly tender !
One finds fresh feelings under change of skies—
   A new horizon brings a newer splendour.

As I love thee, I never loved before ;
   Believe me, Guilo, for I speak most truly.
What though to Romney and to Paul I swore
   The selfsame words ; my heart now worships newly.

We never feel the same emotion twice :
   No two ships ever ploughed the selfsame billow.
The waters change, with every fall and rise ;
   So, Guilo, go contented to thy pillow.

ELLA WHEELER WILCOX

ISAURA

DOST thou not tire, Isaura, of this play ?
　　What play ? Why, this old play of winning
　　　　hearts !
Nay, now, lift not thine eyes in that feigned way ;
　　'Tis all in vain—I know thee, and thine arts.

Let us be frank, Isaura.　I have made
　　A study of thee ; and while I admire
The practised skill with which thy plans are laid,
　　I can but wonder if thou dost not tire.

Why, I tire even of Hamlet and Macbeth !
　　When over-long the season runs, I find
Those master-scenes of passion, blood, and death,
　　After a time, do pall upon my mind.

Dost thou not tire of lifting up thine eyes
　　To read the story thou hast read so oft—
Of ardent glances, and deep quivering sighs,
　　Of haughty faces suddenly grown soft ?

Is it not stale, oh, very stale, to thee,
　　The scene that follows ? Hearts are much the
　　　　same ;
The loves of men but vary in degree—
　　They find no new expressions for the flame.

POEMS OF HOPE

Thou must know all they utter ere they speak,
  As I know Hamlet's part, whoever plays.
Oh, does it not seem sometimes poor and weak?
  I think thou must grow weary of their ways.

I pity thee, Isaura! I would be
  The humblest maiden with her dream untold,
Rather than live a Queen of Hearts, like thee,
  And find life's rarest treasures stale and old.

I pity thee; for now, let come what may,
  Fame, glory, riches, yet life will lack all.
Wherewith can salt be salted? And what way
  Can life be seasoned after love doth pall?

FROM THE GRAVE

WHEN the first sere leaves of the year are falling,
  I heard, with a heart that was strangely thrilled,
Out of the grave of a dead Past calling,
  A voice I fancied for ever stilled.
All through winter, and spring, and summer,
  Silence hung over that grave like a pall;
But, borne on the breath of the last sad comer,
  I listened again to the old-time call.

It is only a love of a bygone season,
  A senseless folly that mocked at me,
A reckless passion that lacked all reason:
  So I killed it, and hid it where none could see.

443

ELLA WHEELER WILCOX

I smothered it first to stop its crying,
  Then stabbed it through with a good sharp blade :-
And cold and pallid I saw it lying,
  And deep—ah ! deep was the grave I made.

But now I know that there is no killing
  A thing like Love, for it laughs at Death.
There is no hushing, there is no stilling
  That which is part of your life and breath.
You may bury it deep, and leave behind you
  The land, the people that knew your slain ;
It will push the sods from its grave, and find you
  On wastes of water or desert plain.

You may hear but tongues of a foreign people,
  You may list to sounds that are strange and new ;
But, clear as a silver bell in a steeple,
  That voice from the grave shall call to you.
You may rouse your pride, you may use your reason,
  And seem for a space to slay Love so ;
But, all in its own good time and season,
  It will rise and follow wherever you go.
You shall sit sometimes, when the leaves are falling,
  Alone in your heart, as I sit to-day,
And hear that voice from your dead Past calling
  Out of the graves that you hid away.

PERFECTNESS

ALL perfect things are saddening in effect.
    The autumn wood robed in its scarlet clothes,
  The matchless tinting on the royal rose
Whose velvet leaf by no least flaw is flecked,
Love's supreme moment, when the soul unchecked
  Soars high as heaven, and its best rapture knows,
  These hold a deeper pathos than our woes,
Since they leave nothing better to expect.

Resistless change, when powerless to improve,
  Can only mar. The gold will pale to gray—
  No thing remains to-morrow as to-day—
The rose will not seem quite so fair, and love
  Must find its measures of delight made less.
  Ah, how imperfect is all Perfectness!

BLEAK WEATHER

DEAR Love, where the red lilies blossomed and grew
  The white snows are falling;
And all through the woods where I wandered with you
  The loud winds are calling;
And the robin that piped to us tune upon tune,
  'Neath the oak you remember,
O'er hilltop and forest has followed the June
  And left us December.

ELLA WHEELER WILCOX

He has left like a friend who is true in the sun
  And false in the shadows ;
He has found new delights in the land where he's gone,
  Greener woodlands and meadows.
Let him go ! what care we ? let the snow shroud the lea,
  Let it drift on the heather ;
We can sing through it all ; I have you, you have me,
  And we'll laugh at the weather.

The old year may die and a new year be born
  That is bleaker and colder :
It cannot dismay us : we dare it, we scorn,
  For our love makes us bolder.
Ah, Robin ! sing loud on your far distant lea,
  You friend in fair weather !
But here is a song sung that's fuller of glee
  By two warm hearts together.

GRACIA

NAY, nay, Antonio ! nay, thou shalt not blame her,
  My Gracia, who hath so deserted me.
Thou art my friend ; but if thou dost defame her
  I shall not hesitate to challenge thee.

" Curse and forget her ? " so I might another
  One not so bounteous natured or so fair ;
But she, Antonio, she was like no other—
  I curse her not, because she was so rare.

POEMS OF HOPE

She was made out of laughter and sweet kisses ;
   Not blood, but sunshine, through her blue veins ran ;
Her soul spilled over with its wealth of blisses—
   She was too great for loving but a man.

None but a god could keep so rare a creature—
   I blame her not for her inconstancy ;
When I recall each radiant smile, and feature,
   I wonder she was so long true to me.

Call her not false or fickle. I, who love her,
   Do hold her not unlike the royal sun,
That, all unmated, roams the wide world over
   And lights all worlds, but lingers not with one.

If she were less a goddess, more a woman,
   And so had dallied for a time with me,
And then had left me, I, who am but human,
   Would slay her, and her newer love, may-be.

But since she seeks Apollo, or another
   Of those lost gods (and seeks him all in vain)
And has loved me as well as any other
   Of her men-loves, why, I do not complain.

ELLA WHEELER WILCOX

THE FAREWELL OF CLARIMONDE

(SUGGESTED BY THE " CLARIMONDE " OF
THEOPHILE GAUTIER)

ADIEU, Romauld ! But thou canst not forget me,
 Although no more I haunt thy dreams at night,
Thy hungering heart for ever must regret me,
 And starve for those lost moments of delight.

Naught shall avail thy priestly rites and duties—
 Nor fears of Hell, nor hopes of Heaven beyond :
Before the Cross shall rise my fair form's beauties—
 The lips, the limbs, the eyes of Clarimonde.

Like gall the wine sipped from the sacred chalice,
 Shall taste to one who knew my red mouth's bliss :
When Youth and Beauty dwelt in Love's own palace
 And life flowed on in one eternal kiss.

Through what strange ways I come, dear heart, to reach
 thee,
 From viewless lands, by paths no man e'er trod 1
I braved all fears, all dangers dared, to teach thee
 A love more mighty than thy love of God.

Think not in all His Kingdom to discover
 Such joys, Romauld, as ours, when fierce yet fond
I clasped thee—kissed thee—crowned thee my one lover :
 Thou canst not find another Clarimonde.

I knew all arts of love : he who possessed me,
　Possessed all women, and could never tire ;
A new life dawned for him who once caressed me
　Satiety itself I set on fire.

Inconstancy I chained : men died to win me ;
　Kings cast by crowns for one hour on my breast,
And all the passionate tide of love within me
　I gave to thee, Romauld.　Wert thou not blest ?

Yet, for the love of God, thy hand hath riven
　Our welded souls.　But not in prayer well conned,
Not in thy dearly-purchased peace of Heaven,
　Canst thou forget those hours with Clarimonde.

IF I SHOULD DIE

RONDEAU

IF I should die, how kind you all would grow.
　In that strange hour I would not have one foe.
　There are no words too beautiful to say
　Of one who goes forevermore away
Across that ebbing tide which has no flow.

With what new lustre my good deeds would glow !
If faults were mine, no one would call them so,
　Or speak of me in aught but praise that day,
　　If I should die.

ELLA WHEELER WILCOX

Ah, friends ! before my listening ear lies low.
While I can hear and understand, bestow
   That gentle treatment and fond love, I pray,
   The lustre of whose late though radiant way
Would gild my grave with mocking light, I know,
    If I should die.

MISALLIANCE

I AM troubled to-night with a curious pain ;
   It is not of the flesh, it is not of the brain,
   Nor yet of a heart that is breaking :
But down still deeper, and out of sight—
In the place where the soul and the body unite—
   There lies the seat of the aching.

They have been lovers, in days gone by ;
But the soul is fickle, and longs to fly
   From the fettering misalliance ;
And she tears at the bonds which are binding her so,
And pleads with the body to let her go,
   But he will not yield compliance.

For the body loves, as he loved in the past
When he wedded the soul ; and he holds her fast,
   And swears that he will not loose her ;
That he will keep her and hide her away
For ever and ever and for a day
   From the arms of Death, the seducer.

POEMS OF HOPE

Ah ! this is the strife that is wearying me—
The strife 'twixt a soul that would be free
　　And a body that will not let her.
And I say to my soul, " Be calm, and wait :
For I tell ye truly that soon or late
　　Ye surely shall drop each fetter."

And I say to the body, " Be kind, I pray ;
For the soul is not of thy mortal clay,
　　But is formed in spirit fashion."
And still through the hours of the solemn night
I can hear my sad soul's plea for flight,
　　And my body's reply of passion.

RED CARNATIONS

ONE time in Arcadie's fair bowers
　　There met a bright immortal band,
To choose their emblems from the flowers
　　That made an Eden of that land.

Sweet Constancy, with eyes of hope,
　　Strayed down the garden path alone
And gathered sprays of heliotrope,
　　To place in clusters at her zone.

True Friendship plucked the ivy green,
　　Forever fresh, forever fair.
Inconstancy with flippant mien
　　The fading primrose chose to wear.

451

ELLA WHEELER WILCOX

One moment Love the rose paused by ;
  But Beauty picked it for her hair.
Love paced the garden with a sigh—
  He found no fitting emblem there.

Then suddenly he saw a flame ;
  A conflagration turned to bloom.
It even put the rose to shame,
  Both in its beauty and perfume.

He watched it, and it did not fade :
  He plucked it, and it brighter grew
In cold or heat, all undismayed,
  It kept its fragrance and its hue.

" Here deathless love and passion sleep,"
  He cried, " embodied in this flower.
This is the emblem I will keep."
  Love wore carnations from that hour.

THE LOST GARDEN

THERE was a fair green garden sloping
    From the south-east side of the mountain-ledge ;
And the earliest tint of the dawn came groping
  Down through its paths, from the day's dim edge.
The bluest skies and the reddest roses
  Arched and varied its velvet sod ;
And the glad birds sang, as the soul supposes
  The angels sing on the hills of God.

POEMS OF HOPE

I wandered there when my veins seemed bursting
  With life's rare rapture, and keen delight ;
And yet in my heart was a constant thirsting
  For something over the mountain-height.
I wanted to stand in the blaze of glory
  That turned to crimson the peaks of snow,
And the winds from the west all breathed a story
  Of realms and regions I longed to know.

I saw on the garden's south side growing
  The brightest blossoms that breathe of June ;
I saw in the east how the sun was glowing,
  And the gold air shook with a wild bird's tune ;
I heard the drip of a silver fountain,
  And the pulse of a young laugh throbbed with glee ;
But still I looked out over the mountain
  Where unnamed wonders awaited me.

I came at last to the western gateway
  That led to the path I longed to climb ;
But a shadow fell on my spirit straightway,
  For close at my side stood grey-beard Time.
I paused, with feet that were fain to linger
  Hard by that garden's golden gate ;
But Time spoke, pointing with one stern finger ;
  " Pass on," he said, " for the day grows late."

And now on the chill grey cliffs I wander ;
  The heights recede which I thought to find,
And the light seems dim on the mountain yonder,
  When I think of the garden I left behind.

ELLA WHEELER WILCOX

Should I stand at last on its summit's splendour,
  I know full well it would not repay
For the fair lost tints of the dawn so tender,
  That crept up over the edge o' day.

I would go back, but the ways are winding,
  If ways there are to that land, in sooth ;
For what man succeeds in ever finding
  A path to the garden of his lost youth ?
But I think sometimes, when the June stars glisten,
  That a rose-scent drifts from far away ;
And I know, when I lean from the cliffs and listen
  That a young laugh breaks on the air like spray.

DROUGHT

WHY do we pity those who weep ?   The pain
    That finds a ready outlet in the flow
  Of salt and bitter tears is blessèd woe,
And does not need our sympathies.   The rain
But fits the shorn field for new yield of grain ;
  While the red brazen skies, the sun's fierce glow,
  The dry, hot winds that from the tropics blow,
Do parch and wither the unsheltered plain.
The anguish that through long, remorseless years
  Looks out upon the world with no relief,
Of sudden tempests or slow dripping tears—
  The still, unuttered, silent, wordless grief
That evermore doth ache, and ache, and ache—
This is the sorrow wherewith hearts do break.

POEMS OF HOPE

THE SADDEST HOUR

THE saddest hour of anguish and of loss
    Is not that season of supreme despair
When we can find no least light anywhere
To gild the dread, black shadow of the Cross.
Not in that luxury of sorrow when
    We sup on salt of tears, and drink the gall
    Of memories of days beyond recall—
Of lost delights that cannot come again.

But when, with eyes that are no longer wet,
    We look out on the great, wide world of men,
And, smiling, lean toward a bright to-morrow,
    Then backward shrink, with sudden keen regret,
    To find that we are learning to forget :
Ah ! then we face the saddest hour of sorrow.

MY HERITAGE

INTO life so full of love was sent,
    That all the shadows which fall on the way
    Of every human being, could not stay,
But fled before the light my spirit lent.

I saw the world through gold and crimson dyes :
    Men sighed, and said, " Those rosy hues will fade
    As you pass on into the glare and shade ! "
Still beautiful the way seems to mine eyes.

455

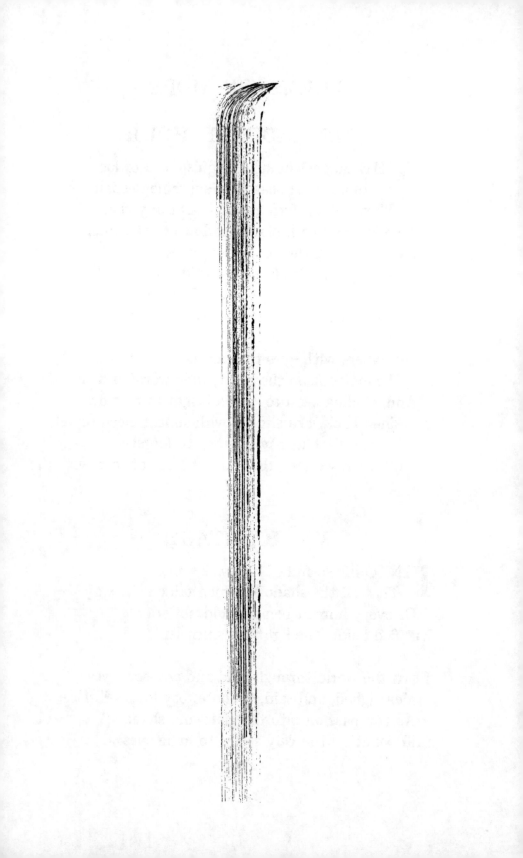

of los

ywhere

he gall

in

r wet
l

t

ELLA WHEELER WILCOX

They said, " You are too jubilant and glad ;
  The world is full of sorrow and of wrong.
  For soon your lips shall breathe forth sighs—not
    song ! "
The day wears on, and yet I am not sad.

They said, " You love too largely, and you must
  Through wound on wound, grow bitter to your kind."
  They were false prophets ; day by day I find
More cause for love, and less cause for distrust.

They said, " Too free you give your soul's rare wine ;
  The world will quaff, but it will not repay."
  Yet into the emptied flagons, day by day,
True hearts pour back a nectar as divine.

Thy heritage ! Is it not love's estate ?
  Look to it, then, and keep its soil well tilled.
  I hold that my best wishes are fulfilled
Because I love so much, and cannot hate.

RESOLVE

BUILD on resolve, and not upon regret,
  The structure of thy future. Do not grope
Among the shadows of old sins, but let
  Thine own soul's light shine on the path of hope
And dissipate the darkness. Moist no tears
Upon the blotted record of lost years,
But turn the leaf, and smile, oh, smile, to see
The fair white pages that remain for thee.

Prate not of thy repentance.   But believe
   The spark divine dwells in thee : let it grow.
That which the upreaching spirit can achieve
   The grand and all creative forces know;
They will assist and strengthen as the light
Lifts up the acorn to the oak-tree's height.
Thou hast but to resolve, and lo ! God's whole
Great universe shall fortify thy soul.

THE TIGER

IN the still jungle of the senses lay
   A tiger soundly sleeping, till one day
A bold young hunter chanced to come that way.

" How calm," he said, " that splendid creature lies,
I long to rouse him into swift surprise ! "
A well aimed arrow, shot from amorous eyes,

And lo ! the tiger rouses up and turns,
A coal of fire his glowing eyeball burns,
His mighty frame with savage hunger yearns.

He crouches for a spring ; his eyes dilate—
Alas ! bold hunter, what shall be thy fate ?
Thou canst not fly, it is too late, too late.

Once having tasted human flesh, ah ! then,
Woe, woe unto the whole rash world of men,
The awakened tiger will not sleep again.

ELLA WHEELER WILCOX

ONLY A SIMPLE RHYME

ONLY a simple rhyme of love and sorrow,
　　Where " blisses " rhymed with " kisses," " heart,"
　　　　with " dart."
Yet, reading it, new strength I seemed to borrow,
　　To live on bravely, and to do my part.

A little rhyme about a heart that's bleeding—
　　Of lonely hours, and sorrow's unrelief.
I smiled at first ; but there came with the reading,
　　A sense of sweet companionship in grief.

The selfishness of my own woe forsaking,
　　I thought about the singer of that song.
Some other breast felt this same weary aching,
　　Another found the summer days too long.

The few sad lines, my sorrow so expressing,
　　I read, and on the singer, all unknown,
I breathed a fervent, though a silent, blessing,
　　And seemed to clasp his hand within my own.

And though fame pass him, and he never know it,
　　And though he never sings another strain,
He has performed the mission of the poet,
　　In helping some sad heart to bear its pain.

LET ME LEAN HARD

LET me lean hard upon the Eternal Breast :
  In all earth's devious ways, I sought for rest
And found it not. I will be strong, said I,
And lean upon myself. I will not cry
And importune all heaven with my complaint,
But now my strength fails, and I fall, I faint :
    Let me lean hard.

Let me lean hard upon the unfailing Arm.
I said I will walk on, I fear no harm,
The spark divine within my soul will show
The upward pathway where my feet should go ;
But now the heights to which I most aspire
Are lost in clouds. I stumble and I tire :
    Let me lean hard.

Let me lean harder yet. That swerveless force
Which speeds the solar systems on their course
Can take, unfelt, the burden of my woe,
Which bears me to the dust and hurts me so.
I thought my strength enough for any fate,
But lo ! I sink beneath my sorrow's weight.
    Let me lean hard.

ELLA WHEELER WILCOX

THE YEAR OUTGROWS THE SPRING

THE year outgrows the spring it thought so sweet
   And clasps the summer with a new delight,
Yet wearied, leaves her languors and her heat
   When cool-browed autumn dawns upon his sight.

The tree outgrows the bud's suggestive grace
   And feels new pride in blossoms fully blown.
But even this to deeper joy gives place
   When bending boughs 'neath blushing burdens groan.

Life's rarest moments are derived from change,
   The heart outgrows old happiness, old grief,
And suns itself in feelings new and strange.
   The most enduring pleasure is but brief.

Our tastes, our needs, are never twice the same.
   Nothing contents us long, however dear.
The spirit in us, like the grosser frame,
   Outgrows the garments which it wore last year.

Change is the watchword of Progression.   When
   We tire of well-worn ways, we seek for new.
This restless craving in the souls of men
   Spurs them to climb, and seek the mountain view.

So let who will erect an altar shrine
   To meek-browed Constancy, and sing her praise ;
Unto enlivening Change I shall build mine,
   Who lends new zest, and interest to my days.

POEMS OF HOPE

AT ELEUSIS

I AT Eleusis, saw the finest sight,
    When early morning's banners were unfurled.
  From high Olympus, gazing on the world,
The ancient gods once saw it with delight.
Sad Demeter had in a single night
    Removed her sombre garments! and mine eyes
    Beheld a 'broidered mantle in pale dyes
Thrown o'er her throbbing bosom.   Sweet and clear
There fell the sound of music on mine ear.
    And from the South came Hermes, he whose lyre
    One time appeased the great Apollo's ire.
The rescued maid, Persephone, by the hand,
    He led to waiting Demeter, and cheer
And light and beauty once more blessed the land

COURAGE

THERE is a courage, a majestic thing
    That springs forth from the brow of pain, full-
        grown,
  Minerva-like, and dares all dangers known,
And all the threatening future yet may bring ;
Crowned with the helmet of great suffering,
    Serene with that grand strength by martyrs shown,
    When at the stake they die and make no moan,
And even as the flames leap up are heard to sing.

ELLA WHEELER WILCOX

A courage so sublime and unafraid,
　It wears its sorrows like a coat of mail ;
And Fate, the archer, passes by dismayed,
　Knowing his best barbed arrows needs must fail
To pierce a soul so armoured and arrayed
　That Death himself might look on it and quail.

THE WHEEL OF THE BREAST

THROUGH rivers of veins on the nameless quest
　The tide of my life goes hurriedly sweeping,
Till it reaches that curious wheel o' the breast,
The human heart, which is never at rest.
　Faster, faster, it cries, and leaping,
Plunging, dashing, speeding away,
The wheel and the river work night and day.

I know not wherefore, I know not whither
　This strange tide rushes with such mad force ;
It glides on hither, it slides on thither,
　Over and over the selfsame course,
　With never an outlet and never a source ;
And it lashes itself to the heat of passion
And whirls the heart in mill-wheel fashion.

I can hear in the hush of the still, still night,
　The ceaseless sound of that mighty river ;

POEMS OF HOPE

I can hear it gushing, gurgling, rushing,
  With a wild, delirious strange delight,
  And a conscious pride in its sense of might,
As it hurries and worries my heart for ever.

And I wonder oft as I lie awake,'
  And list to the river that seethes and surges
  Over the wheel that it chides and urges,—
I wonder oft if that wheel will break
  With the mighty pressure it bears, some day,
  Or slowly and wearily wear away.

For little by little the heart is wearing,
Like the wheel of the mill, as the tide goes tearing
  And plunging hurriedly through my breast,
  In a network of veins on a nameless quest,
From and forth, unto unknown oceans,
Bringing its cargoes of fierce emotions,
  With never a pause or an hour for rest.

A PICTURE

I STROLLED last eve across the lonely down,
  One solitary picture struck my eye,
  A distant ploughboy stood against the sky—
How far he seemed, above the noisy town !

ELLA WHEELER WILCOX

Upon the bosom of a cloud the sod
  Laid its bruised cheek, as he moved slowly by,
  And, watching him, I asked myself if I
In very truth stood half as near to God.

DAWN

DAY'S sweetest moments are at dawn;
    Refreshed by his long sleep, the Light
Kisses the languid lips of Night,
Ere she can rise and hasten on.
All glowing from his dreamless rest
He holds her closely to his breast,
Warm lip to lip and limb to limb,
Until she dies for love of him.

SUNSET

I SAW the day lean o'er the world's sharp edge,
  And peer into night's chasm, dark and damp.
High in his hand he held a blazing lamp,
Then dropped it, and plunged headlong down the ledge.

With lurid splendour that swift paled to grey,
I saw the dim skies suddenly flush bright.
'Twas but the expiring glory of the light
Flung from the hand of the adventurous day.

POEMS OF HOPE

A MEETING

QUITE carelessly I turned the newsy sheet ;
 A song I sang, full many a year ago,
Smiled up at me, as in a busy street
 One meets an old-time friend he used to know.

So full it was, that simple little song,
 Of all the hope, the transport, and the truth,
Which to the impetuous morn of life belong,
 That, once again, I seemed to grasp my youth.

So full it was of that sweet, fancied pain
 We woo and cherish ere we meet with woe.
I felt, as one who hears a plaintive strain
 His mother sang him in the long ago.

Up from the grave, the years that lay between
 That song's birthday and my stern present, came
Like phantom forms, and swept across the scene,
 Bearing their broken dreams of love and fame.

Fair hopes and bright ambitions that I knew
 In that old time, with their ideal grace,
Shone for a moment, then were lost to view,
 Behind the dull clouds of the commonplace.

With trembling hands I put the sheet away ;
 Ah, little song ! the sad and bitter truth
Struck like an arrow when we met that day !
 My life has missed the promise of its youth.

ELLA WHEELER WILCOX

TWIN-BORN

HE who possesses virtue at its best,
  Or greatness in the true sense of the word,
  Has one day started even with that herd
Whose swift feet now speed, but at sin's behest.
It is the same force in the human breast
  Which makes men gods or demons.   If we gird
  Those strong emotions by which we are stirred
With might of will and purpose, heights unguessed
  Shall dawn for us ; or if we give them sway
We can sink down and consort with the lost.
All virtue is worth just the price it cost.
  Black sin is oft white truth, that missed its way.
And wandered off in paths not understood.
Twin-born I hold great evil and great good.

HIDDEN GEMS

WE know not what lies in us, till we seek.
  Men dive for pearls—they are not found on shore ;
The hillsides, most unpromising and bleak,
  Do sometimes hide the ore.

Go, dive in the vast ocean of thy mind,
  O man ! far down below the noisy waves,
Down in the depths and silence thou mayst find
  Rare pearls and coral caves.

POEMS OF HOPE

Sink thou a shaft into a mine of thought ;
　Be patient, like the seekers after gold,
Under the rocks and rubbish lieth what
　May bring thee wealth untold.

Reflected from the vasty Infinite,
　However dulled by earth, each human mind
Holds somewhere gems of beauty and of light
　Which, seeking, thou shalt find.

A FABLE

SOME cawing Crows, a hooting Owl,
　A Hawk, a Canary, an old Marsh Fowl,
　One day all met together,
To hold a caucus and settle the fate
Of a certain bird (without a mate),
　A bird of another feather.

" My friends," said the Owl, with a look most wise,
" The Eagle is soaring too near the skies,
　In a way that is quite improper ;
Yet the world is praising her, so I'm told,
And I think her actions have grown so bold
　That some of us ought to stop her."

" I have heard it said," quoth Hawk, with a sigh,
" That young lambs died at the glance of her eye,
　And I wholly scorn and despise her.

467

ELLA WHEELER WILCOX

This, and more, I am told they say—
And I think that the only proper way
   Is never to recognise her."

" I am quite convinced," said Crow, with a caw,
" That the Eagle minds no moral law,
   She's a most unruly creature."
" She's an ugly thing," piped Canary Bird ;
" Some call her handsome — it's so absurd—
   She hasn't a decent feature."

Then the old Marsh Hen went hopping about,
She said she was sure—*she* hadn't a doubt—
   Of the truth of each bird's story ;
And she thought it a duty to stop her flight,
To pull her down from her lofty height,
   And take the gilt from her glory.

But, lo ! from a peak on the mountain grand
That looks out over the smiling land
   And over the mighty ocean,
The Eagle is spreading her splendid wings—
She rises, rises, and upward swings,
   With a slow, majestic motion.

Up in the blue of God's own skies,
With a cry of rapture, away she flies,
   Close to the Great Eternal :
She sweeps the world with her piercing sight—
Her soul is filled with the infinite
   And the joy of things supernal.

POEMS OF HOPE

Thus rise forever the chosen of God,
The genius-crowned or the power-shod,
  Over the dust-world sailing ;
And back, like splinters blown by the winds,
Must fall the missiles of silly minds,
  Useless and unavailing.

PRAYER

I DO not undertake to say
  That literal answers come from Heaven,
But I know this—that when I pray
  A comfort, a support is given
That helps me rise o'er earthly things
  As larks soar up on airy wings.

In vain the wise philosopher
  Points out to me my fabric's flaws,
In vain the scientists aver
  That " all things are controlled by laws."
My life has taught me day by day
That it availeth much to pray.

I do not stop to reason out
  The why and how. I do not care,
Since I know this, that when I doubt,
  Life seems a blackness of despair,
The world a tomb ; and when I trust,
Sweet blossoms spring up in the dust.

Since I know in the darkest hour,
    If I lift up my soul in prayer,
Some sympathetic loving Power
    Sends hope and comfort to me there.
Since balm is sent to ease my pain,
What need to argue or explain ?

Prayer has a sweet refining grace,
    It educates the soul and heart.
It lends a lustre to the face,
    And by its elevating art
It gives the mind an inner sight
That brings it near the Infinite.

From our gross selves it helps us rise
    To something which we yet may be.
And so I ask not to be wise,
    If thus my faith is lost to me.
Faith that with angel's voice and touch,
Says " Pray, for prayer availeth much."

BOUND AND FREE

COME to me, Love ! Come on the wings of the
    wind !
Fly as the ring-dove would fly to his mate !
Leave all your cares and your sorrows behind !
    Leave all the fears of your future to Fate !

ELLA WHEELER WILCOX

Come ! and our skies shall be glad with the gold
  That paled into grey when you parted with me.
Come ! but remember that, just as of old,
  You must be bound, Love, and I must be free.

Life has lost savour since you and I parted ;
  I have been lonely, and you have been sad.
Youth is too brief to be sorrowful-hearted—
  Come ! and again let us laugh and be glad.
Lips should not sigh that are fashioned to kiss—
  Breasts should not ache that joy's secret have found.
Come ! but remember, in spite of all this,
  I must be free, Love, while you must be bound.

You must be bound to be true while you live,
  And I keep my freedom for ever, as now.
You must ask only for that which I give—
  Kisses and love-words, but never a vow.
Come ! I am lonely, and long for your smile,
  Bring back the lost lovely Summer to me !
Come ! but remember, remember the while,
  That you must be bound, Love, and I must be free.

A REMINISCENCE

I SAW the wild honey-bee kissing a rose,
  A wee one, that grows
Down low on the bush, where her sisters above
  Cannot see all that's done
  As the moments roll on,
Nor hear all the whispers and murmurs of love.

They flaunt out their beautiful leaves in the sun,
  And they flirt, every one,
With the wild bees who pass, and the gay butterflies.
  And that wee thing in pink—
  Why, they never once think
That she's won a lover right under their eyes.

It reminded me, Kate, of a time—you know when!
  You were so petite then,
Your dresses were short, and your feet were so small.
  Your sisters, Maud-Belle
  And Madeline—well,
They *both* set their caps for me, after that ball.

How the blue eyes and black eyes smiled up in my face!
  'Twas a neck-and-neck race,
Till that day when you opened the door in the hall,
  And looked up and looked down,
  With your sweet eyes of brown,
And *you* seemed so tiny, and *I* felt so tall.

Your sisters had sent you to keep me, my dear,
  Till they should appear.
Then you were dismissed like a child in disgrace.
  How meekly you went!
  But your brown eyes, they sent
A thrill to my heart, and a flush to my face.

We always were meeting some way after that.
  You hung up my hat,

POEMS OF CHEER

hall meet beneath God's arching skies,
 While suns shall blaze, or stars shall gleam,
nd looking in each other's eyes
 Shall hold the past but as a dream.

ut round and perfect and complete,
 Life like a star shall climb the height,
s we two press with willing feet
 Together toward the Infinite.

nd still behind the space between,
 As back of dawns the sunbeams play,
here shines the face I have not seen,
 Whose smile shall wake my world to-day.

PLATONIC

I KNEW it the first of the Summer—
 I knew it the same at the end—
That you and your love were plighted,
 But couldn't you be my friend?
Couldn't we sit in the twilight,
 Couldn't we walk on the shore,
With only a pleasant friendship
 To bind us, and nothing more?

There was never a word of nonsense
 Spoken between us two,
Though we lingered oft in the garden
 Till the roses were wet with dew,

475

ELLA WHEELER WILCOX

And got it again when I finished my call.
　Sixteen, and so sweet !
　Oh, those cute little feet !
Shall I ever forget how they tripped down the hall ?

Shall I ever forget the first kiss by the door,
　Or the vows murmured o'er,
Or the rage and surprise of Maud-Bell ?　Well-a-day,
　How swiftly time flows !
　And who would suppose
That a *bee* could have carried me so far away ?

A GIRL'S FAITH

ACROSS the miles that stretch between,
　　Through days of gloom or glad sunlight,
There shines a face I have not seen
　Which yet doth make my world more bright.

He may be near, he may be far,
　Or near or far I cannot see,
But faithful as the morning star
　He yet shall rise and come to me.

What though fate leads us separate ways,
　The world is round and time is fleet.
A journey of a few brief days,
　And face to face we two shall meet.

Shall meet beneath God's arching skies,
  While suns shall blaze, or stars shall gleam,
And looking in each other's eyes
  Shall hold the past but as a dream.

But round and perfect and complete,
  Life like a star shall climb the height,
As we two press with willing feet
  Together toward the Infinite.

And still behind the space between,
  As back of dawns the sunbeams play,
There shines the face I have not seen,
  Whose smile shall wake my world to-day.

PLATONIC

I KNEW it the first of the Summer—
  I knew it the same at the end—
That you and your love were plighted,
  But couldn't you be my friend?
Couldn't we sit in the twilight,
  Couldn't we walk on the shore,
With only a pleasant friendship
  To bind us, and nothing more?

There was never a word of nonsense
  Spoken between us two,
Though we lingered oft in the garden
  Till the roses were wet with dew,

ELLA WHEELER WILCOX

We touched on a thousand subjects—
  The moon and the stars above ;
But our talk was tinctured with science,
  With never a hint of love.

" A wholly platonic friendship,"
  You said I had proved to you,
" Could bind a man and a woman
  The whole long season through,
With never a thought of folly,
  Though both are in their youth."
What would you have said, my lady,
  If you had known the truth ?

Had I done what my mad heart prompted—
  Gone down on my knees to you.
And told you my passionate story
  There in the dusk and dew ;
My burning, burdensome story,
  Hidden and hushed so long,
My story of hopeless loving—
  Say, would you have thought it wrong ?

But I fought with my heart and conquered,
  I hid my wound from sight ;
You were going away in the morning,
  And I said a calm good-night.

But now, when I sit in the twilight,
  Or when I walk by the sea,
That friendship quite " platonic "
  Comes surging over me.

And a passionate longing fills me
   For the roses, the dusk and the dew,—
For the beautiful Summer vanished—
   For the moonlit talks—and you.

BY AND BYE

"BY and bye" the maiden sighed—"by and bye
   He will claim me for his bride.
Hope is strong and time is fleet ;
Youth is fair, and love is sweet.
Clouds will pass that fleck my sky.
He will come back by and bye—by and bye."

"By and bye," the soldier said—"by and bye,
After I have fought and bled,
I shall go home from the wars,
Crowned with glory, seamed with scars.
Joy will flash from some one's eye
When she greets me by and bye—by and bye."

"By and bye," the mother cried—"by and bye.
Strong and sturdy at my side,
Like a staff supporting me,
Will my bonnie baby be.
Break my rest, then, wail and cry—
Thou'lt repay me by the bye—by and bye."

ELLA WHEELER WILCOX

Fleeting years of time have sped—hurried by—
Still the maiden is unwed ;
All unknown the soldier lies,
Buried under alien skies ;
And the son, with blood-shot eye,
Saw his mother starve and die.
God in Heaven ! dost Thou on high,
Keep the promised by and bye—by and bye ?

AN AFTERNOON

I AM stirred by the dream of an afternoon
   Of a perfect day—though it was not June ¡
The lilt of winds, and the droning tune
   That a busy city was humming.

And a bronze-brown head, and lips like wine
Leaning out through the window-vine
A-list for steps that were maybe mine—
   Eager steps that were coming.

I can see it all, as a dreamer may—
The tender smile on your lips that day,
And the glow on your cheek as we rode away
   Into the golden weather.

And a love-light shone in your eyes of brown—
I swear there did !—as we drove down
The crowded avenue out of the town
   Through shadowy lanes, together :

Drove out into the sunset-skies
That glowed with wonderful crimson dyes !
And with soul and spirit, and heart and eyes
   We silently drank their splendour.

But the golden glory that lit the place
Was not alone from the sunset's grace—
For I saw in your fair, uplifted face
   A light that was wondrously tender.

I say I saw it. And yet to-day
I ask myself, in a cynical way,
Was it only a part you had learned to play,
   To see me act the lover ?

And I curse myself for a fool. And yet
I would willingly die without one regret
Could I bring back the day whose sun has set—
   And you—and live it over.

ROMNEY

NAY, Romney, nay—I will not hear you say
   Those words again: "I love you, love you sweet!"
You are profane—blasphemous. I repeat,
You are no actor for so grand a play.

You love with all your heart ? Well, that may be ;
   Some cups are fashioned shallow. Should I try
   To quench my thirst from one of those, when dry—
I who have had a full bowl proffered me—

ELLA WHEELER WILCOX

A new bowl brimming with a draught divine,
  One single taste thrilled to the finger-tips ?
  Think you I even care to bathe my lips
With this poor sweetened water you call wine ?

And though I spilled the nectar ere 'twas quaffed,
  And broke the bowl in wanton folly, yet
  I would die of my thirst ere I would wet
My burning lips with any meaner draught.

So leave me, Romney.   One who has seen a play
  Enacted by a star cannot endure
  To see it rendered by an amateur.
You know not what Love is—now go away !

NO SPRING

UP from the South come the birds that were banished,
    Frightened away by the presence of frost.
Back to the vale comes the verdure that vanished,
  Back to the forest the leaves that were lost.
Over the hillside the carpet of splendour
  Folded through Winter, Spring spreads down again ;
Along the horizon, the tints that were tender,
  Lost hues of Summer time, burn bright as then.

Only the mountains' high summits are hoary,
  To the ice-fettered river the sun gives the key.
Once more the gleaming shore lists to the story
  Told by an amorous Summer-kissed sea.

POEMS OF CHEER

All things revive that in Winter-time perished,
  The rose buds again in the light o' the sun,
All that was beautiful, all that was cherished,
  Sweet things and dear things and all things—save one.

Late, when the year and the roses were lying
  Low with the ruins of Summer and bloom,
Down in the dust fell a love that was dying,
  And the snow piled above it, and made it a tomb.
Lo! now! the roses are budded for blossom—
  Lo! now! the Summer is risen again.
Why dost thou bud not, O Love of my bosom?
  Why dost thou rise not, and thrill me as then?

Life without love is a year without Summer,
  Heart without love is a wood without song.
Rise then, revive then, thou indolent comer,
  Why dost thou lie in the dark earth so long?
Rise! ah, thou canst not! the rose-tree that sheddest
  Its beautiful leaves, in the Spring time may bloom,
But of cold things the coldest, of dead things the deadest,
  Love buried once, rises not from the tomb.

Green things may grow on the hillside and heather.
  Birds seek the forest and build there and sing.
All things revive in the beautiful weather,
  But unto a dead love there cometh no Spring.

ELLA WHEELER WILCOX

TWO

ONE leaned on velvet cushions like a queen—
　　To see him pass, the hero of an hour,
Whom men called great.　She bowed with languid mien,
　And smiled, and blushed, and knew her beauty's
　　power.

One trailed her tinselled garments through the street
　　And thrust aside the crowd, and found a place
So near, the blooded courser's prancing feet
　　Cast sparks of fire upon her painted face.

One took the hot-house blossoms from her breast,
　　And tossed them down as he went riding by,
And blushed rose-red, to see them fondly pressed
　　To bearded lips, while eye spoke unto eye.

One, bold and hardened with her sinful life,
　　Yet shrank and shivered painfully, because
His cruel glance cut keener than a knife,
　　The glance of him who made her what she was.

One was observed, and lifted up to fame,
　　Because the hero smiled upon her ! while
One who was shunned and hated, found her shame
　　In basking in the death-light of his smile.

MIDSUMMER

AFTER the May time, and after the June time,
  Rare with blossoms and perfumes sweet,
Cometh the round world's royal noontime,
  The red midsummer of blazing heat,
When the sun, like an eye that never closes,
  Bends on the earth its fervid gaze,
And the winds are still, and the crimson roses
  Droop and wither and die in its rays.

Unto my heart has come that season,
  O, my lady, my worshipped one,
When over the stars of Pride and Reason
  Sails Love's cloudless, noonday sun.
Like a great red ball in my bosom burning
  With fires that nothing can quench or tame,
It glows till my heart itself seems turning
  Into a liquid lake of flame.

The hopes half shy, and the sighs all tender,
  The dreams and fears of an earlier day,
Under the noontide's royal splendour,
  Droop like roses and wither away.
From the hills of doubt no winds are blowing,
  From the isle of pain no breeze is sent.
Only the sun in a white heat glowing
  Over an ocean of great content.

ELLA WHEELER WILCOX

Sink, O, my soul, in this golden glory,
  Die, O, my heart, in thy rapture-swoon,
For the Autumn must come with its mournful story,
  And Love's midsummer will fade too soon.

ÆSTHETIC

IN a garb that was guiltless of colours
    She stood, with a dull, listless air—
A creature of dumps and of dolours,
    But most undeniably fair.

The folds of her garments fell round her,
    Revealing the curve of each limb ;
Well proportioned and graceful I found her,
    Although quite alarmingly slim.

From the hem of her robe peeped one sandal—
    " High Art " was she down to her feet ;
And though I could not understand all
    She said, I could see she was sweet.

Impressed by her limpness and languor,
    I proffered a chair near at hand ;
She looked back a mild sort of anger—
    Posed anew, and continued to stand.

Some praises I next tried to mutter
    Of the fan that she held to her face ;
She said it was " utterly utter,"
    And waved it with languishing grace.

484

I then, in a strain quite poetic,
  Begged her gaze on the bow in the sky.
She looked—said its curve was " æsthetic,"
  But the " tone was too dreadfully high."

Her lovely face, lit by the splendour
  That glorified landscape and sea,
Woke thoughts that were daring and tender :
  Did her thoughts, too, rest upon me ?

" Oh, tell me," I cried, growing bolder,
  " Have I in your musings a place ? "
" Well, yes," she said over her shoulder,
  " I was thinking of nothing in space."

PLEA TO SCIENCE

O SCIENCE, reaching backward through the distance,
  Most earnest child of God,
Exposing all the secrets of existence,
  With thy divining rod,
I bid thee speed up to the heights supernal,
  Clear thinker, ne'er sufficed ;
Go seek and bind the laws and truths eternal,
  But leave me Christ.

Upon the vanity of pious sages
  Let in the light of day.
Break down the superstitions of all ages—
  Thrust bigotry away ;

485

ELLA WHEELER WILCOX

Stride on and bid all stubborn foes defiance,
  Let Truth and Reason reign.
But I beseech thee, O Immortal Science,
  Let Christ remain.

What canst thou give to help me bear my crosses,
  In place of Him, my Lord ?
And what to recompense for all my losses,
  And bring me sweet reward ?
Thou couldst not with thy clear, cold eyes of reason,
  Thou couldst not comfort me
Like one who passed through that tear-blotted season,
  In sad Gethsemane !

Through all the weary, wearing hours of sorrow,
  What word that thou hast said
Would make me strong to wait for some to-morrow
  When I should find my dead ?
When I am weak and desolate, and lonely—
  And prone to follow wrong ?
Not thou, O Science—Christ, my Saviour, only
  Can make me strong.

Thou art so cold, so lofty, and so distant,
  Though great my need might be,
No prayer, however constant and persistent,
  Could bring thee down to me.
Christ stands so near, to help me through each hour,
  To guide me day by day.
O Science, sweeping all before thy power—
  Leave Christ, I pray !

RESPITE

THE mighty conflict, which we call existence,
    Doth wear upon the body and the soul.
Our vital forces wasted in resistance,
    So much there is to conquer and control.

The rock which meets the billows with defiance
    Undaunted and unshaken day by day,
In spite of its unyielding self-reliance,
    Is by the warfare surely worn away.

And there are depths and heights of strong emotions
    That surge at times within the human breast,
More fierce than all the tides of all the oceans
    Which sweep on ever in divine unrest.

I sometimes think the rock worn with adventures,
    And sad with thoughts of conflicts yet to be,
Must envy the frail reed which no one censures,
    When overcome 'tis swallowed by the sea.

This life is all resistance and repression.
    Dear God, if in that other world unseen,
Not rest, we find, but new life and progression,
    Grant us a respite in the grave between.

487

ELLA WHEELER WILCOX

" LEUDEMANNS-ON-THE-RIVER "

TOWARD even when the day leans down
  To kiss the upturned face of night,
Out just beyond the loud-voiced town
  I know a spot of calm delight.
Like crimson arrows from a quiver
  The red rays pierce the waters flowing
  While we go dreaming, singing, rowing,
To Leudemanns-on-the-River.

The hills, like some glad mocking-bird,
  Send back our laughter and our singing,
While faint—and yet more faint is heard
  The steeple bells all sweetly ringing.
Some message did the winds deliver
  To each glad heart that August night,
  All heard, but all heard not aright
By Leudemanns-on-the River.

Night falls as in some foreign clime
  Between the hills that slope and rise.
So dusk the shades at landing time,
  We could not see each other's eyes.
We only saw the moonbeams quiver
  Far down upon the stream ! that night
  The new moon gave but little light
By Leudemanns-on-the-River.

How dusky were those paths that led
  Up from the river to the hall.
The tall trees branching overhead
  Invite the early shades that fall.
In all the glad blithe world, oh, never
    Were hearts more free from care than when
    We wandered through those walks, we ten,
By Leudemanns-on-the-River.

So soon, so soon, the changes came,
  This August day we two alone,
On that same river not the same,
  Dream of a night for ever flown.
Strange distances have come to sever
    The hearts that gaily beat in pleasure,
    Long miles we cannot cross or measure—
From Leudemanns-on-the-River.

We'll pluck two leaves, dear friend, to-day.
  The green, the russet ! seems it strange
  So soon, so soon, the leaves can change !
Ah, me ! so runs all life away.
This night wind chills me, and I shiver ;
  The Summer-time is almost past.
  One more good-bye—perhaps the last
To Leudemanns-on-the-River.

ELLA WHEELER WILCOX

A DREAM

THAT was a curious dream ; I thought the three
    Great planets that are drawing near the sun
  With such unerring certainty, begun
To talk together in a mighty glee.
They spoke of vast convulsions which would be
    Throughout the solar system—the rare fun
    Of watching haughty stars drop, one by one,
And vanish in a seething vapour sea.

I thought I heard them comment on the earth—
    That small dark object—doomed beyond a doubt.
    They wondered if live creatures moved about
Its tiny surface, deeming it of worth.
    And then they laughed—'twas such a ringing shout
That I awoke and joined too in their mirth.

MY HOME

THIS is the place that I love the best,
    A little brown house, like a ground-bird's nest,
Hid among grasses, and vines and trees,
Summer retreat of the birds and bees.

The tenderest light that ever was seen
Sifts through the vine-made window screen—
Sifts and quivers, and flits and falls
On home-made carpets and gray-hung walls.

POEMS OF CHEER

All through June, the west wind free
The breath of the clover brings to me.
All through the languid July day
I catch the scent of the new-mown hay.

The morning glories and scarlet vine
Over the doorway twist and twine ;
And every day, when the house is still,
The humming-bird comes to the window-sill.

In the cunningest chamber under the sun
I sink to sleep when the day is done ;
And am waked at morn, in my snow-white bed,
By a singing-bird on the roof o'erhead.

Better than treasures brought from Rome
Are the living pictures I see at home—
My aged father, with frosted hair,
And mother's face, like a painting rare.

Far from the city's dust and heat,
I get but sounds and odours sweet.
Who can wonder I love to stay,
Week after week, here hidden away,
In this sly nook that I love the best—
The little brown house, like a ground-bird's nest ?

ELLA WHEELER WILCOX

I DREAM

OH, I have dreams. I sometimes dream of Life
　　In the full meaning of that splendid word.
　Its subtle music which few men have heard,
Though all may hear it, sounding through earth's strife.
Its mountain heights by mystic breezes kissed,
　　Lifting their lovely peaks above the dust ;
　　Its treasures which no touch of time can rust,
Its emerald seas, its dawns of amethyst,
　　Its certain purpose, its serene repose,
　　Its usefulness, that finds no hour for woes.
　　　　This is my dream of Life.

Yes, I have dreams. I ofttimes dream of Love
　　As radiant and brilliant as a star.
　　As changeless, too, as that fixed light afar
Which glorifies vast worlds of space above.
Strong as the tempest when it holds its breath,
　　Before it bursts in fury ; and as deep
　　As the unfathomed seas, where lost worlds sleep.
And sad as birth, and beautiful as death.
　　As fervent as the fondest soul could crave,
　　Yet holy as the moonlight on a grave.
　　　　This is my dream of Love.

Yes, yes, I dream. One oft-recurring dream,
　　Is beautiful and comforting and blest.
　　Complete with certain promises of rest,
Divine content, and ecstasy supreme.

When that strange essence, author of all faith,
   That subtle something, which cries for the light,
   Like a lost child who wanders in the night,
Shall solve the mighty mystery of Death,
   Shall find eternal progress, or sublime
   And satisfying slumber for all time.
      This is my dream of Death.

DREAMS

THANK God for dreams ?   I, desolate and lone,
   In the dark curtained night did seem to be
The centre where all golden sun-rays shone,
   And, sitting there, held converse sweet with thee.
No shadow lurked between us ; all was bright
   And beautiful as in the hours gone by ;
I smiled, and was rewarded by the light
   Of olden days soft beaming from thine eye.
Thank God, thank God for dreams !

I thought the birds all listened ; for thy voice
   Pulsed through the air like beat of silver wings.
It made each chamber of my soul rejoice
   And thrilled along my heart's tear-rusted strings.
As some devout and everprayerful nun
   Tells her bright beads, and counts them o'er and o'er,
Thy golden words I gathered, one by one,
   And slipped them into memory's precious store.
Thank God, thank God for dreams !

ELLA WHEELER WILCOX

My lips met thine in one ecstatic kiss.
  Hand pressed in hand, and heart to heart we sat.
Why even now I am surcharged with bliss—
  With joy supreme, if I but think of that.
No fear of separation or of change
  Crept in to mar our sweet serene content.
In that blest vision, nothing could estrange
  Our wedded souls, in perfect union blent.
Thank God, thank God for dreams !

Thank God for dreams ! when nothing else is left.
  When the sick soul, all tortured with its pain,
Knowing itself forever more bereft,
  Finds waiting hopeless and all watching vain,
When empty arms grow rigid with their ache,
  When eyes are blinded with sad tides of tears,
When stricken hearts do suffer yet not break,
  For loss of those who come not with the years—
Thank God, thank God for dreams !

SLIPPING AWAY

SLIPPING away—slipping away !
  Out of our brief year slips the May ;
And Winter lingers, and Summer flies ;
And Sorrow abideth, and Pleasure dies ;
And the days are short, and the nights are long ;
And little is right, and much is wrong.

POEMS OF CHEER

Slipping away is the Summer-time ;
It has lost its rhythm and lilting rhyme—
For the grace goes out of the day so soon,
And the tired head aches in the glare of noon,
And the way seems long to the hills that lie
Under the calm of the western sky.

Slipping away are the friends whose worth
Lent a glow to the sad old earth :
One by one they slip from our sight ;
One by one their graves gleam white ;
Or we count them lost by the crueller death
Of a trust betrayed, or a murdered faith.

Slipping away are the hopes that made
Bliss out of sorrow, and sun out of shade ;
Slipping away is our hold on life ;
And out of the struggle and wearing strife,
From joys that diminish, and woes that increase,
We are slipping away to the shores of Peace.

LITTLE BLUE HOOD

EVERY morning and every night
There passes our window near the street
A little girl with an eye so bright,
    And a cheek so round and a lip so sweet !
The daintiest, jauntiest little miss
That ever anyone longed to kiss.

495

ELLA WHEELER WILCOX

She is neat as wax and fresh to view,
And her look is wholesome and clean and good.
Whatever her gown, her hood is blue,
   And so we call her " Little Blue Hood,"
For we know not the name of the dear little lass,
But we call to each other to see her pass,

" Little Blue Hood is coming now ! "
   And we watch from the window while she goes by,
She has such a bonny, smooth, white brow,
   And a fearless look in her long-lashed eye ;
And a certain dignity wedded to grace,
Seems to envelop her form and face.

Every morning, in sun or rain,
   She walks by the window with sweet, grave air,
And never guesses behind the pane
   We two are watching and thinking her fair ;
Lovingly watching her down the street,
Dear Little Blue Hood, bright and sweet.

Somebody ties that hood of blue
   Under the face so fair to see,
Somebody loves her, beside we two,
   Somebody kisses her—why can't we ?
Dear Little Blue Hood, fresh and fair,
Are you glad we love you, or don't you care ?

POEMS OF CHEER

WHAT HAPPENS

WHEN thy hand touches mine, through all the mesh
　　Of intricate and interlacèd veins
Shoot swift delights that border on keen pains :
Flesh thrills to thrilling flesh.

When in thine eager eyes I look to find
　　A comrade to my thought, thy ready brain
Delves down and makes its inmost meaning plain :
Mind answers unto mind.

When hands and eyes are hid by seas that roll
　　Wide wastes between us, still so near thou art　·
I count the very pulses of thy heart :
Soul speaketh unto soul.

So every law, or human or divine,
In heart and brain and spirit makes thee mine.

POEMS OF THE WEEK

SUNDAY

LIE still and rest, in that serene repose
　　That on this holy morning comes to those
Who have been burdened with the cares which make
The sad heart weary and the tired head ache.
　　　　Lie still and rest—
　　God's day of all is best.

ELLA WHEELER WILCOX

MONDAY

Awake! arise! Cast off thy drowsy dreams!
Red in the East, behold the Morning gleams.
" As Monday goes, so goes the week," dames say,
Refreshed, renewed, use well the initial day.
  And see! thy neighbour
  Already seeks his labour.

TUESDAY

Another morning's banners are unfurled—
Another day looks smiling on the world.
It holds new laurels for thy soul to win;
Mar not its grace by slothfulness or sin.
  Nor sad, away,
  Send it to yesterday.

WEDNESDAY

Half-way unto the end—the week's high moon.
The morning hours do speed away so soon!
And, when the noon is reached, however bright,
Instinctively we look towards the night.
  The glow is lost
  Once the meridian cross'd.

THURSDAY

So well the week has sped, hast thou a friend?
Go spend an hour in converse. It will lend
New beauty to thy labours and thy life
To pause a little sometimes in the strife.
  Toil soon seems rude
  That has no interlude.

POEMS OF CHEER

FRIDAY

From feasts abstain ; be temperate, and pray ;
Fast if thou wilt ; and yet, throughout the day,
Neglect no labour and no duty shirk ;
Not many hours are left thee for thy work—
    And it were meet
    That all should be complete.

SATURDAY

Now with the almost finished task make haste ;
So near the night thou hast no time to waste.
Post up accounts, and let thy Soul's eyes look
For flaws and errors in Life's ledger-book.
    When labours cease,
    How sweet the sense of peace !

TWO SAT DOWN

TWO sat down in the morning time,
    One to sing and one to spin.
All men listened the song sublime—
    But no one listened the dull wheel's din.

The singer sat in a pleasant nook,
    And sang of a life that was fair and sweet,
While the spinner sat with a steadfast look
    Busily plying her hands and feet.

ELLA WHEELER WILCOX

The singer sang on with a rose in her hair,
   And all men listened her dulcet tone ;
And the spinner spun on with a dull despair
   Down in her heart as she sat alone.

But lo ! on the morrow no one said
   Aught of the singer or what she sang,
Men were saying : " Behold this thread,"
   And loud the praise of the spinner rang.

The world has forgotten the singer's name—
   Her rose is faded, her songs are old ;
But far o'er the ocean the spinner's fame
   Yet is blazoned in lines of gold.

GHOSTS

THERE are ghosts in the room.
   As I sit here alone, from the dark corners there
They come out of the gloom,
And they stand at my side and they lean on my chair.

   There's the ghost of a Hope
That lighted my days with a fanciful glow,
   In her hand is the rope
That strangled her life out.   Hope was slain long ago.

   But her ghost comes to-night
With its skeleton face and expressionless eyes,
   And it stands in the light,
And mocks me, and jeers me with sobs and with sighs.

There's the ghost of a Joy,
A frail, fragile thing, and I prized it too much,
  And the hands that destroy
Clasped it close, and it died at the withering touch.

There's the ghost of a Love,
Born with joy, reared with hope, died in pain and unrest,
  But he towers above
All the others—this ghost ; yet a ghost at the best,

I am weary, and fain
Would forget all these dead : but the gibbering host
  Make my struggle in vain—
In each shadowy corner there lurketh a ghost.

FLEEING AWAY

MY thoughts soar not as they ought to soar,
    Higher and higher on soul-lent wings ;
But ever and often, and more and more
  They are dragged down earthward by little things,
By little troubles and little needs,
As a lark might be tangled among the weeds.

My purpose is not what it ought to be,
  Steady and fixed, like a star on high,
But more like a fisherman's light at sea ;
  Hither and thither it seems to fly—
Sometimes feeble, and sometimes bright,
Then suddenly lost in the gloom of night.

ELLA WHEELER WILCOX

My life is far from my dream of life—
  Calmly contented, serenely glad ;
But, vexed and worried by daily strife,
  It is always troubled, and ofttimes sad—
And the heights I had thought I should reach one day
Grow dimmer and dimmer, and farther away.

My heart finds never the longed-for rest ;
  Its worldly striving, its greed for gold,
Chilled and frightened the calm-eyed guest
  Who sometimes sought me in days of old ;
And ever fleeing away fom me
Is the higher self that I long to be.

FOES

THANK Fate for foes ! I hold mine dear
    As valued friends. He cannot know
The zest of life who runneth here
    His earthly race without a foe.

I saw a prize. " Run," cried my friend ;
  " 'Tis thine to claim without a doubt."
But ere I half-way reached the end
  I felt my strength was giving out.

My foe looked on the while I ran ;
  A scornful triumph lit his eyes.
With that perverseness born in man,
  I nerved myself, and won the prize.

POEMS OF CHEER

All blinded by the crimson glow
   Of sin's disguise, I tempted Fate.
" I knew thy weakness ! " sneered my foe,
   I saved myself, and baulked his hate.

For half my blessings, half my gain,
   I needs must thank my trusty foe ;
Despite his envy and disdain,
   He serves me well where'er I go.

So may I keep him to the end,
   Nor may his enmity abate ;
More faithful than the fondest friend,
   He guards me ever with his hate.

FRIENDSHIP

DEAR friend, I pray thee, if thou wouldst be proving
   Thy strong regard for me,
Make me no vows.   Lip-service is not loving ;
   Let thy faith speak for thee.

Swear not to me that nothing can divide us—
   So little such oaths mean.
But when distrust and envy creep beside us,
   Let them not come between.

Say not to me the depths of thy devotion
   Are deeper than the sea ;
But watch, lest doubt or some unkind emotion
   Embitter them for me.

ELLA WHEELER WILCOX

Vow not to love me ever and for ever—
  Words are such idle things ;
But when we differ in opinions, never
  Hurt me by little stings.

I'm sick of words : they are so lightly spoken,
  And spoken, are but air.
I'd rather feel thy trust in me unbroken
  Than list thy words so fair.

If all the little proofs of trust are heeded,
  If thou art always kind,
No sacrifice, no promise will be needed
  To satisfy my mind.

OVER THE MAY HILL

ALL through the night-time, and all through the day-
    time,
  Dreading the morning and dreading the night,
Nearer and nearer we drift to the May-time
  Season of beauty and season of blight,
Leaves on the linden, and sun on the meadow,
  Green in the garden, and bloom everywhere,
Gloom in my heart, and a terrible shadow,
  Walks by me, sits by me, stands by my chair.

Oh, but the birds by the brooklet are cheery,
  Oh, but the woods show such delicate greens,
Strange how you droop and how soon you are weary—
  Too well I know what that weariness means.

But how could I know in the crisp winter weather
  (Though sometimes I noticed a catch in your breath),
Riding and singing and dancing together,
  How could I know you were racing with death ?

How could I know when we danced until morning,
  And you were the gayest of all the gay crowd—
With only that shortness of breath for a warning,
  How could I know that you danced for a shroud ?
Whirling and whirling through moonlight and starlight,
  Rocking as lightly as boats on the wave,
Down in your eyes shone a deep light—a far light,
  How could I know 'twas the light to your grave ?

Day by day, day by day, nearing and nearing,
  Hid under greenness, and beauty and bloom,
Cometh the shape and the shadow I'm fearing,
  " Over the May hill " is waiting your tomb.
The season of mirth and of music is over—
  I have danced my last dance, I have sung my last song,
Under the violets, under the clover,
  My heart and my love will be lying ere long.

RIVER AND SEA

WE stood by the river that swept
  In its glory and grandeur away ;
But never a pulse of me leapt,
  And you wondered at me that day.

ELLA WHEELER WILCOX

We stood by the lake as it lay
   With its dimpled face turned to the light ;
Was it strange I had nothing to say
   To so fair and enchanting a sight ?

I look on your tresses of gold—
   You are fair and a thing to be loved—
Do you think I am heartless and cold
   That I look and am wholly unmoved ?

One answer, dear friend, I will make
   To the questions your eyes ask of me :
" Talk not of the river or lake
   To those who have looked on the sea."

AQUILEIA

[On the election of the Roman Emperor Maximus, by the Senate,
A.D. 238, a powerful army, headed by the Thracian giant Maximus,
laid siege to Aquileia. Though poorly prepared for war, the con-
stancy of her citizens rendered her impregnable. The women of
Aquileia cut off their hair to make ropes for the military engines.
The small body of troops was directed by Chrispinus, a Lieutenant
of the Senate. Apollo was the Deity supposed to protect them.—
Gibbon's Roman History.]

" THE ropes, the ropes ! Apollo send us ropes,"
   Chrispinus cried, " or death attends our hopes."
Then panic reigned, and many a mournful sound
Hurt the cleft air ; for where could ropes be found ?

AQUILEIA

POEMS OF CHEER

Up rose a Roman mother ; tall was she
As her own son, a youth of noble height.
A little child was clinging to her knee—
She loosed his twining arms and put him down.
And her dark eyes flashed with a sudden light.

How like a queen she stood ! her royal crown,
The rich dark masses of her splendid hair,
Just flecked with spots of sunshine here and there,
Twined round her brow ; 'twas like a coronet,
Where gems of gold lie bedded deep in jet.

She loosed the comb that held the shining strands,
And threaded out the meshes with her hands.
The purple mass fell to her garment's hem.
A queen new clothed without her diadem
She stood before her subjects.

                   " Now," she cried,
" Give me thy sword, Julianus ! " And her son
Unsheathed the blade (that had not left his side
Save when it sought a foeman's blood to shed),
Awed by her regal bearing, and obeyed.
With the white beauty of her firm fair hand,
She clasped the hilt ; then severed one by one,
Her gold-flecked purple tresses. Strand on strand
Free e'en as foes had fallen by that blade,
Robbed of its massive wealth of curl and coil,
Yet like some antique model, rose her head
In all its classic beauty.

                                        " See ! " she said,
And pointed to the shining mound of hair ;
" Apollo makes swift answer to thy prayer,
Chrispinus.   Quick ! now, soldiers, to thy toil ! "
Forth from a thousand throats what seemed one voice
Rose shrilly, filling all the air with cheer.
" Lo ! " quoth the foe, " our enemies rejoice ! "
Well might the Thracian giant quake with fear !

For while skilled hands caught up the gleaming threads
And bound them into cords, a hundred heads
Yielded their beauteous tresses to the sword,
And cast them down to swell the precious hoard.

Nor was the noble sacrifice in vain ;
Another day beheld the giant slain.

ALL MAD

" HE is mad as a hare, poor fellow,
        And should be in chains," you say.
I haven't a doubt of your statement,
    But who isn't mad, I pray ?
Why, the world is a great asylum,
    And people are all insane,
Gone daft with pleasure and folly,
    Or crazed with passion and pain.

POEMS OF CHEER

The infant who shrieks at a shadow,
  The child with his Santa Claus faith,
The woman who worships Dame Fashion,
  Each man with his notions of death,
The miser who hoards up his earnings,
  The spendthrift who wastes them too soon,
The scholar grown blind in his delving,
  The lover who stares at the moon,

The poet who thinks life a pæan,
  The cynic who thinks it a fraud,
The youth who goes seeking for pleasure,
  The preacher who dares talk of God,
All priests with their creeds and their croaking,
  All doubters who dare to deny,

The gay who find aught to wake laughter,
  The sad who find aught worth a sigh,
Whoever is downcast or solemn,
  Whoever is gleeful and glad,
Are only the dupes of delusions—
  We are all of us—all of us mad.

WISHES FOR A LITTLE GIRL

WHAT would I ask the kindly fates to give
    To crown her life, if I could have my way?
My strongest wishes would be negative,
  If they would but obey.

509

ELLA WHEELER WILCOX

Give her not greatness.   For great souls must stand
  Alone and lonely in this little world ;
Cleft rocks that show the great Creator's hand,
  Thither by earthquakes hurled.

Give her not genius.   Spare her the cruel pain
  Of finding her whole life a prey for daws ;
Of hearing with quickened sense and burning brain
  The world's sneer-tinged applause.

Give her not perfect beauty's gifts.   For then
  Her truthful mirror would infuse her mind
With love for self, and for the praise of men,
  That lowers woman-kind.

But make her fair and comely to the sight,
  Give her more heart than brain, more love than pride,
Let her be tender-thoughted, cheerful, bright,
  Some strong man's star and guide.

Not vainly questioning why she was sent
  Into this restless world of toil and strife,
Let her go bravely on her way, content
  To make the best of life.

POEMS OF CHEER

THE NEW AND OLD CENTURIES

A CURIOUS vision on mine eyes enfurled
In the deep night.   I saw, or seemed to see,
Two Centuries meet, and sit down *vis-à-vis*
Across the great round-table of the world.
One with suggested sorrows in his mien,
And on his brow the furrowed lines of thought,
And one whose glad expectant presence brought
A glow and radiance from the realms unseen.

Hand clasped with hand, in silence for a space,
The Centuries sat ; the sad old eyes of one
(As grave paternal eyes regard a son)
Gazing upon that other eager face.
And then a voice, as cadenceless and gray
As the sea's monody in winter-time,
Mingled with tones melodious as the chime
Of bird choirs singing in the dawns of May.

THE OLD CENTURY SPEAKS

By you Hope stands.   With me Experience walks,
Like a fair jewel in a faded box.
In my tear-rusted heart sweet pity lies
For all the dreams that look forth from your eyes,
And those bright-hued ambitions, which I know
Must fall like leaves and perish in Time's snow
(Even as my soul's garden stands bereft)
I give you pity ! 'tis the one gift left.

ELLA WHEELER WILCOX

THE NEW CENTURY

Nay, nay, good friend! not pity, but Godspeed.
Here in the morning of my life I need
Counsel, and not condolence ; smiles, not tears,
To guide me through the channels of the years.
Oh! I am blinded by the blaze of light
That shines upon me from the Infinite.
Blurred is my vision by the close approach
To unseen shores whereon the times encroach.

THE OLD CENTURY

Illusion, all illusion.   List and hear
The godless cannons booming far and near,
Flaunting the flag of Unbelief, with Greed
For pilot, lo! the pirate age in speed
Bears on to ruin.   War's most hideous crimes
Besmirch the record of these modern times.
Degenerate is the world I leave to you—
My happiest speech to earth will be—adieu.

THE NEW CENTURY

You speak as one too weary to be just.
I hear the guns—I see the greed and lust.
The death throes of a giant evil fill
The air with riot and confusion.   Ill
Ofttimes makes fallow ground for Good, and Wrong
Builds Right's foundation when it grows too strong.
Pregnant with promise is the hour, and grand
The trust you leave in my all-willing hand.

POEMS OF CHEER

THE OLD CENTURY

As one who throws a flickering taper's ray
To light departing feet, my shadowed way
You brighten with your faith.   Faith makes the man.
Alas! that my poor foolish age outran
Its early trust in God.   The death of art
And progress follows when the world's hard heart
Casts out religion.   'Tis the human brain
Men worship now, and heaven, to them, means—gain.

THE NEW CENTURY

Faith is not dead, though priest and creed may pass.
For thought has leavened the whole unthinking mass,
And man looks now to find the God within.
We shall talk more of love, and less of sin,
In this new era.   We are drawing near
Unatlassed boundaries of a larger sphere.
With awe I wait till Science leads us on
Into the full effulgence of its dawn.

POSSESSION

THAT which we had we still possess,
   Though leaves may drop and stars may fall;
No circumstance can make it less
   Or take it from us, all in all.

ELLA WHEELER WILCOX

That which is lost we did not own ;
   We only held it for a day—
A leaf by careless breezes blown ;
   No fate could take our own away.

I hold it as a changeless law
   From which no soul can sway or swerve,
We have that in us which will draw
   Whate'er we need or most deserve.

Even as the magnet to the steel
   Our souls are to our best desires ;
The Fates have hearts and they can feel—
   They know what each true life requires.

We think we lose when we most gain ;
   We call joys ended ere begun ;
When stars fade out do skies complain,
   Or glory in the rising sun ?

No fate could rob us of our own—
   No circumstance can make it less ;
What time removes was but a loan,
   For what was ours we still possess.

FLOODS

IN the dark night, from sweet refreshing sleep
  I wake to hear outside my window-pane
The uncurbed fury of the wild spring rain,
And weird winds lashing the defiant deep,
And roar of floods that gather strength, and leap
Down dizzy, wreck-strewn channels to the main.
I turn upon my pillow, and again
Compose myself for slumber.
                               Let them sweep;
I once survived great floods, and do not fear,
Though ominous planets congregate, and seem
To foretell strange disasters.

                               From a dream—
Ah! dear God! such a dream!—I woke to hear,
Through the dense shadows lit by no stars' gleam,
The rush of mighty waters on my ear.
Helpless, afraid, and all alone, I lay;
The floods had come upon me unaware.

I heard the crash of structures that were fair;
The bridges of fond hopes were swept away
By great salt waves of sorrow. In dismay
I saw by the red lightning's lurid glare
That on the rock-bound island of despair
I had been cast. Till the dim dawn of day

5I5

ELLA WHEELER WILCOX

I heard my castles falling, and the roll
Of angry billows bearing to the sea
The broken timbers of my very soul.
Were all the pent-up waters from the whole
Stupendous solar system to break free,
There are no floods now that can frighten me.

INDEX OF FIRST LINES

INDEX OF FIRST LINES

518

INDEX OF FIRST LINES

519

INDEX OF FIRST LINES

INDEX OF FIRST LINES

INDEX OF FIRST LINES

INDEX OF FIRST LINES

523

INDEX OF FIRST LINES

INDEX OF FIRST LINES

INDEX OF FIRST LINES

INDEX OF FIRST LINES

Printed by BALLANTYNE, HANSON & Co.
Edinburgh & London

CPSIA information can be obtained
at www.ICGtesting.com
Printed in the USA
LVHW082133030319
609363LV00020B/407/P

9 781333 299897